I. Hammond Morris

The Teaching of Drawing

I. Hammond Morris

The Teaching of Drawing

ISBN/EAN: 9783337166069

Printed in Europe, USA, Canada, Australia, Japan

Cover: Foto ©Thomas Meinert / pixelio.de

More available books at **www.hansebooks.com**

THE
TEACHING OF DRAWING

BY

I. H. MORRIS, Art Master

AUTHOR OF
'GEOMETRICAL DRAWING' AND 'PRACTICAL PLANE AND SOLID GEOMETRY'

THIRD EDITION

LONDON
LONGMANS, GREEN, AND CO.
AND NEW YORK: 15 EAST 16th STREET
1894

All rights reserved

PREFACE

THE OBJECT of this manual is to provide a fairly complete course of methodical teaching in drawing, as required in Elementary schools by the Department of Science and Art. It is universally admitted by all who have either to supervise or to examine the work done in schools, that there is abundant room for improvement in the method of teaching this important subject.

The methods, hints, and suggestions given, are the outcome of an extensive practical experience in Elementary Schools, Art Night Classes, and Schools of Art; and although doubtless familiar to some, the author ventures to hope that they will be of material assistance to many who may not have had the opportunity of receiving a special training in drawing.

The book contains about 700 illustrations, which have been specially drawn for the purpose. The Freehand examples, which are mostly shown in stages, may be divided into three sections, viz., Conventional Ornament, Plant Forms, and Common Objects. Many are original drawings, others are based upon examples from the Illustrated Syllabus, Dyce's Drawing Book, Examination Tests, Casts of Ornament, &c. They are selected to illustrate definite principles which the teacher may readily apply to other figures. Considerable space is devoted to the teaching of Scale Drawing, Model Drawing, and Solid Geometry, as these parts of the subject require the most skilful and intelligent teaching.

Especial attention is directed to the large number of specimen lessons. These are given chiefly with a view of affording assistance to young teachers and those who may not have had much practical acquaintance with the subject.

I. H. M.

SHEFFIELD : *August* 1893.

CONTENTS

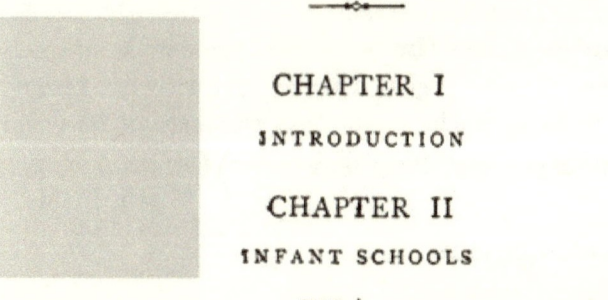

CHAPTER I

INTRODUCTION

PAGE
1

CHAPTER II

INFANT SCHOOLS

	PAGE		PAGE
CODE REQUIREMENTS	3	OBJECTS COMPOSED OF UPRIGHT AND LEVEL LINES	12
APPARATUS	4		
USE OF CRAYONS	5	SLANTING LINES AND PATTERNS COMPOSED OF UPRIGHT, LEVEL, AND SLANTING LINES	16
UPRIGHT LINES	6		
LEVEL LINES	7		
COMBINATIONS OF UPRIGHT AND LEVEL LINES	8	OBJECTS	20
FRETS	10		

CHAPTER III

STANDARD I

SYLLABUS AND APPARATUS	23	LESSON. THE SQUARE	33
INTRODUCTORY LESSON	24	DICTATED DRAWING. DIAMETERS AND DIAGONALS	34
METHOD OF USING PENCIL AND RULER	26	LINES INTERSECTING AT RIGHT ANGLES	35
LESSON. HORIZONTAL LINES	27		
VERTICAL, OBLIQUE, AND PARALLEL LINES	29	BISECTION AND TRISECTION OF THE RIGHT ANGLE	37
ARRANGEMENT OF THE DRAWING	30	EXAMPLES	39
		MEMORY DRAWING	42
ANGLES	31		

CHAPTER IV

STANDARD II

	PAGE		PAGE
SYLLABUS AND APPARATUS	43	CURVES AND COMMON OB-	
RULER WORK. PARALLELS	45	JECTS	48
PERPENDICULARS . .	46		

CHAPTER V

STANDARD III

	PAGE		PAGE
SYLLABUS	52	DRAWING OF GEOMETRICAL	
FREEHAND DRAWING OF		FIGURES WITH RULERS	68
CURVED FIGURES .	52	LESSON	69
,, FIRST STAGE . .	53	EXAMPLES	71
,, SECOND STAGE . .	53	TRIANGLES	76
,, THIRD STAGE . .	55	ZIGZAGS	78
,, LESSON . . .	58	THE HEXAGON . . .	79
EXAMPLES	61	LESSON	81
FREEHAND DRAWING OF		THE OCTAGON . . .	82
RIGHT-LINED FORMS .	66	THE PENTAGON . . .	83

CHAPTER VI

FREEHAND DRAWING. STANDARDS IV-VII

	PAGE		PAGE
LESSON	86	LESSON	104
EXAMPLES. STANDARD IV	89	EXAMPLES. STANDARD VI	116
,, ,, V	99	,, ,, VII	128
METHOD OF DRAWING			
VASES	99		

CHAPTER VII

SCALE DRAWING. STANDARD IV

	PAGE		PAGE
SYLLABUS AND APPARATUS	134	DRAWING ON SQUARED	
INTRODUCTORY LESSON .	136	PAPER	147
CONSTRUCTION OF SCALES .	137	ENLARGING OR REDUCING	
LESSON	138	A GIVEN FIGURE. .	151
EXAMPLES	140	LESSON	151
DRAWING TO SCALE ON		TESTS	154
PLAIN PAPER . .	142		

CHAPTER VIII

PLANE GEOMETRY. STANDARDS V AND VII

	PAGE		PAGE
SYLLABUS AND APPARATUS.		TESTS	164
STANDARD V . .	156	SYLLABUS. STANDARD VII	166
LESSON	158	TESTS	167
EXAMPLES	159		

CHAPTER IX

SOLID GEOMETRY. STANDARDS VI AND VII

SYLLABUS AND APPARATUS.		PENDICULAR NOR	
STANDARD VI .	172	PARALLEL TO THE V.P.	185
HOW TO MAKE MODELS .	173	PLANE FIGURES . . .	187
PLAN AND ELEVATION .	176	SECTIONS . . .	189
SOLIDS STANDING ON A		TESTS	194
FACE	180	SYLLABUS. STANDARD VII	197
LESSON I . . .	180	EASY POSITIONS OF THE	
LESSON II . . .	181	CIRCLE, CYLINDER, AND	
LESSON III . .	182	CONE . . .	197
SOLIDS STANDING ON AN		THE CIRCLE . . .	198
EDGE	183	THE CYLINDER AND CONE .	200
I. EDGE PERPENDICULAR TO		SECTIONS. THE SPHERE .	201
THE V.P. . . .	183	,, THE CYLINDER	202
II. EDGE PARALLEL TO THE		,, THE CONE .	203
V.P.	183	TESTS	205
III. EDGE NEITHER PER-			

CHAPTER X

MODEL DRAWING. STANDARDS V AND VI

SYLLABUS. STANDARD V .	208	THE CYLINDER, AXIS VER-	
INTRODUCTORY LESSONS 209	211	TICAL. FIRST LESSON .	218
ARRANGEMENT OF THE		,, AXIS HORI-	
MODELS . . .	212	ZONTAL. LESSON .	220
THE CUBE. FIRST LESSON .	212	THE CONE	223
,, SECOND LESSON	214	THE BOX, OPEN BOOK, CY-	
,, THIRD LESSON .	215	LINDER AND BOARD,	
COMMON ERRORS . .	215	CONE AND SLATE, JAR,	
THE SQUARE PRISM, FRAME,		JUGS, GALLON BOTTLE,	
BOX, SLATE AND BOOK	216	ROLLER, SAUCEPAN .	224

	PAGE		PAGE
THE HEXAGONAL PRISM. AXIS VERTICAL. LESSONS	229	THE CYLINDRICAL RING	236
		VASES	237
		SYLLABUS. STANDARD VI.	242
,, AXIS HORIZONTAL	231	GROUPS AND COMMON OBJECTS	242
THE TRIANGULAR PRISM, PYRAMIDS	234		

CHAPTER XI

LIGHT AND SHADE. STANDARD VII

SYLLABUS	248	THE VASE	256
MATERIALS	248	SHADING FROM CASTS	256
FIRST LESSON	249	METHOD OF SHADING THE CAST	259
SECOND ,, THE CUBE	251		
THE CYLINDER	254		

CHAPTER XII

THE ELEMENTARY DRAWING CERTIFICATE

REQUIREMENTS FOR FIRST CLASS CERTIFICATE	262	ELEMENTARY STAGE MODEL	263
REQUIREMENTS FOR SECOND CLASS CERTIFICATE	262	ELEMENTARY STAGE OF SHADING FROM CASTS	266
ELEMENTARY STAGE FREEHAND	263	ELEMENTARY STAGE OF PRACTICAL PLANE AND SOLID GEOMETRY	267

THE
TEACHING OF DRAWING

CHAPTER I

INTRODUCTION

Now that Drawing is practically compulsory ' for boys in schools for older scholars,' as a condition of earning the annual grants, it is absolutely necessary that it should be taught intelligently, systematically, and thoroughly. By intelligent teaching is meant the training of the eye to see, the mind to think, and the hand to carry out the representation of the forms seen, or the conceptions formed in the mind. Drawing taken without method is neither useful nor interesting to the pupil, whereas when well taught it is the most pleasurable and fascinating subject taught in our schools, providing, as it does, a complete change from the ordinary routine of school work, and calling into exercise faculties which otherwise would not be properly developed.

It is now a well-established fact, based upon actual experience, that with very few exceptions all children may be taught to draw. They will not all arrive at the same pitch of efficiency—some can only crawl while others walk or even run. The advantages of a training in drawing from an educational point of view alone are quite sufficient to justify its position as a most important branch of school work. The powers of the eye, the hand, and the mind are all more fully developed ; habits of neatness and careful observation are formed, ability to perceive and appreciate beauty of form is cultivated, and the imaginative and inventive faculties are all fostered and increased. In addition to these points, we may mention its great importance in connection with industrial and commercial pursuits. It is the one part of technical education that can be well and easily done in ordinary schools.

To secure success the teacher must be enthusiastic in the work, and continually adding to his or her own store of art knowledge, or the work will become mechanical and uninteresting. Collective teaching from the blackboard will do more than anything else to stimulate the teacher's energy, and as large copies are now chiefly used for testing the work done, and the necessities of schools require large numbers to be taught simultaneously, it has now become imperative that the same methods so successfully used in teaching other subjects should be applied to drawing. The old plan of giving out copies and the teacher going round to each pupil individually, is rapidly and deservedly becoming a thing of the past. The advantages of blackboard teaching are so obvious that they scarcely need repetition : the great saving in teaching all the class the same thing at the same time, the ease with which errors can be pointed out and difficulties illustrated, the demonstration of proper methods of procedure, the stating of the reasons for the various steps taken, and the fact that the pupil is encouraged to try and imitate what he sees the teacher doing, are reasons quite sufficient to justify its adoption. The teacher is also enabled to more effectively supervise the work done, and can grade his lessons so that one naturally follows from the principles last taught.

I would here point out that it is not at all necessary that the teacher of drawing in an elementary school should be an artist : extensive practical experience has clearly shown that the ordinary teachers of the school, even when not possessed of much artistic ability, can by preparation and careful attention to good methods produce excellent results in the elementary work.

CHAPTER II

INFANT SCHOOLS

DRAWING in infant schools is somewhat beyond the scope of this book, which is written more with a view of dealing with the teaching of drawing as required in schools for older scholars by the Science and Art Department, and which the teachers must necessarily thoroughly master to meet the requirements and earn the grants. This money payment hampers and restricts in many ways, by confining all to one hard and fast line. Many would like to vary the course or introduce fresh matter, but there is not time to do both, and to earn the payments it is necessary to keep to the beaten track.

In infant schools this is not the case to so great an extent, the teacher having a little more freedom of choice. The Code now offers a grant of one shilling on the average attendance of the boys if drawing be satisfactorily taught, and as drawing is now obligatory for boys in schools for older scholars, it certainly appears more rational that the infant boys should draw instead of practising needlework. In circular 291 to H. M. Inspectors the Education Department states, '*That drawing may be taught to boys in infant schools on the lines of the Froebel system. Slates ruled with crossed lines, making squares a quarter of an inch wide, should be used, and on them the children should be made to draw perpendicular, horizontal, and diagonal lines.*

'*Interest may be given to the exercise by making figures or patterns out of the combinations developed in this practice; but the main object of the teaching should be the training of the hand to execute with nicety and precision, and the eye to discern degrees of variation in the straight lines from the perpendicular or hori-*

zontal, and to compare *and judge the relative lengths of the* lines *and the angles made by their junction.'*

Article 98*b* of the new Code prescribes *simple geometrical drawing* as one of the employments which best satisfy the third of the requirements necessary to obtain the highest grant.

Drawing can be readily carried out without much additional expense: the children simply require chequered slates ruled in squares about a quarter of an inch wide, and the teacher a blackboard ruled with red lines forming squares two inches in width. Red lines are preferable to white, as the chalk marks can be more easily distinguished. Cards and copies are only necessary for the use of the teacher, and those should be selected which show patterns and representations of objects treated in the flat—that is, showing only length and breadth. Copies showing thickness should not be taken, as infants are quite incapable either of understanding or representing these successfully.

There are numerous Kindergarten books and cards published from which the teacher may select the material for the lessons, which may also be made a powerful aid in teaching number and imparting general information.

In the following suggestive course, the patterns are largely based upon the Department's circular, as there is plenty of instructive and interesting matter embodied in the three positions of lines, upright, level, and slanting, and the great variety of combinations that may be made from them.

Endless and wearisome repetition of lines in any particular position should be avoided, as the child will probably draw the second line quite as accurately as the twentieth. The lines may also be varied in length and symmetrically arranged so as to form a simple pattern from the beginning, thus adding variety and interest to the lesson as well as training the eye in habits of observation. The examples given are not intended to be exhaustive, but merely indicative of the method of procedure. A few suggestive questions and hints are here and there given as a guide to young teachers.

The children should be taught to draw the lines from top to bottom, and from left to right. In beginning a copy, the teacher should mark the position of one of the left hand corners by a small dot on the board; this should be repeated on the slates by the pupils. The number of squares required for the line should be counted and a small dot made to indicate the end of the line. The two dots should now be joined. This method should be followed throughout, as the pupils work more accurately and systematically by this means.

As the children advance to the drawing of simple patterns, portions of the copy may be emphasised by shading, as shown in figs. 49, 50, &c. This adds to the appearance of the drawing, and is valuable as a means of directing attention to the shapes of the spaces. As further progress is made, **crayons** or **coloured** chalks may be used. For example, if the shaded spaces in figs. 49, 50, &c., are suitably coloured, a great charm is added to the work. In other copies, two colours might be used, thus producing a very pleasing effect.

Upright Lines

Question on the kind of line. '*Straight.*' '***Upright.***' Illustrate what 'upright' means by a piece of string with a weight attached. Elicit plenty of examples, and take the walls as a basis. Explain use of plumb line in building a wall. Why

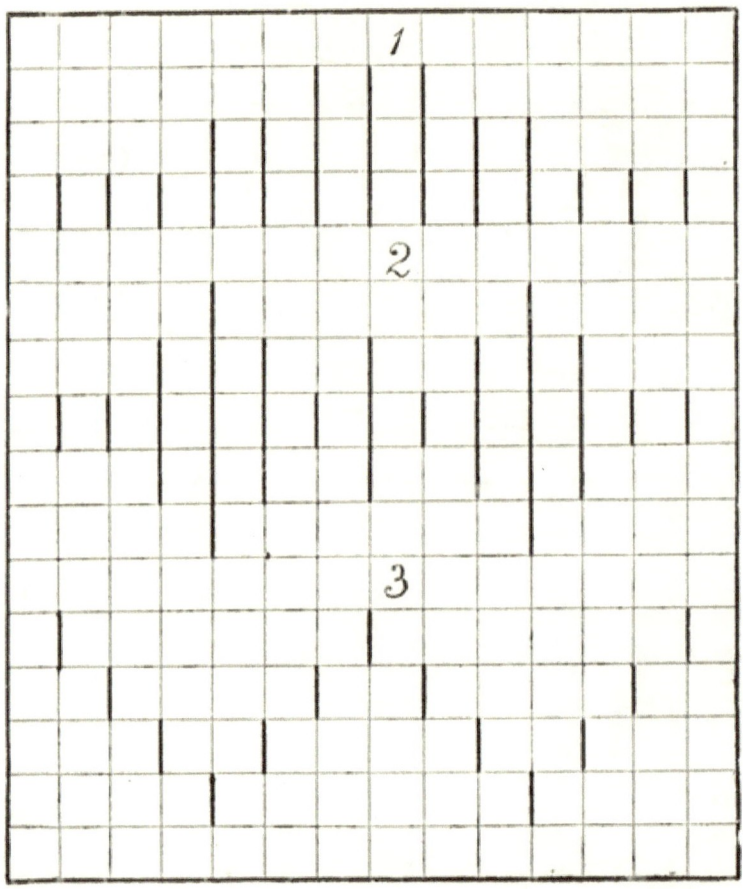

must the wall be upright? Illustrate with a pile of books or wooden bricks, showing that they will fall if not upright. What are the walls made of? What is the man called who builds with bricks, &c.? How long is the first line? How many of the first make one of the third? How many lines are there? How many are of the same length? &c.

Level Lines

Proceed in a similar manner to that suggested in dealing with upright lines.

Take the floor as the object of comparison. Elicit the various parts of the room and furniture that are level.

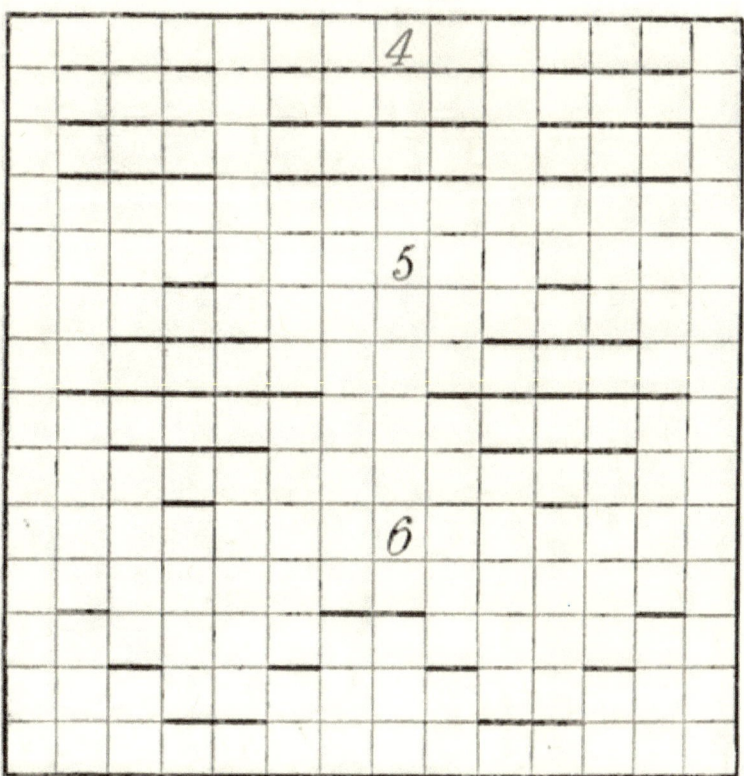

Show with a glass of water that the surface of the water is always level, while the surfaces of solids will remain in whatever position the object may be placed.

Recapitulate the facts concerning upright and level lines, and give plenty of illustrations.

Combinations of **Upright** and Level **Lines**

How many upright lines in fig. 10? How many level ones? How many lines altogether? What is the figure? What do we call the point where two sides meet? How many corners

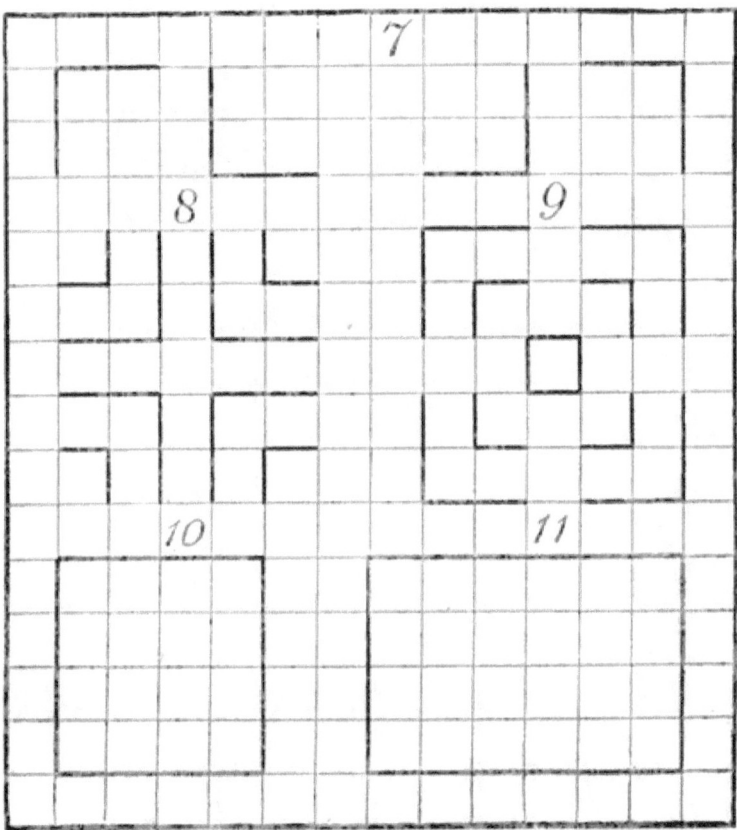

are there? Are they all alike? Elicit plenty of illustrations showing how common this corner is. Show that there are corners of different sizes, and let the children test whether the corners are right angles, by fitting in a book or a slate. Explain why fig. 11 is not a square, and draw it in different positions.

Infant Schools

Fret patterns afford a great variety of pleasing exercises, and give excellent practice in cultivating habits of observation and accuracy.

Plenty of illustrations showing the use of this ornament in

the decoration of borders of oilcloths, carpets, wall-papers, &c., can be easily shown, thus adding interest to the lesson.

The numbers placed beside the lines show the order in which they should be drawn. To make this perfectly clear, fig. 19 is shown in its three, and fig. 20 in its five, separate stages of development. Each of these steps marks a stage

Infant Schools

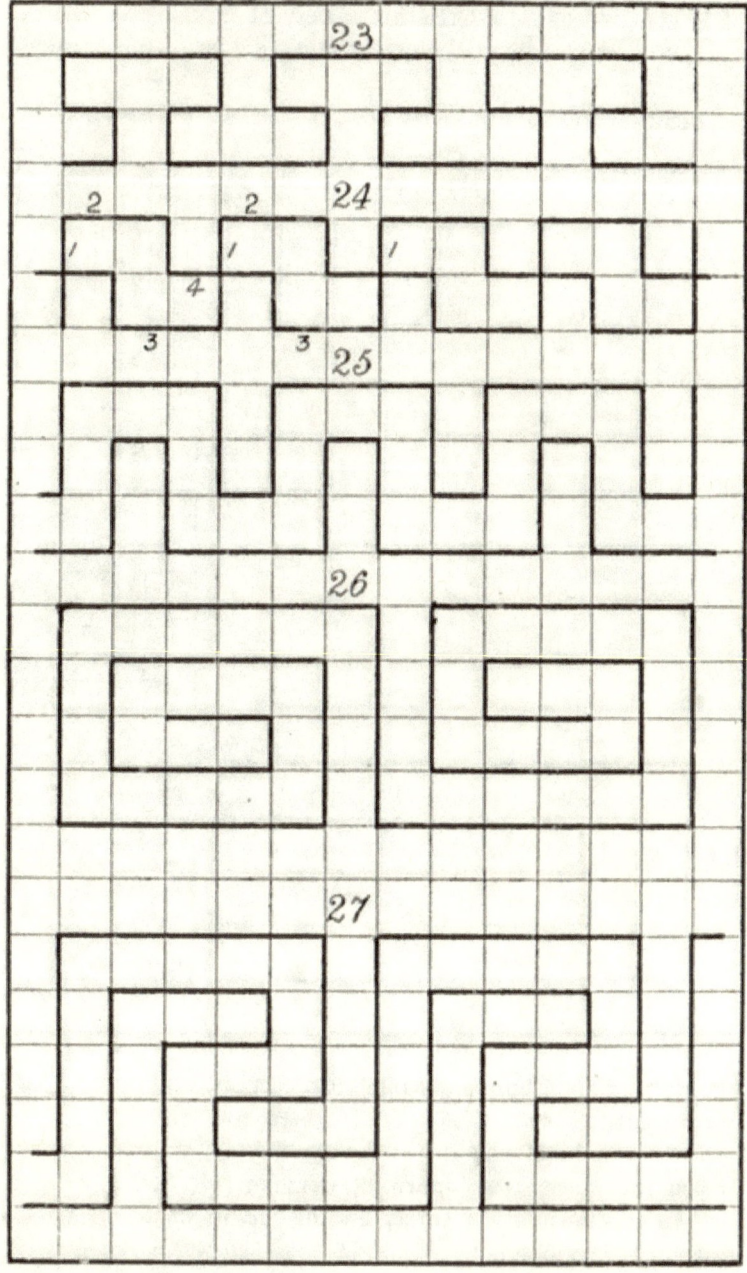

when the slates should be examined, and forms a complete copy in itself, increasing in difficulty towards the last. The

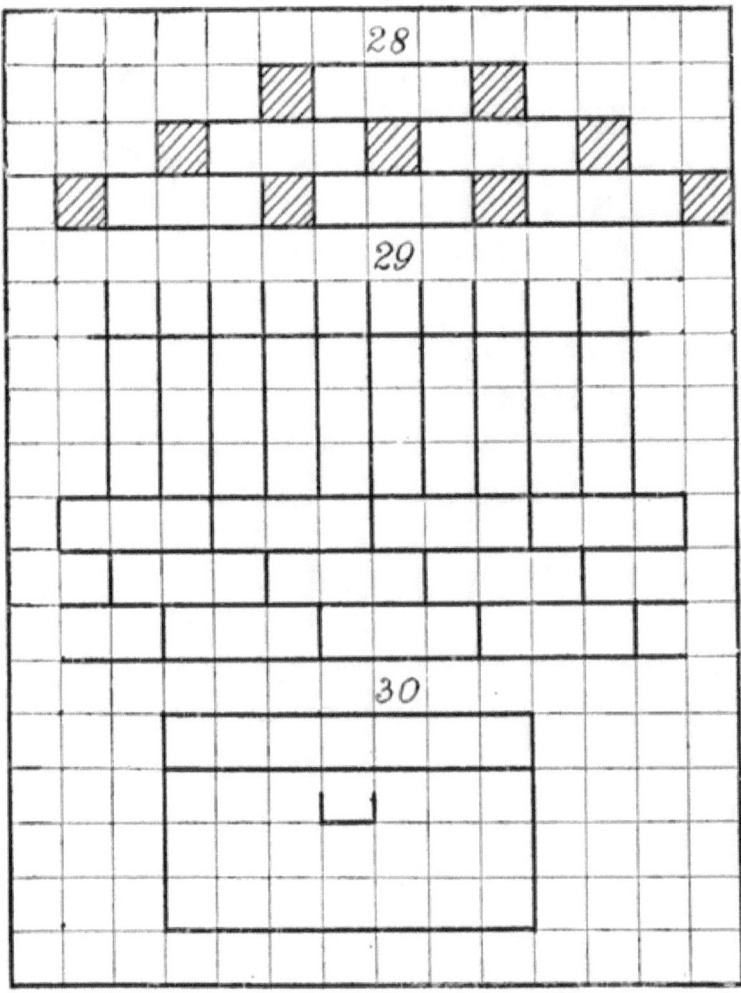

children also are being unconsciously trained in the proper method of building up a pattern.

The various objects should all be explained and questioned upon for a few minutes; for example in fig. 29, after ascertaining what object is represented, these other points might be noticed:—What are the palings made of? How many are there? How are they held up? What do they stand upon? What colour are the bricks? What else are bricks used for? What

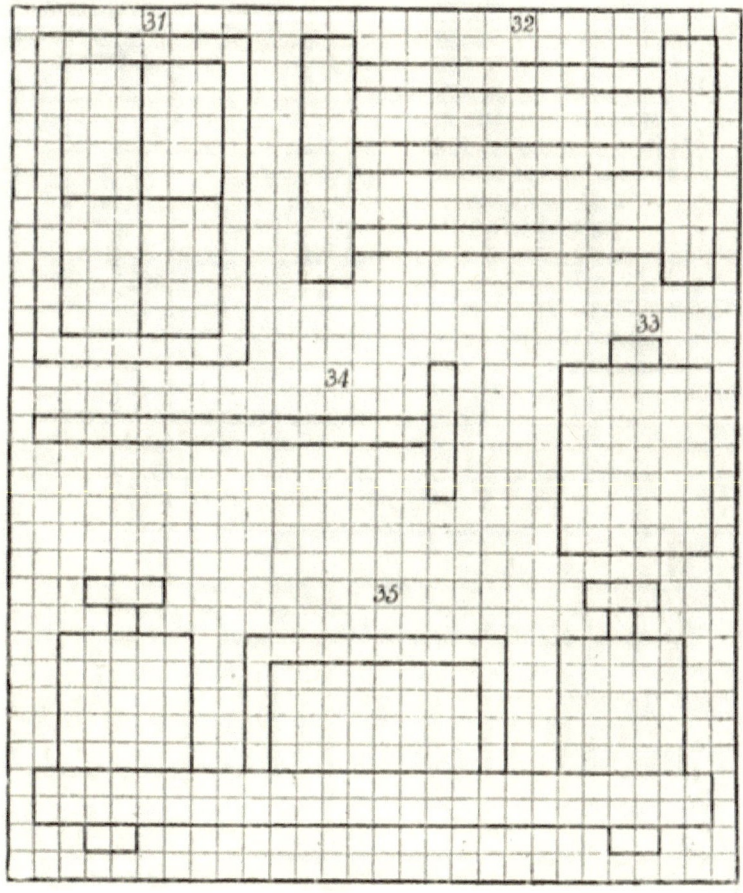

is the man called who builds the wall? How does he get the wall upright? What sort of lines do the rows of bricks make? &c. These are merely suggestions as to the manner in which interest may be aroused and the general intelligence of the class increased.

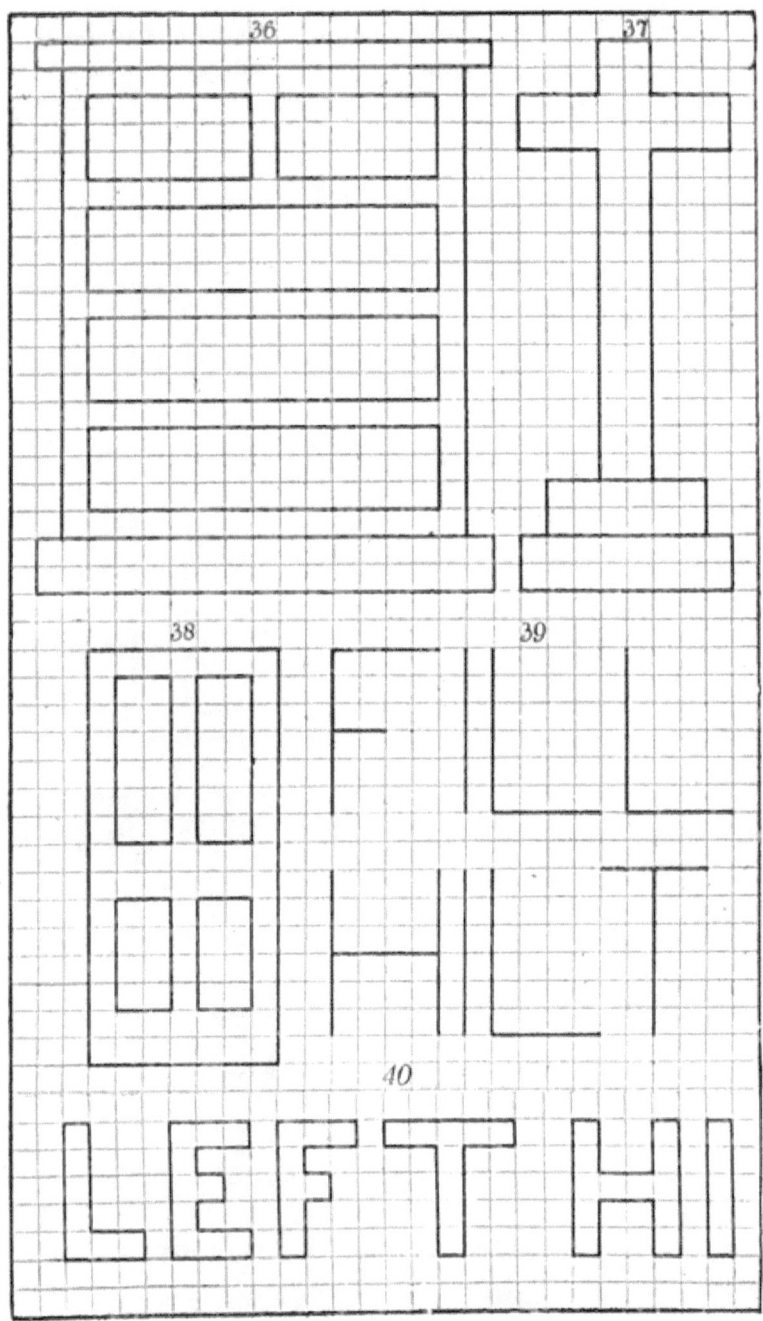

How many sides has the window in fig. 31? What is the window fixed in? What is the frame made of? What is the

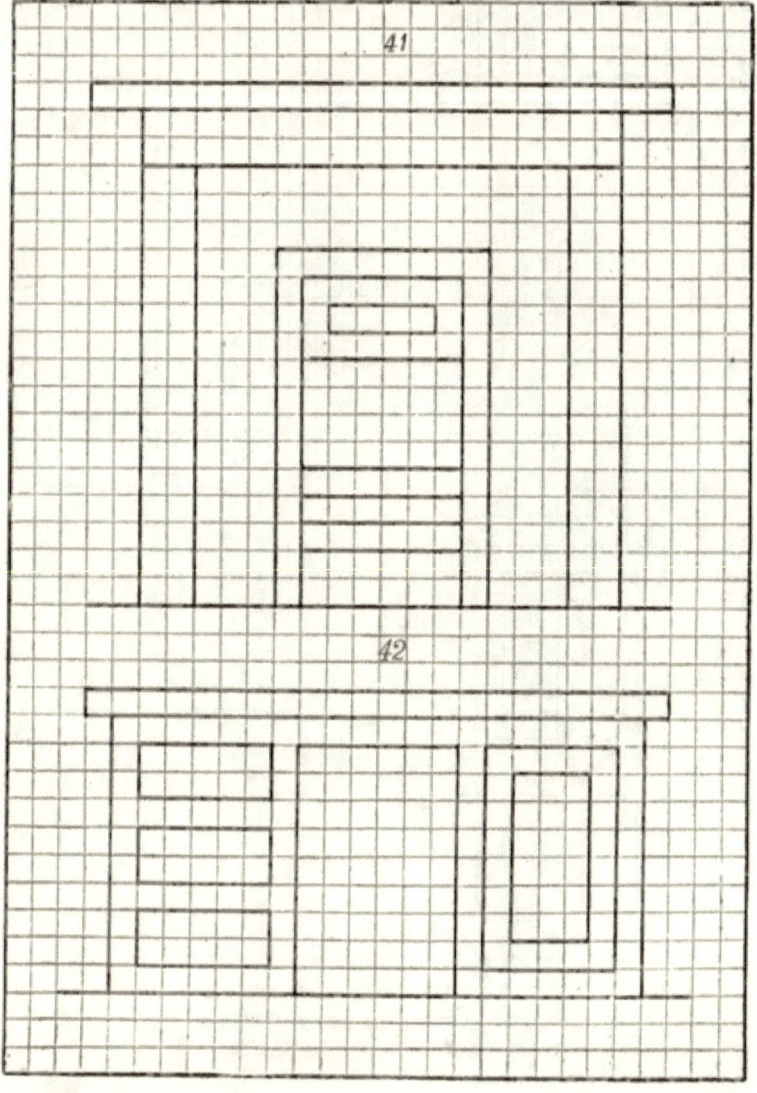

window for? Why is glass used? Why would not wood do? Question on the number of panes, position of the lines, shape of the corners, &c.

Slanting Lines

These are more difficult to draw, and at first should only be short. They greatly increase the variety of the patterns and the skill of the children, as they are now compelled to do with-

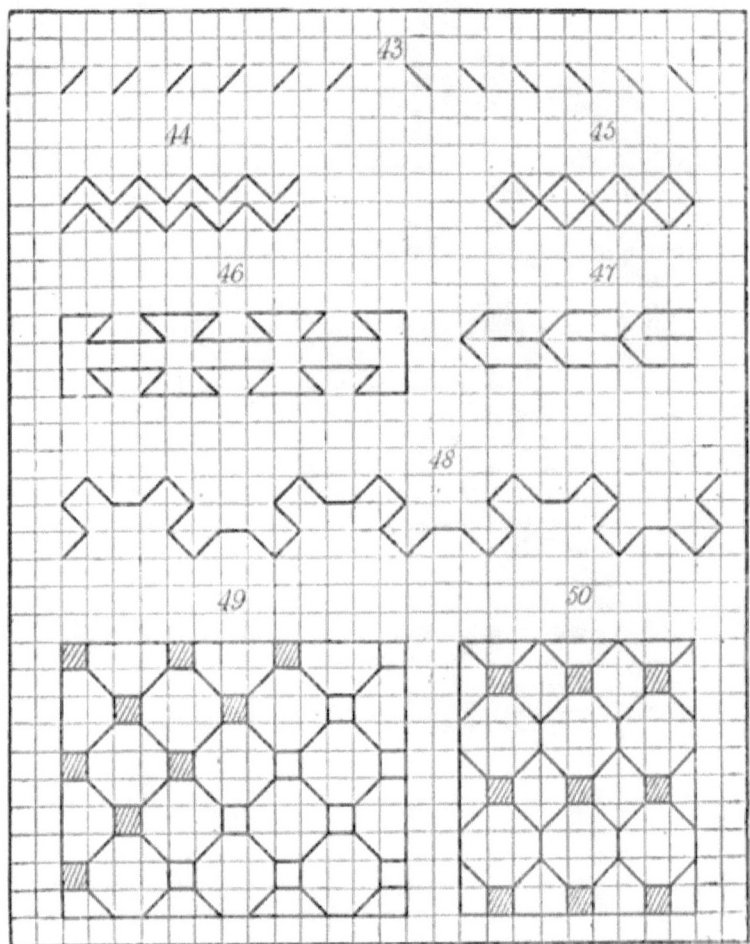

out the line to guide the pencil. The roof is a good illustration to use as a starting-point. The fact that lines slant both ways should be clearly shown.

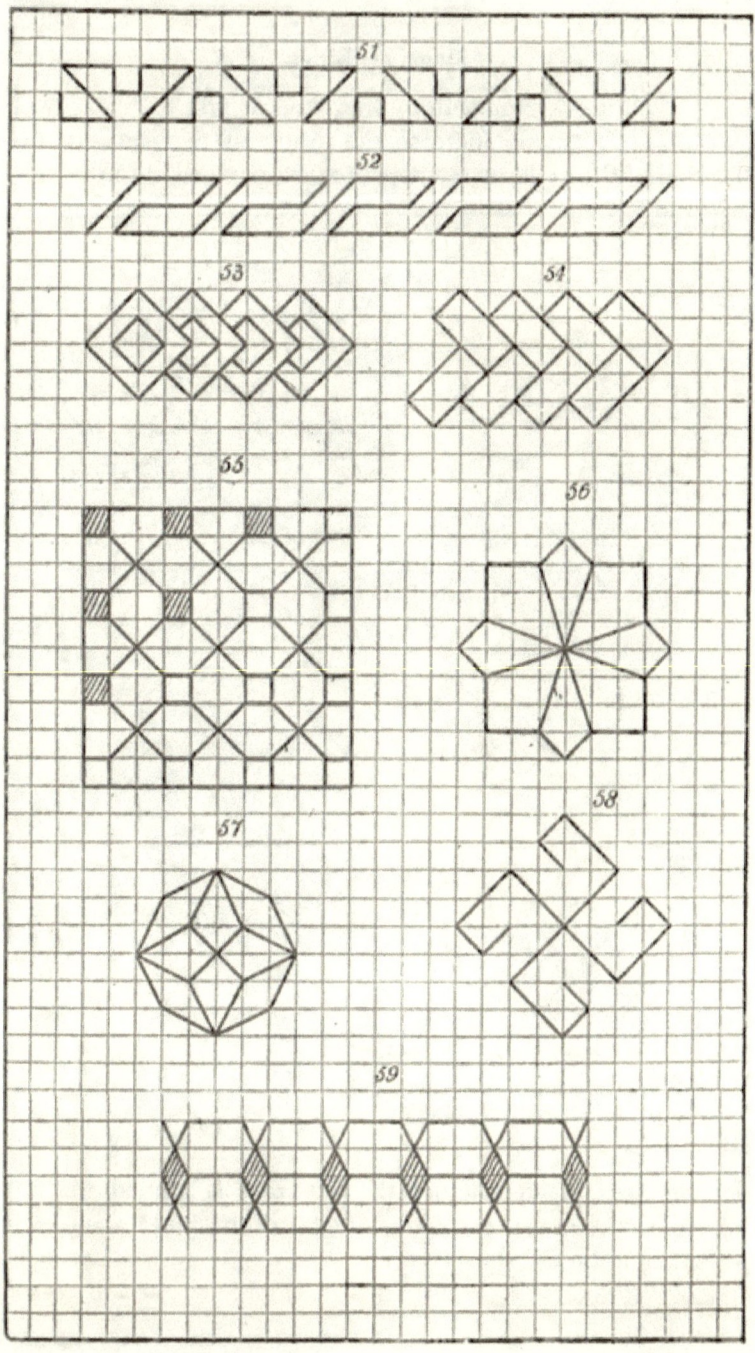

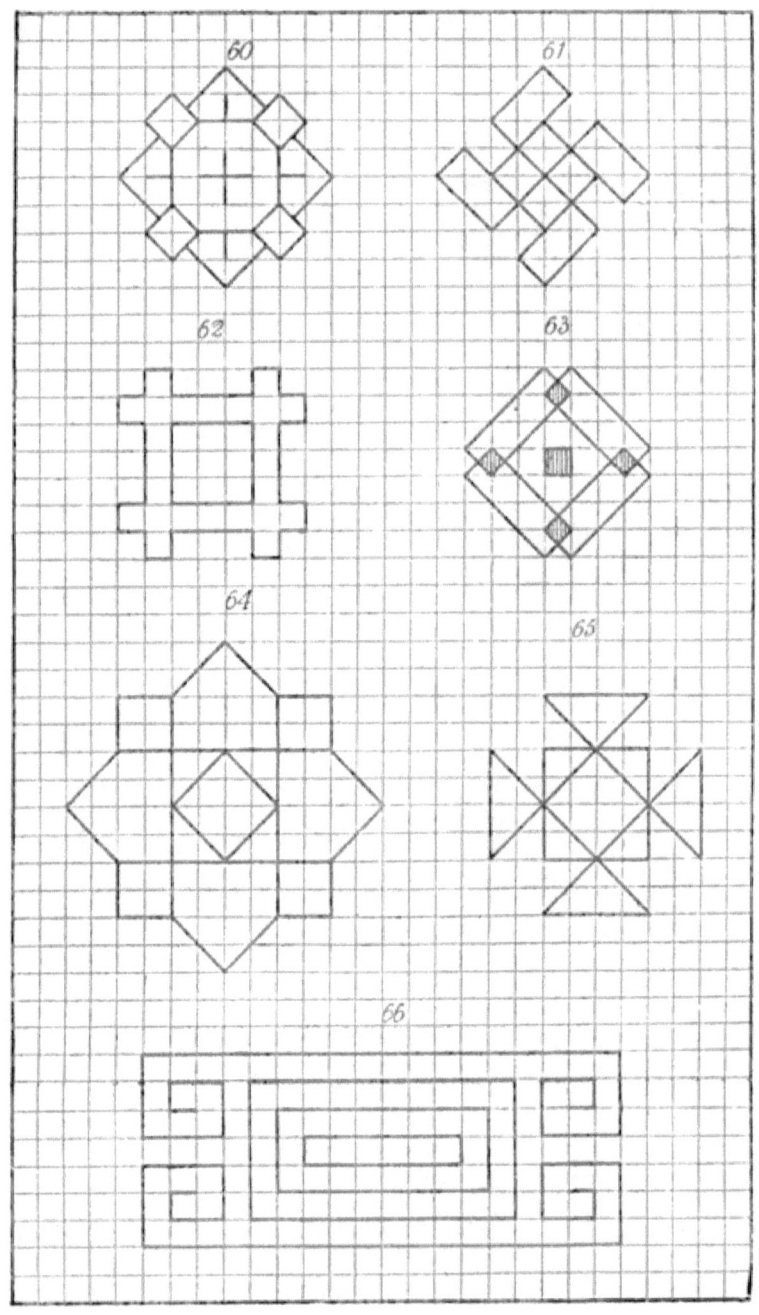

Infant Schools

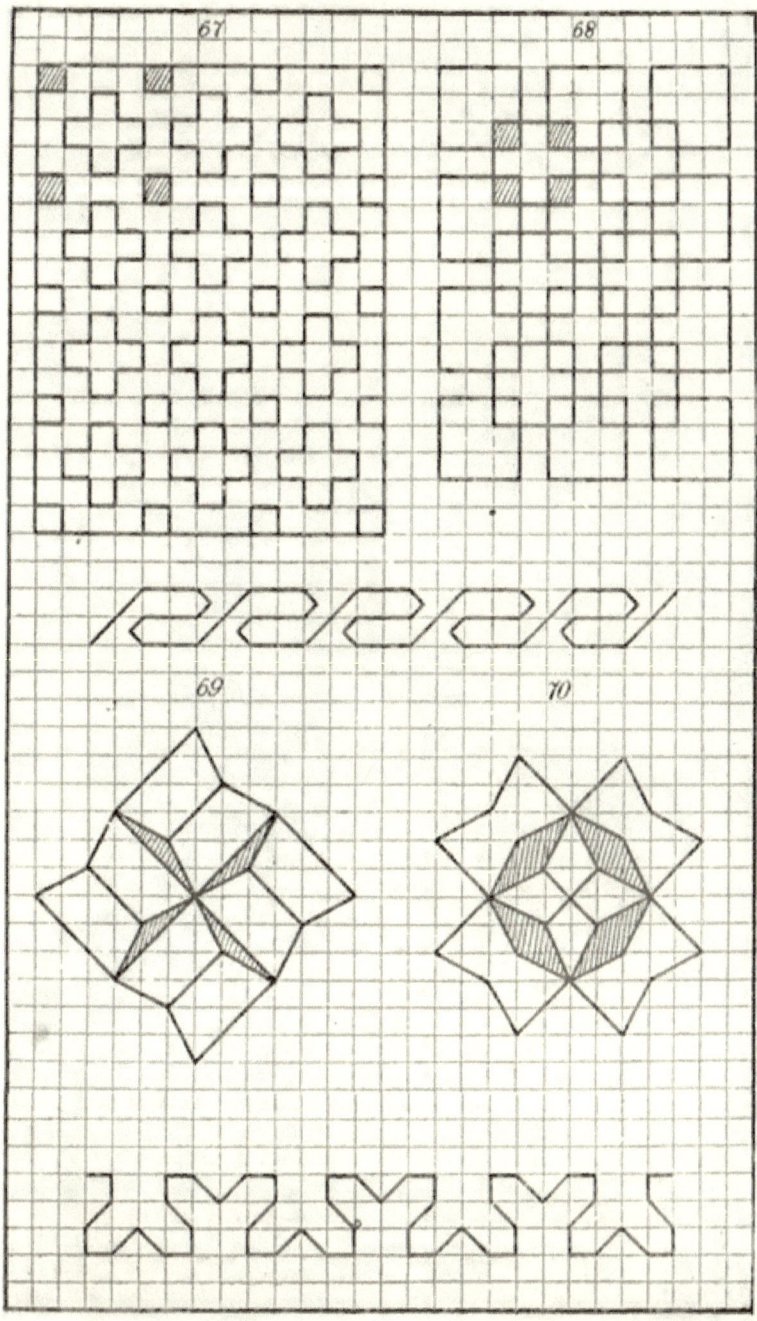

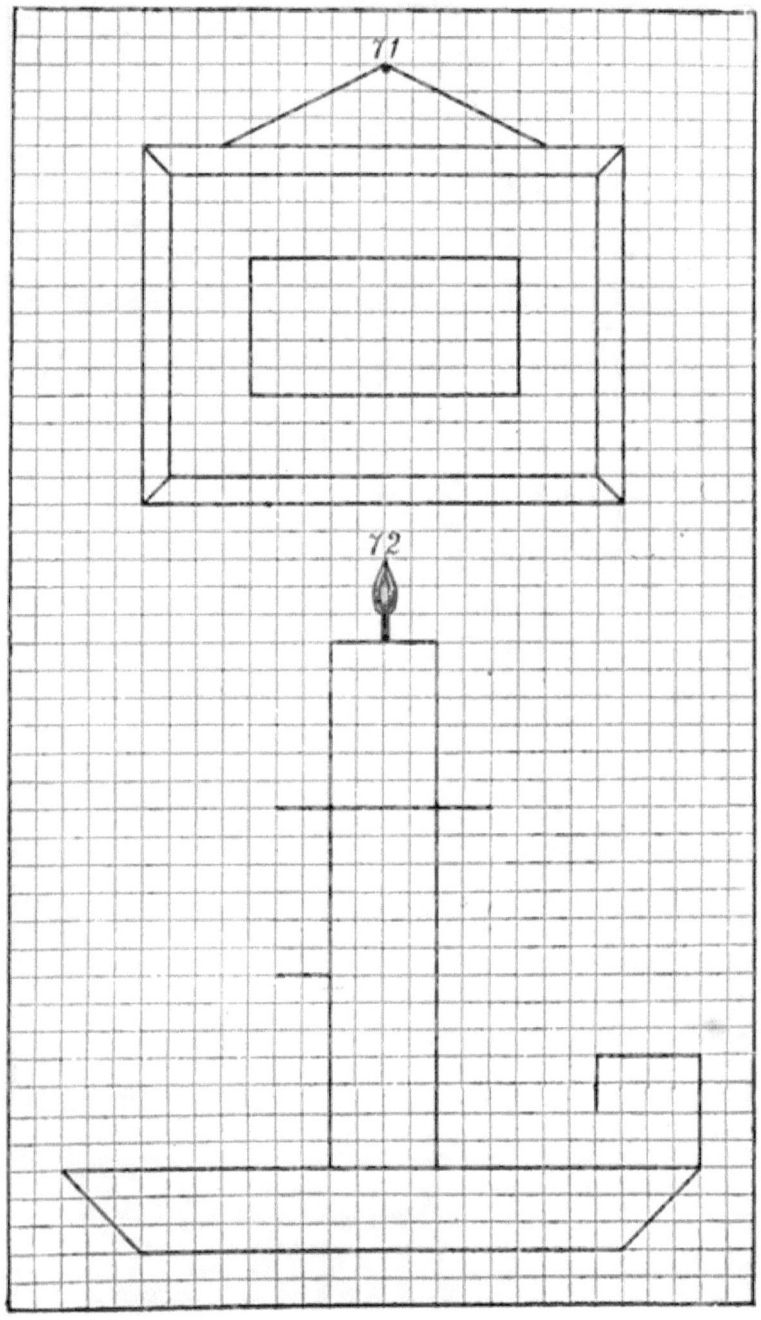

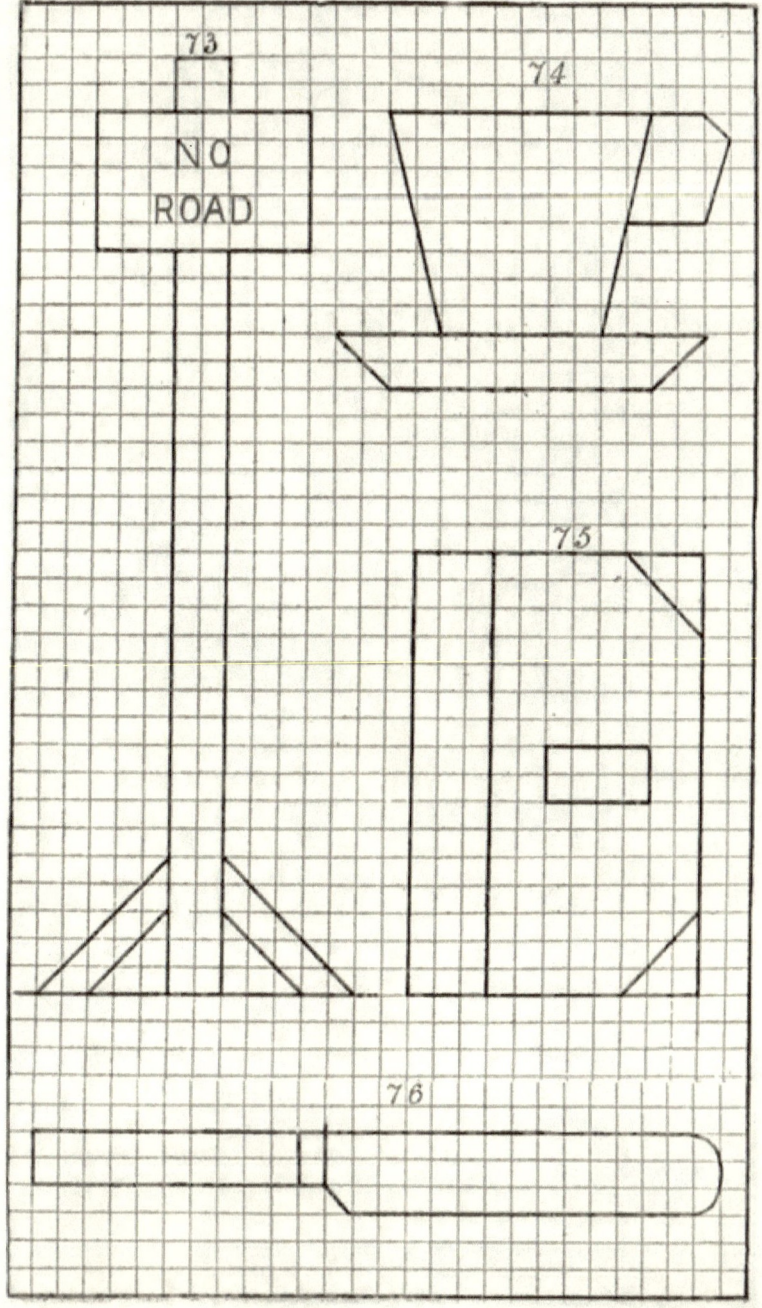

CHAPTER III

STANDARD I

Syllabus.—*Drawing, freehand and with the ruler, of lines, angles, parallels, and the simplest right-lined forms, such as some of those given in Dyce's Drawing Book.* (*To be drawn on slates.*)

The syllabus for this standard is not very difficult, and at first sight may appear rather monotonous. It will require on this account great variety of questioning, and copious illustrations showing the practical application of the examples drawn. When taught with intelligence the work is very interesting and popular with the children.

The **teacher** will require :—
1. **Large Blackboard** with a dull surface.
2. **Chalk**, sharpened to a chisel point.
3. **Large T-Square**, not less than three feet in length, divided into feet and inches. One with the blade *screwed* on the stock is preferable, especially for using with the set-squares.
4. **Demonstration Sheets.**—These save the teacher's time, and enable the pupils to see at once the object they are going to draw. If the sheets are not provided, a sketch of the copy should be placed at one corner of the board previous to the commencement of the lesson.

The **children** will require :—
1. **Slates** about ten inches by seven inches, one side of which *must* be plain.
2. **Slate-Pencils** of good quality (the bad ones scratch the slates and break easily), which should always be well sharpened and used for **drawing** only. When less than three inches in

length, they should not be used unless with a holder, as a short pencil cannot be used with freedom.

3. **Rulers.**—These should be marked in inches, and if used for this standard only, halves and quarters will be the only subdivisions needed. They should not exceed nine inches in length, the edge should be bevelled, the scale marks and figures should be clear and distinct, with the inch marks running quite across the ruler from edge to edge.

Introductory Lesson

Before children can begin to use the ruler, it is absolutely necessary that they should thoroughly understand the meaning of the various marks upon it. This may be made not only an instructive, but also an exceedingly interesting lesson to young children. The questioning must be smart and definite, and accompanied with plenty of practical applications of the various points elicited. The following lesson is suggestive of the manner in which the subject should be dealt with.

It must be carefully borne in mind that the children are young, and only beginning, and are therefore capable of receiving information in but small quantities, and when expressed in the clearest and simplest language. Similar lessons will be found to be frequently necessary in the early stages of teaching the subject.

What is this? '*It is a ruler.*'

(Insist upon the answer being given in the form of a sentence as far as possible.)

What can you tell me about its edges? '*They are straight.*'

Show a round ruler. Elicit that the ruler used for drawing with is flat.

Why is it flat? '*It can be kept firmly on the slate.*'

Elicit other examples of flat surfaces.

Are the two flat surfaces of the ruler alike? '*No.*'

What is the difference between them? '*One side has marks and figures upon it.*'

Are the marks all alike?

How many long marks are there?

The teacher should now draw a representation of the ruler on the board, and place the long marks upon it, as indicated on the children's rulers.

How many parts do the long marks divide the ruler into?

Note.—This is a very important question, and the difference between the marks and the parts should be clearly shown, as it is a very common error for children, even in the higher standards, to confuse the marks with the parts which they separate. If there be any difficulty fold a strip of paper into as many parts as there are on the ruler, cut them up, and let the children count them.

What do you notice near the marks? '*Figures.*'

Name the figures. Explain that the figures indicate the number of parts that the ruler is divided into, and that each of these parts is called an inch.

How many inches make a foot? Show a foot ruler.

How many feet high is the door?

Take other illustrations, and let the objects be rapidly measured after the children have first estimated the distances.

How many inches long is the book? Measure it.

How many inches can you span? &c.

How many half-pennies can be placed on the ruler? (Half-penny = 1 inch in diameter.)

Now let the children mark several points, *a*, *b*, *c*, *d*, on the left hand side of their slates. From *a* draw a line 2 inches, from *b* 4 inches, from *c* 5 inches, and from *d* 6 inches in length respectively.

The slates should be shown, and rapidly scanned after each line has been drawn.

The teacher now returns to the blackboard representation of the ruler, and marks the half-inches.

How many parts have I divided the inch into?

What would you call each part?

Hold up your rulers and count each half-inch, pointing them out with your pencils.

How many half-inches is the whole ruler divided into?

Now mark points as before, and draw lines of $2\frac{1}{2}$, $4\frac{1}{2}$, $6\frac{1}{2}$, and $1\frac{1}{2}$ inches in length respectively.

Next mark the **quarter-inches,** and proceed in a similar manner.

Smaller divisions should not be taken for this standard. If the children are carefully and systematically taught after this fashion, there will be no difficulty as to the practical use of the ruler.

Method of Using the Pencil and Ruler.—The ruler must always be placed with the bevelled edge upwards, and held firmly in position with the fingers well distributed, and placed near the *centre* of the ruler, as shown in the illustration, and *not at the end*.

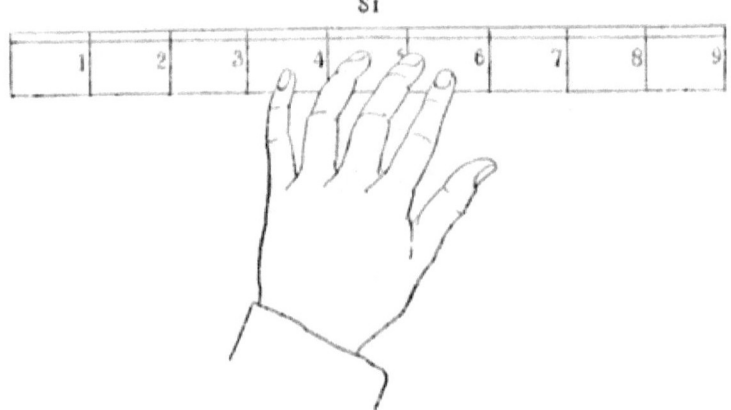

The pencil should be held sloping at about an angle of 60°, with its *point close to the edge* of the ruler. In ruling the lines be careful to insist that the pupils always rule along the *upper edge*, and from *left to right* or from *top to bottom*.

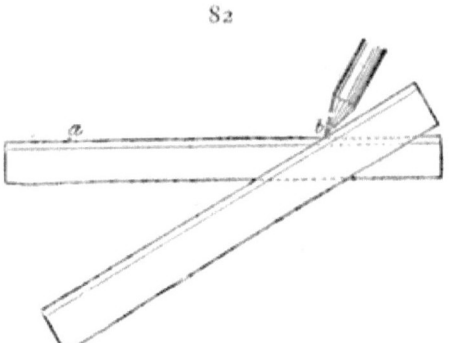

The teacher should show carefully the method of joining two points. Place two points, *a* and *b*, on the board, and place the point of the chalk on *b*; now place the bevelled edge of the ruler against the point of the chalk, keep the chalk firm, and move the end of the ruler up until it reaches point *a*. Hold the ruler firm, remove the chalk to *a*, and rule the line. This is rather difficult for beginners, but it will save a considerable amount of time and trouble if persevered with at first. Examples should now be given until the children can join the points readily.

Care must be taken that the points to be joined are not covered up by the ruler. The teacher may now give the definition. **A** straight line *is the shortest distance between two points.*

The opportunity should be taken here to show that all lines drawn with the ruler are straight lines, no matter what their direction may be, as children frequently confuse the term *straight* with *level* and *upright*.

Lengthening Lines.—To lengthen a line the pencil and ruler should be used in the same manner as in joining two points. Place the pencil on the line, adjust the ruler as in fig. 82, and rule to the required length without showing the joining.

First Drawing Exercise.—The children may now proceed to the first exercise suggested in the 'Illustrated Syllabus,' viz. :—To draw a number of parallel lines in various positions.

1. **Horizontal Lines.**—Mark two points, *a* and *b*, one inch and a half from the top of the slate, and through these points rule a line four inches long, as shown in the previous exercise. Set off distances of one inch with the ruler from each end of the line, *ab*. [Place the ruler for setting off the distances, as shown in fig. 83, with the inch mark on the line ; the distances can then be quickly marked without moving the ruler.] Rule the lines firmly and evenly, and insist upon all leaving the line when ruled. *Allow no rubbing out.* It is far better to leave the line when ruled, even if not quite accurate, than to attempt to alter it by rubbing out, as the children not only

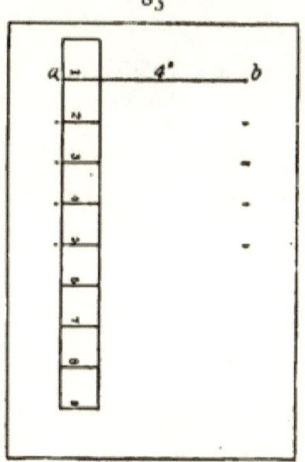

smudge the slate, but waste time by getting behind with their work.

Commendation must be freely distributed, as little children especially are stimulated to greater emulation by judicious praise. Four or five lines only should be drawn at first, or the exercise becomes wearisome. A short lesson with plenty of questions and illustrations is the most profitable.

Questions of the following character are suggested.

How many lines are there?

What sort of lines are they? '*They are straight lines.*'

What is a straight line? '***The shortest distance** between two points.*'

How long is each of the lines?

What else can you tell me about them? '*They are all the same length.*'

Explain the term 'equal.'

What position are the lines in? '*Level.*'

Explain the meaning of 'level,' and show how the surface of water keeps level even when the vessel containing it is tilted to one side.

Tell me something else that is level. '*The floor.*'

Elicit numerous other examples.

What else can you tell me about the lines, besides being straight, equal, and level? '*They are the same distance apart.*'

Explain the term 'parallel.'

What is parallel to the floor? '*The ceiling.*'

Educe plenty of examples, such as opposite walls, edges of books, slates, desks, boards, windows, railway lines, &c.

The definition of parallel lines may now be given.

The term *horizontal* may be used as well as level; children use it quite as readily. The meaning of horizon must be clearly given, and if the children live near, or have been to the sea-side, they will have no difficulty in realising what the horizon is.

All the terms used should be put on the board, and copied by the pupils, but it is not desirable to write up definitions for young children. Frequent questioning is more interesting, and secures the desired result just as well.

2. **Vertical Lines.**—Show that lines may be in other positions besides being level by referring to the walls, roofs, &c. Draw upright or vertical lines in a similar manner to that adopted for the horizontal lines in fig. 83.

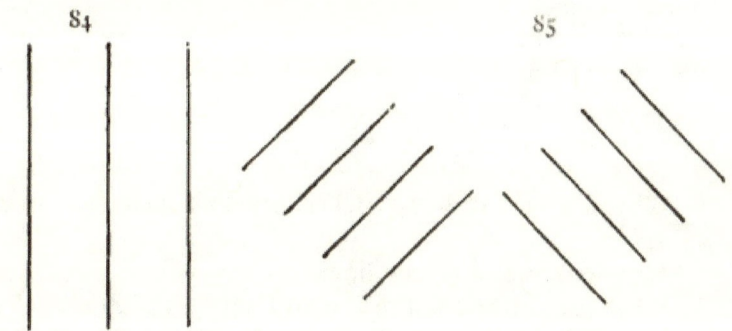

3. **Oblique Lines.**—Draw in a similar fashion to the preceding, and show that they may slope either way. It will probably be easier for the children to turn the slate into a sloping position with a corner towards them in doing this exercise.

The floor and the walls give two useful comparisons for horizontal and vertical lines. The use of the plumb line by workmen should be referred to, and it should be used to test whether objects in the room, or lines on the blackboard, are vertical.

It is now very good practice to let the children draw parallel lines by judging the distance with the eye only. To do this, let them first mark the points for the left-hand end of the lines only before ruling.

Freehand Drawing of Parallel Lines.—The children will now be fairly familiar with the ruler and the various terms relating to lines, and may proceed to the real difficulty, viz.—the drawing of straight lines without the aid of the ruler. In teaching, it is undoubtedly much easier to do the ruled copy first, and then proceed to the freehand. At examinations the freehand is generally required to be drawn first.

The pencil should be held freely, not close to the point, and making an acute angle with the slate. The points for the first line should then be marked, and the child taught to guide his pencil by noticing the top of the slate. Then, after carefully taking the pencil across from point to point without marking the slate, the line should be *lightly* drawn across without joinings or stopping. The hand must not lie upon the slate, but the little finger may just touch to ensure steadiness to the hand. Now mark the position of the next line, and draw it in a similar manner. The lines in the earlier lessons should not be drawn too long. Practice will enable the children to draw longer lines successfully. If the ends of the parallel lines be joined a simple pattern is at once formed, and additional interest is thereby given to the lesson.

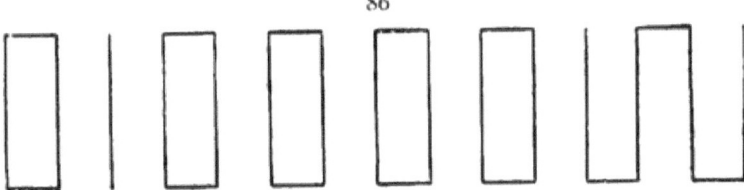

86

Arrangement of the **Drawing**.—It is perhaps advisable to call attention here to the arrangement of the drawing on the slates. Some inspectors prefer the ruler and freehand drawings to be both on the same side of the slate, others require each drawing to fill the slate. The latter plan is much more difficult,

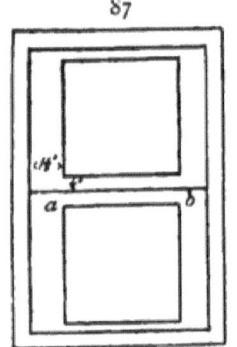

87

as the lines run to a considerable length, but it has the advantage of securing much better and bolder work.

If the two are required on the same side, divide the slate into two parts by setting off five inches from the top, at each side of the slate, and ruling a line across. Now, if the figure required be a square of four inch sides, let the children draw the first line half-an-inch from the dividing line, commencing about one and a half inches from the left-hand side of the slate. This will ensure the drawing being placed nicely on the slate, thus adding considerably to its appearance, and also training the children to place their work symmetrically. If the freehand drawing be the same figure, first **draw the top line** *ab*, the square above forming a guide.

When, however, only one drawing is required on each side, reserve the plain side of the slate for the freehand, and work the ruled drawing on the other side. The position of the drawing on the slate must always be thought out **before beginning**. A six-inch square placed as in **fig. 88** is certainly more effective than one placed as in fig. 89.

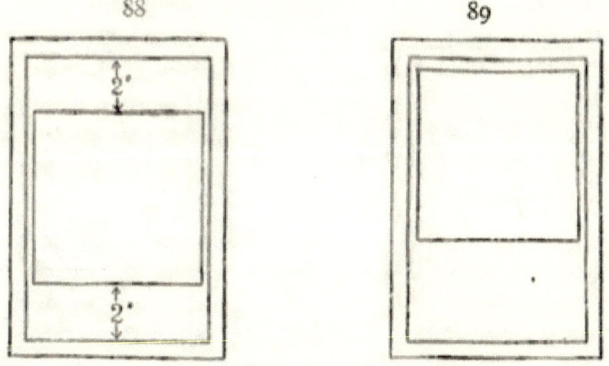

Angles.—These should now be taken and drawn in various positions, both **freehand** and with the ruler, and arranged on the slates according to the methods suggested.

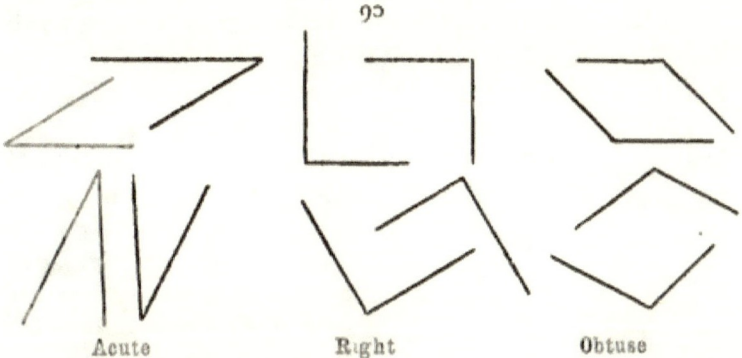

Acute　　　　　Right　　　　　Obtuse

The children must be able to recognise and draw the angles in any position.

In explaining the three **kinds** of angles it **is** advisable to commence with the *right* angle, and show that it is the corner made by the *upright* wall meeting the *level* floor, and that the largest angle of the set-square will exactly fit it. Numerous examples should now be elicited and tested with the set-square. The fact should be pointed out that all right angles are equal, irrespective of the length or position of the lines forming them. The term **perpendicular** may now be explained, and the difference **between** vertical and perpendicular pointed out, that whereas *vertical* means upright and refers to one position of the line only, *perpendicular* means that a line is at right angles to some **other** line and **may be in** any position. This is an exceedingly common error, and should be clearly explained and well illustrated. A **perpendicular line** may now be defined as *a straight line at right angles* to another straight line.

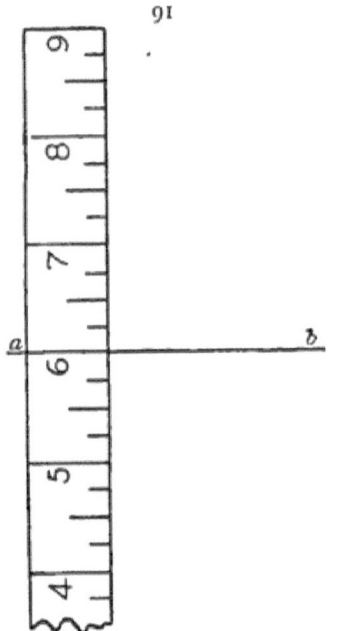

91

Acute and Obtuse angles should be defined as being respectively *less* or *greater* than a right angle. An open book furnishes a ready illustration ; open it at a right angle and test it with the set-square, and then obtain the acute and obtuse angles. The fact should be constantly before the pupil that the lengths of the lines forming the angle do not regulate its size.

Construction of **the right angle.**—On paper the set-square should always be used, but on slates it will probably be found more convenient to use the ruler only, as the slate frame prevents the set-square from being used easily. To construct a right angle with the aid of the ruler only, first draw *ab* (fig. 91). Now place the ruler so that one of the marks showing the inches, which runs right across the ruler at right angles to its edges, exactly coincides with the line *ab* A perpendicular may now be drawn of any given length. It is most essential that the teacher should see that the line on the ruler exactly coincides with the line first drawn.

The Square

Directly the construction of the right angle is understood, its combinations may at once be proceeded with. The square affords a large number of exercises, as a great variety of simple patterns may be made from it. The position of the starting line should receive careful attention; this will, of course, depend upon the size of the square to be drawn. The remarks on the 'arrangement of the drawing,' **figs. 87, 88,** and **89,** will make clear what is necessary to be done. The teacher must always see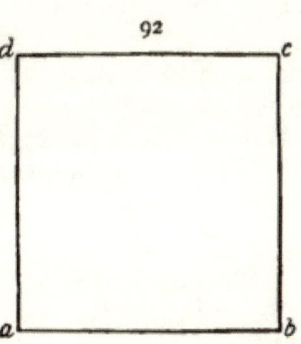
that the starting line is properly placed. To draw the square commence with line *ab*, placed as previously directed; now place the ruler as in fig. 91 and obtain *ad* and *bc*. Make them equal to *ab*, and complete the figure by joining *d* with *c*. Plenty of questions should be given as the drawing proceeds, which should be recapitulated and supplemented at the end of the lesson.

What sort of a line is *ab*? '*Straight and also horizontal.*'

Then, if *ab* be horizontal, what will be the position of *ad*? '*Vertical.*'

What other line in the figure is vertical?

What else do you notice about *ad* and *bc*? '*They are parallel.*'

In what position is *dc*?

If *ad* be at right angles to *ab*, what else may be said about it? '*It is perpendicular to ab.*'

How many right angles does the figure contain?

How many equal sides?

What is the figure called?

D

Then a **square** *is a figure with four equal sides and four equal angles.*

Particular attention must be given to the *firmness and even thickness* of the lines, and to the accuracy of the joinings at the angles.

The square should now be drawn *freehand*, following the same method, but starting from the middle line as suggested in fig. 87.

Dictation of Drawing.—This is an exceedingly useful exercise, as it keeps all the class together, stimulates the intelligence, compels the children to think and act promptly, and affords an excellent method of testing whether the work has been thoroughly mastered. The following examples will show what is meant : the teacher can, of course, vary them in an infinite variety of ways.

1. Mark a point near the bottom of the slate one inch from the left hand side. From this point draw a horizontal line, five inches long. From each end of the line draw upright lines four inches long. Join the ends of these lines.

2. Draw a vertical line four inches long down the middle of the slate. From the top of this line draw a line to the left at right angles to it, and two inches long. Find the middle of the vertical line with your ruler. Join this point with the end of the two-inch line.

3. Draw a square of six-inch sides. Find the middle of each side with your ruler. Join the middle point of the bottom side of the square with the middle point of the side parallel to it.

Diameters and Diagonals.—The **diameter** of a square *is a line joining the centres of the opposite sides.*

93

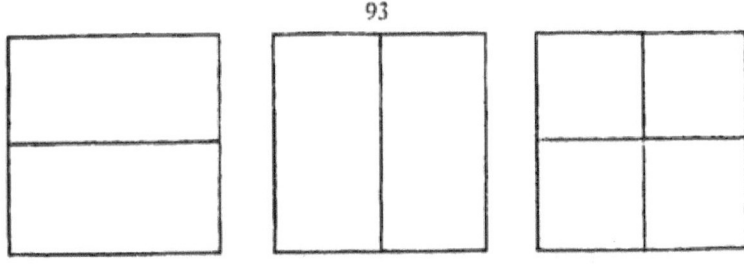

In drawing the ruled examples, bisect the sides with the aid of the ruler. In the freehand the sides of the square must be carefully bisected by trial.

The **diagonal** *joins the opposite corners*, and is much more difficult to draw, the tendency being to curve the line outwards from the hand.

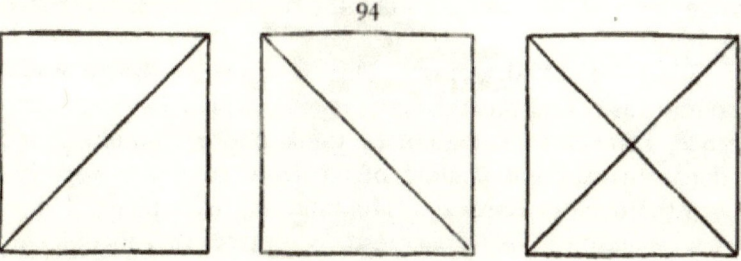

94

The pencil should be carried across from corner to corner without touching the slate before putting in the line. It will assist the beginner if the slate be turned so that the diagonals would be in a horizontal position. It is not, however, a good plan to allow the children to turn their slates or papers to any great extent, as after practice they can draw the line just as readily in one direction as another, and greater power and freedom in using the pencil is acquired by keeping the paper in the same position.

Lines Intersecting at Right Angles

Fig. 95.—First draw the vertical line. Bisect it and draw

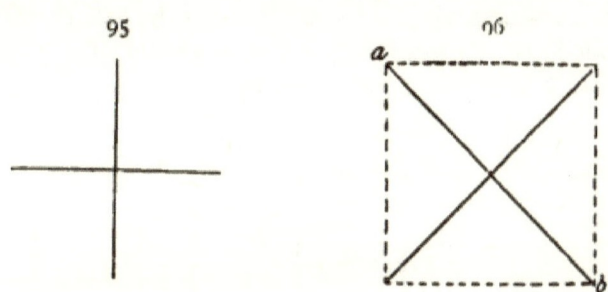

the horizontal line, using the ruler to get the right angle as in fig. 91. For the *freehand* proceed in a similar manner.

Fig. 96.—The square shown in dotted line should be very

lightly drawn, and the diagonals inserted. In the *freehand* example, the square should then be carefully cleaned out. If, however, the length of the lines were given, then first draw *ab*, sloping as nearly as possible in the given position, and obtain the other line at right angles to it, in the same manner as in the preceding figure.

Fig. 97.—Draw the dotted square, insert the diameters and diagonals, and for the *freehand* clean out the parts shown in dotted line, taking care to leave all the lines of equal length.

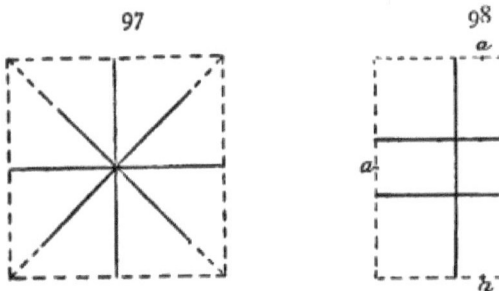

Fig. 98.—Draw the square, set off the widths either from the centres, *a*, of the sides, or from the angles, whichever may be most convenient : the distance between the lines and the size of the square will determine this. For the *freehand*, the best plan will be to set off the distance on each side of the point *a*, and then draw the lines.

Fig. 99.—Draw the square, set off equal distances on each side from the angles, and join the points. This figure is occasionally set to be drawn without the aid of the square. It then forms a most difficult exercise. The best way to proceed is to fix point *a* in the middle of the slate. Incline the slate and mark points *b* and *c* in the same line as *a*, and equidistant from it. Through *b* and *c* draw parallel lines. Obtain *de* at right angles to *bc*, and make *ad* and *ae* equal to *ac* and *ab*. Through *d* and *e* draw lines at right angles to the other lines. Or the small square formed by the intersec-

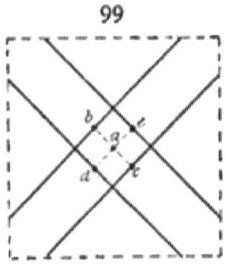

tion of the lines may be drawn first, and its sides produced equally on each side.

The Bisection and Trisection of the Right Angle

These problems should now be taken. The right angle may be **bisected** by completing the square and drawing the diagonal; afterwards cleaning out the portions in dotted line (fig. 100). A better and easier plan is to use the 45° set-square. First, obtain the right angle, and then use the ruler and set-square as shown in fig. 101.

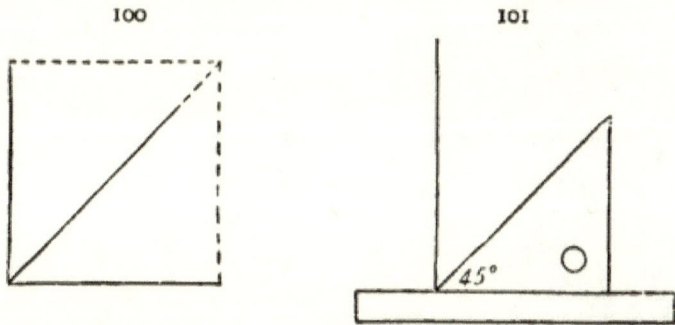

To **trisect** the right angle the set-square with the angle of 30° should be used, as it is the only really quick and accurate method by which the operation can be performed. The only point that requires careful watching is to see that the lines are drawn true from the angle. The method of procedure is as

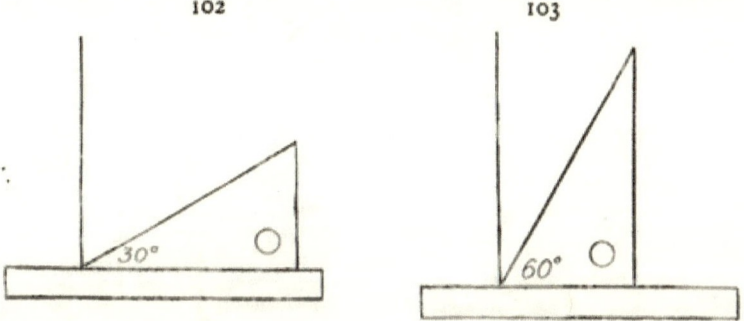

follows. Draw the right angle as large as the space will allow. Place the ruler as in fig. 102, but not too close to the line. Adjust the set-square with the angle of 30° as shown, and rule a line. Now reverse the set-square (still keeping the ruler firmly in its place), place it with the angle of 60° in the right angle, and rule the second line (fig. 103). This problem should be practised by the pupils several times, until they can do it readily and quickly.

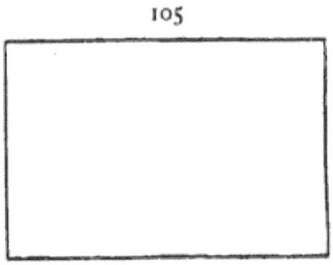

For *freehand*, this is an exceedingly difficult copy. The simplest plan is to estimate the widths between the lines, by marking points *a* and *b*, and drawing from them short lines to the angle. If the distances appear correct, then produce the lines. Children require to perform this operation a number of times before they can estimate the distances with accuracy.

The Rectangle

This figure will present no fresh difficulties to the pupils after the square has been dealt with.

Various exercises are now given, many of which have been set for examination. The teacher can multiply these in a variety of ways. It is not so necessary for the pupils to practise a large number of exercises, as to thoroughly understand the best methods of obtaining lines in particular directions with ease and accuracy.

The dotted lines show the construction necessary to obtain the lines of the figure. They should not be drawn by the pupils.

Fig. 139.—The square in this position is much more difficult to draw. It is necessary to obtain the diagonals first. Draw *ab* of the required length. Bisect it with the ruler, and draw *cd* at right angles. Make *cd* equal to *ab*, and join the ends of

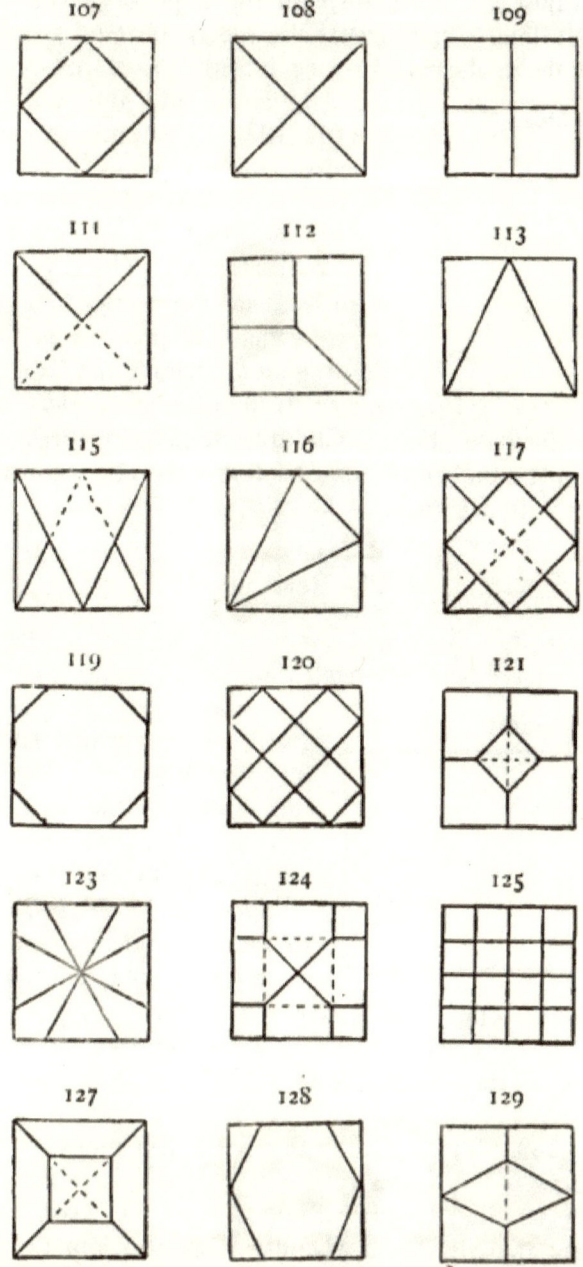

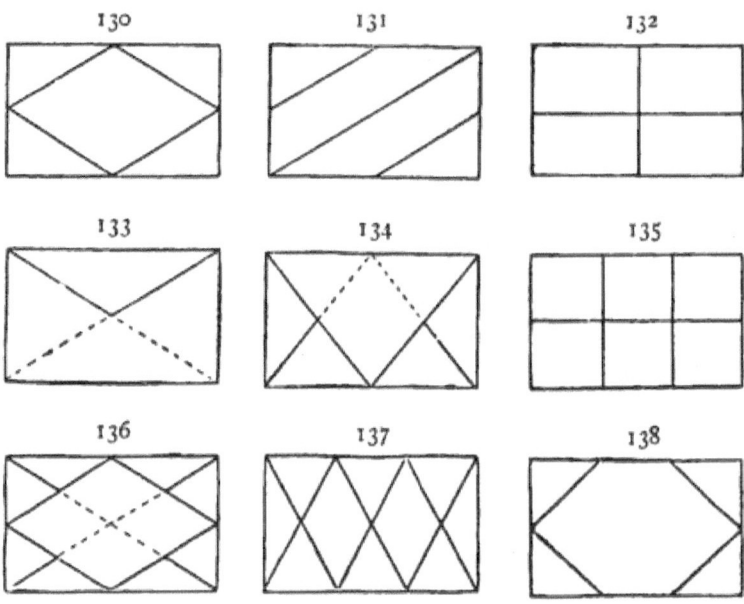

the lines. The construction lines should not be rubbed out in these figures.

Fig. 140.—Draw the diagonals as before, and complete the square. To obtain the lines ac and bd, the distances, eg and gf

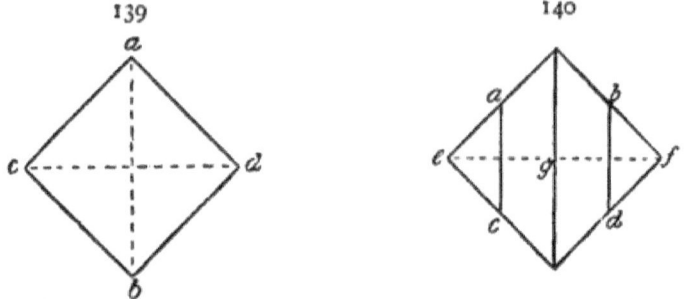

must be bisected with the ruler, and the lines drawn perpendicular to ef. If the diagonals are given, the dimensions of the sides of the square are not known, and cannot be directly bisected with the ruler. Care must be taken to see that ac and bd are drawn exactly perpendicular to ef.

The interior of the square may be filled up in a variety of ways.

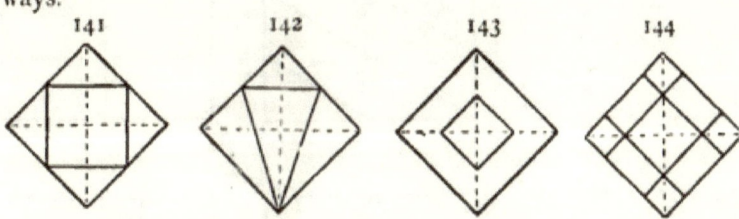

Fig. 145.—Draw a square. Insert the diameters, and afterwards clean out the part shown in dotted line.

Fig. 146.—Draw a rectangle with its sides in the proportion of three to two. Divide the longer sides into three, and

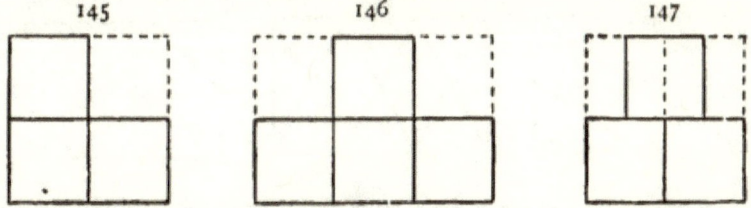

the shorter into two equal parts. Draw the lines cutting the figure into six equal squares. Clean out the parts shown by dotted lines.

Fig. 147.—This may be done as shown by the dotted lines, or the two bottom squares may be drawn first, the centres of their top lines found, and the top square constructed. For *freehand* the first method is much better, as the correct proportions of the squares are more easily obtained.

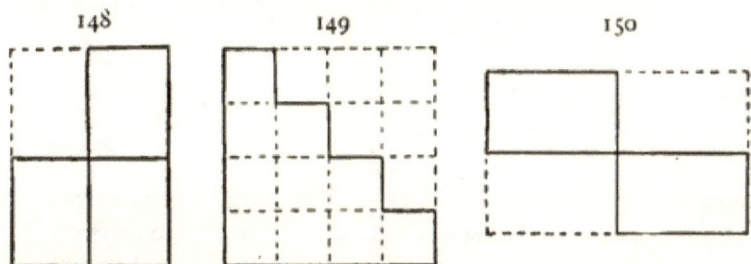

The construction lines show the method in the above figures.

Memory Drawing

This is a valuable aid in every standard towards securing really intelligent work. The best plan to adopt is to let the pupils draw from memory the copy taken in the previous lesson. This need not be a long exercise, and it will test whether the methods used have been thoroughly understood, as well as strengthen the pupil's powers of observation. In the upper standards special attention should be paid to knowledge of the analysis of the copy. It is not at all important that the pupil should remember every little detail ; it is the power of blocking in the masses correctly that needs cultivation.

CHAPTER IV

STANDARD II

Syllabus.—*The same as for Standard I, but on paper.*

The **teacher** will require two large set-squares in addition to the apparatus for Standard I.

The **children** will require:—

1. **Paper.**—This should be of the regulation size, 11 by 7¼ inches, with a smooth unglazed surface. There is a diversity of opinion as to which is the more convenient form to use, books or paper. Many teachers prefer to use loose sheets, as they are more easily manipulated, while on the other hand books are decidedly cleaner, and as a rule children are proud of a well filled book.

2. **Pencils.**—The most suitable pencils are the hexagonal-shaped, as they do not roll off the desks. Cheap pencils are not necessarily the most economical; pencils with crumbling leads or hard wood only produce bad work and cause vexation to both teachers and scholars. The marks of various makers differ in degree of hardness, H and F in some are as soft as HB in others. On the whole HB when not too soft is the most useful pencil to adopt. Pencils must always be kept well pointed, as it is impossible to secure accurate and neat work unless this is attended to. A sharp knife is the best instrument to use, although some of the pencil sharpeners produce a fair point.

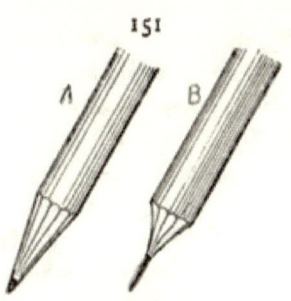

Fig. 151.—*A* shows the form the point should take; when cut as in *B* the point breaks almost directly. It is a very useful

plan to point the pencil at both ends, as the pupil is then provided with a good point throughout the lesson.

Indiarubber.—This should be white and flexible. If the piece be cut in halves along its length it is more useful, as it bends easier, and there is less waste. It should not be used for the ruler drawing, and very sparingly for freehand in the lower standards.

Set-squares.—Those having angles of 45° and 60° are the only ones needed. They should be of good size, large enough to draw 6-inch lines, and about $\frac{1}{8}$ inch thick; they will not then readily break.

Directions.—The same methods of procedure as given for Standard I are equally applicable here. The only additional points to be illustrated will be the improved constructions obtained by the use of the set-squares. The same kind of oral questioning must accompany each lesson, and additional skill in answering and giving illustrations should be required.

The **character of the line** used should receive special attention, as bad habits formed at the beginning are exceedingly difficult to eradicate. For the *ruler* work a good, bold, firm line should be adopted, so that the figure stands out well from the *construction* lines, which should be put in as *lightly* as possible. In the *freehand*, which will probably need more time than the ruler work, the sketching in must be done very lightly and carefully; the pupil should always first indicate the ends of the lines before drawing them, and after passing the pencil carefully between them several times to obtain a general idea of the direction, finally draw the line with one clean, light stroke. The teacher must keep a sharp watch to see that the pencil is held properly. The fingers must not be too near the point, nor in a cramped position. When the copy has been carefully sketched in, the construction lines should be rubbed out, the whole figure cleaned with the indiarubber, and afterwards finished with a clean even line. By lining in, it is not meant that the line should be blackened over (thus frequently spoiling the drawing), but carefully putting in an even line and improving the shape and finish of the copy. Many condemn the use of indiarubber entirely in this Standard, but with care it may be advantageously used to clean up the copy. The cuffs of the pupils' coats should be turned up, and not allowed to rub over the lines drawn, or to soil the paper. Cleanliness must be strictly enforced, or the work will be a continuous source of vexation to the teacher.

Ruler Work

Parallels.—Place the ruler in a vertical position, and hold it firmly with the thumb and third finger of the left hand. Now adjust the set-square as shown, placing one edge in a line

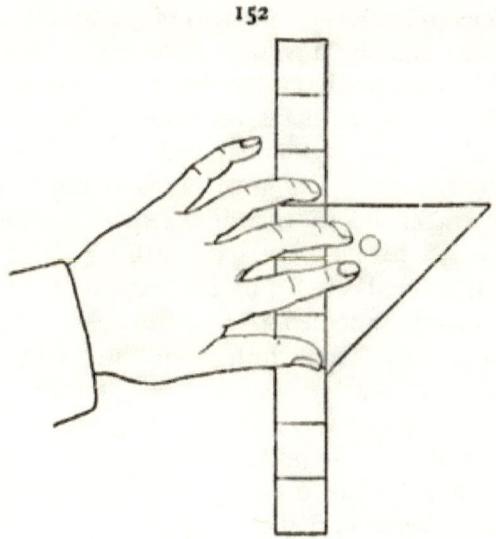

152

with one of the inch marks on the ruler, and taking care to impress upon the pupil the necessity of keeping the other edge touching the ruler throughout its length. Keep the set-square in position by pressing it firmly with the first and second fingers, and rule a line. If the set-square be now slipped with the right hand to the next inch mark while the ruler is still held in position with the left hand, parallels one inch apart will be obtained. Repeat the exercise with parallels 2 inches and $\frac{1}{2}$ inch apart.

Vertical and oblique parallels may now be drawn in a similar manner. Attention should be directed to the fact that while one edge of the set-square gives horizontal lines, the other edge will give oblique lines, but not the same distance apart.

The teacher will find that it will amply repay for the trouble taken, to teach the uses of the set-squares at this early stage; as not only can the figures be drawn more accurately, but the difficulty will be overcome for the other standards; and the work of Standard III will be made easier, more interesting, and more pleasurable to the pupils. Constant vigilance, care, and patience must be exercised when the set-squares are first used; the method of using them must be repeatedly shown on the blackboard, and every pupil must be supervised to see that the proper way of handling them is thoroughly comprehended. A very common error to guard against is the attempt to draw the lines without keeping one edge of the set-square touching the ruler. The children may also be shown that it is not absolutely necessary for the set-square to be of this particular shape; any right-angled figure, such as a slate or book, will also give parallels and perpendiculars.

Perpendiculars.—Exercises in setting up perpendiculars from points in lines in various positions, such as those suggested in fig. 153, should now be given. Dictated exercises may be used here with advantage.

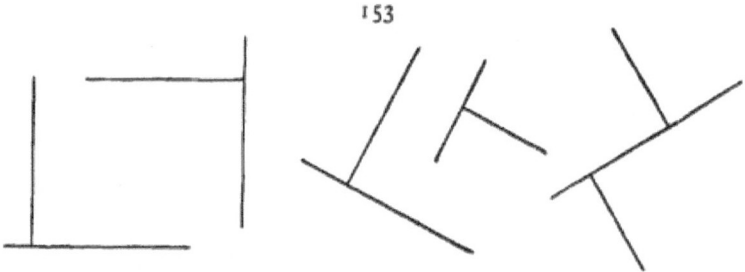

153

All right angles should now be set up, bisected, and trisected by using the set-squares.

The reason for these processes may be demonstrated here

with advantage. Describe a large circle on the board, and draw two diameters at right angles to each other. Fit the set-square into each of the four angles formed, and show that each is a right angle. Now explain that as we use long measure to determine the length of an object, avoirdupois to determine the weight, and other measures to determine content, time, area, &c., so we use a measure to determine the size of an angle. Each one of these right angles is divided into 90 parts by lines drawn from the angle, and the width of the very sharp angle thus formed is called a degree. This may be easily illustrated by describing a large circle on paper and dividing it into four right angles. Divide one of the right angles into nine equal

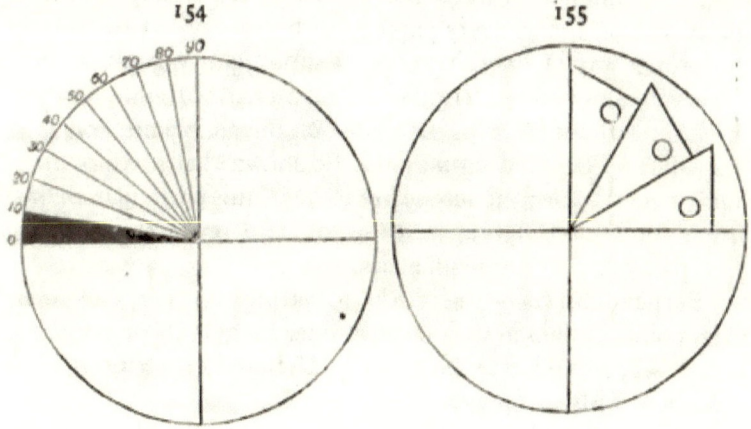

divisions, and subdivide one of these divisions into ten, thus showing the actual size of a degree. If the space between the lines be blackened in as shown in the angle of 10°, **fig. 154**, it will be more readily comprehended. Now take three set-squares, place them with their smallest angles fitting into the right angle. The reason for using the set-square for trisecting a right angle will at once be seen. The number of degrees in the small angle may be elicited, and if two set-squares be removed it will be found that the larger angle of one set square will exactly fit in place of the two, thus giving the angle of 60°. In the same manner two of the 45° set-squares may be shown to fit the same right angle, and consequently one of them would bisect it.

Introduction of Curves and the Drawing of Common Objects.—The Illustrated Syllabus suggests that:—'In order to interest the children it is advisable to teach them to draw as early as possible from actual objects, such as the doors, windows, furniture and apparatus of the school-room. It will also be found quite possible and very desirable to go beyond the foregoing standards in teaching. Thus freehand drawing of bold curves may be introduced in Standards I and II; and exercises may be advantageously given in all standards in drawing from memory.'

With regard to the drawing of **common objects**, they should only be drawn in the flat, and from the teacher's directions; they then form a valuable introduction to the scale drawing of Standard IV. Examples similar to the end elevation of a desk, fig. **156**, the block letters, and many of the simple objects suggested in the Infants' course form good examples. The teacher, however, should carefully work out the measurements beforehand, so that the drawing may not appear distorted.

Freehand curves may be easily introduced without interfering with the other work. The squares and oblongs already drawn can be utilised as a framework for the curves. The cleverer children will in many lessons be able to insert the curves while the others are finishing the ordinary copy. The following examples illustrate a few of the ways in which this may be carried out. The same copies may also be utilised for the work of Standard III at the commencement of the year.

The drawing of **simple patterns** should be followed up here as frequently as possible, as it encourages originality among the children and is a pleasing variation from the other

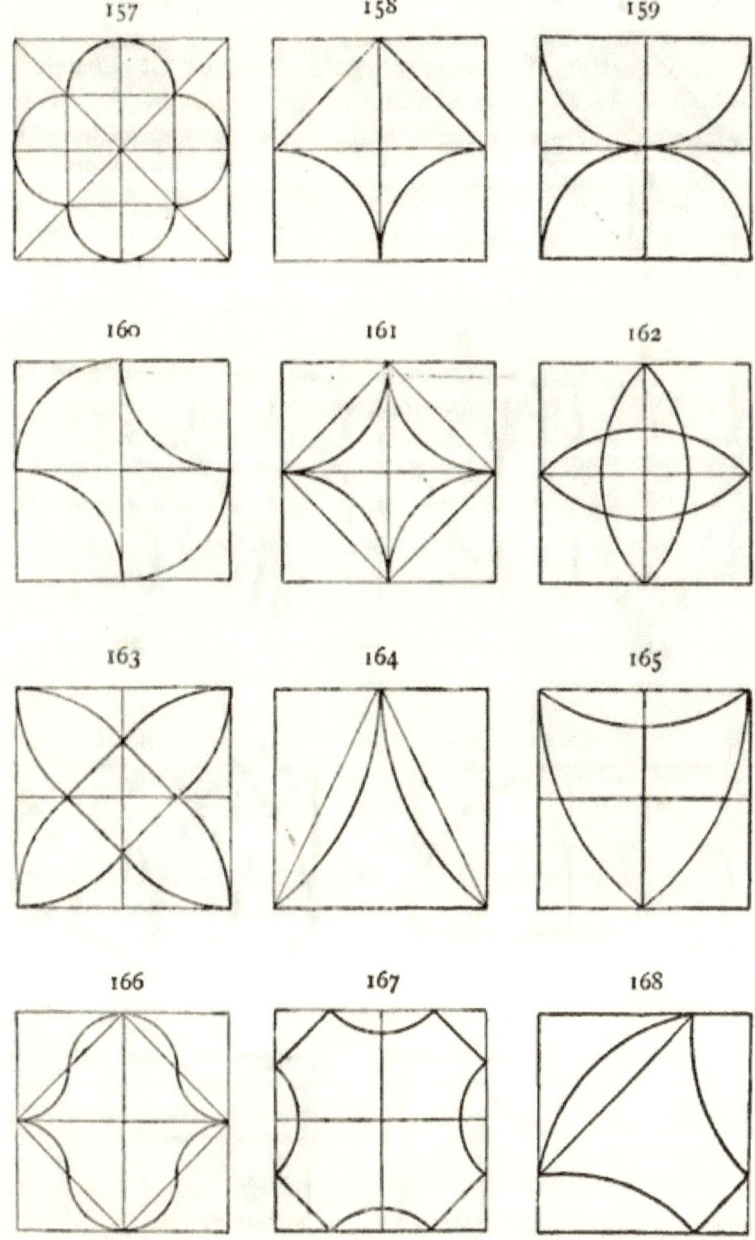

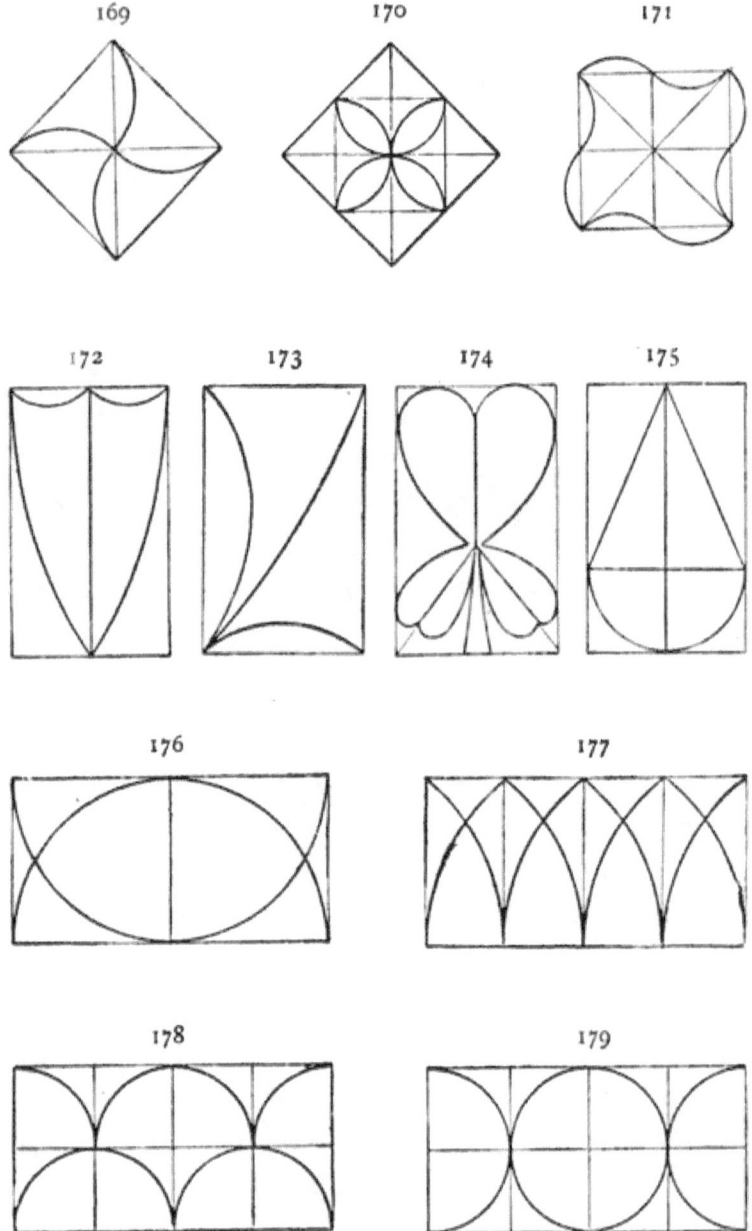

work. If the children are allowed to colour the pattern, as suggested on page 5, a wonderful degree of interest will be created in the work. Examples such as those given in the Infants' course, **figs. 45–70,** are suitable for this purpose. The squared paper of ordinary exercise books answers very well for drawing upon.

CHAPTER V

STANDARD III

Syllabus.—(*a*) *Freehand drawing of regular forms and curved figures from the flat.*

(*b*) *Simple geometrical figures with rulers.*

These right-lined figures to be drawn freehand and also with rulers.

These requirements then resolve themselves into three parts.

I. Freehand drawing of curved figures, which I have divided into three stages.

II. Freehand drawing of right-lined forms.

III. Drawing of geometrical figures with rulers.

The same **apparatus** will be required as for Standard II.

I. FREEHAND DRAWING OF CURVED FIGURES

This is by far the most important and also the most difficult part of the course for this Standard, and will require a greater amount of time than the geometrical drawing. The pupil must be trained to rely more upon his own powers. Hitherto the figures dealt with have been regular in form, and the proportion, or relation which one part of the drawing bears to the other, has been obtained by the help of the ruler, or from definite instructions furnished by the teacher. The pupil must now be shown how to analyse and understand the principles of construction upon which the copy is based, and how to obtain the proper proportions between its various parts. If these important principles are well grounded at this stage, the freehand and model drawing of the upper standards, upon which so much depends, will be executed with much greater correctness, ease, and pleasure.

First Stage.—As the pupils are now thoroughly familiar with the drawing of rectangular forms, it will be found much easier to introduce curved forms by using these rectangular forms as aids. The curves should not be drawn very large at first, as simple curves when too large are very awkward for the beginner to draw; nor is it advisable to spend too long a time over them, as, though they are very necessary, and give excellent training in freedom of hand and knowledge of form, they are somewhat uninteresting to the pupil. They should be drawn about the size suggested on the figures, and the construction lines, which must be indicated very lightly, may be allowed to remain, the most important point at this stage being to secure good curves.

Figs. 180-190.—The pupils must be shown from the blackboard how to obtain the curves with one careful sweep, after the pencil has been carried several times over the paper, so that the general direction of the curve may be obtained before marking it in. On no account must the pupil be allowed to draw the line thickly or in little bits. Adhere as far as possible to the rule already laid down viz., *to draw from left to right and from top to bottom.*

Some teachers prefer to use slates in the first instance, but this is open to great objection and is an encouragement to careless work, as alterations may be made so readily; whereas one of the most important points to inculcate is that when a line is drawn it should not need much alteration, and must remain. The knowledge that the line cannot be easily removed compels the pupil to think where it must be placed, and thus gives confidence and begets carefulness.

Second Stage.—In the next series of examples the construction lines must be carefully cleaned out, and the figure, after being correctly sketched, should be rubbed out until only a faint line is visible. The drawing should then be carefully *lined in* with a sharp pencil; and here it is again pointed out that the lining in is for the purpose of obtaining an even, con-

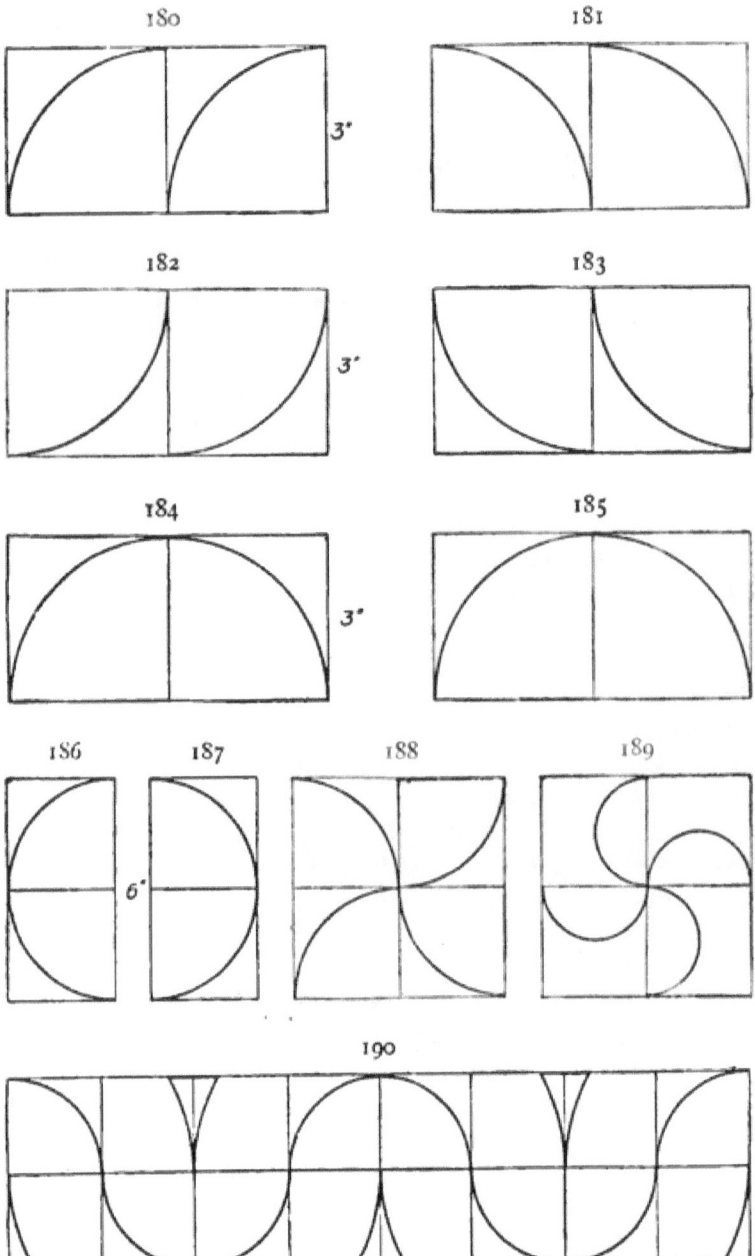

tinuous line, and an improvement in the shape and finish of the copy.

The pupil should be taught here how to divide a line into three equal parts, a much more difficult process than dividing it into two. The following method given by Mr. Taylor in his excellent book on 'Elementary Art Teaching' is exceedingly

191

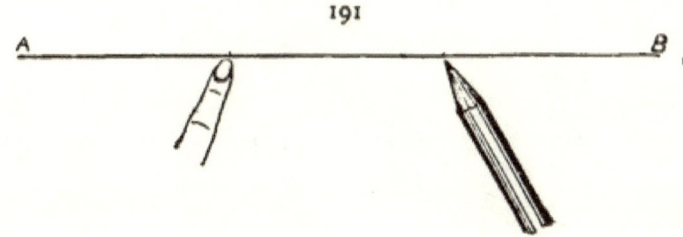

useful. If *AB* be the line to be trisected, then place a finger of the left hand on the line at the same time with the pencil which is to mark the first division; by this means the equality of the three parts may be more easily judged.

Figs. 192-200 are all based on the circle, and should be drawn without the aid of squares. The light lines show the necessary construction. Care should be taken to see that the semicircles run into each other at their junction with a continuous line without showing any angle. About six inches is a convenient size for the longest line in these examples, which should all be carefully *lined in* when drawn.

Third Stage.—Before beginning the next series of examples, which are of the same character as examination tests, the pupil must be taught how to measure, by means of the pencil, objects which are not accessible. This is a most useful and necessary exercise, and should be continually used to ascertain the relationship between the various parts of the copy. Great care and patience will be needed on the teacher's part to see that the method is clearly understood, as the pupil's future progress is largely dependent upon this. Directly the method has been mastered, the power of self-reliance is greatly increased, and it becomes quite exceptional to find the proportion of the figure inaccurate.

56 The Teaching of Drawing

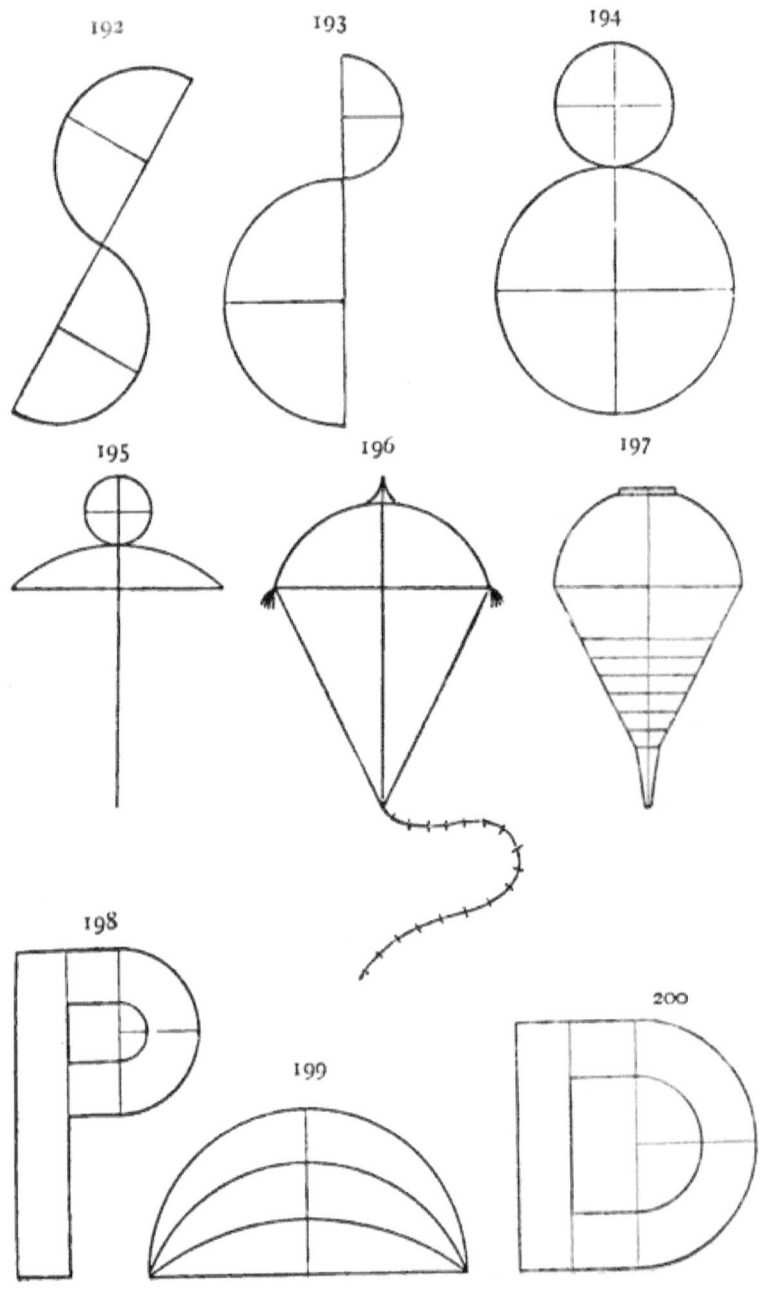

Begin by measuring objects in the room—such as windows, boards, &c.—that can be seen in a similar position by the bulk of the class : taking care always to ask the children to estimate first the relative sizes by means of the eye, and afterwards verify them by measuring with the pencil.

Suppose the example selected be a window, then the method of proceeding would be somewhat as follows :—

Which is the greater, the height or the width of the window?

How much greater is the height than the width?

After obtaining approximately accurate replies, show how to verify with the pencil.

Hold the pencil horizontally at *arm's length*, close one eye, and let the end of the pencil be held in a line with the side (*A*) of the window (fig. 201). Keep this end steady, and slip the thumb along the pencil until it is in line with the other side (*B*) of the window. The distance between the end of the pencil and the thumb nail will represent the actual width of the window as seen by the pupil. (Take care to see that *the pencil is held at right angles to the arm*.) Let the pupils hold up their pencils, still keeping the thumb in position. The teacher will then see at a glance whether the distance has been correctly gauged. Now step this distance vertically up the window. The pupils will readily see that this method furnishes them with a ready means of testing the proportions of their drawing. After a few other measurements of various objects, the best plan is to take lines on the blackboard, comparing them with the board and with each other as follows :—

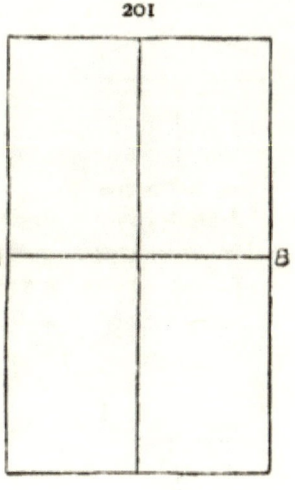

Draw *AB* (fig. 202). Compare it with the height of the board. Lengthen the line to *C*.

Where is point *B*? '*A little below the half.*'
How do you know this?
Compare *CD* with *AC*.

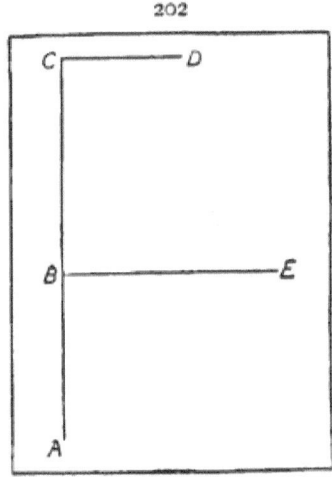

How many times can *CD* be set off on *AC*?

Then what part is *CD* of *AC*? '*A little less than one-third.*'

Compare *BE* with *AC*. '*A little more than half.*'

Similar exercises should frequently be given at the commencement until the method is thoroughly comprehended. In all cases let the comparison be made first with the eye and afterwards verified with the pencil.

A **typical lesson** is given here to show how to apply the method advantageously. Such lessons are frequently required at the examination.

Apparatus.—*Demonstration sheet or a drawing of the figure to be placed before the class, pencils, paper, &c.*

What is the copy like? '*A leaf.*'

What shape is the leaf? '*Like a triangle.*'

What line shall I draw first? '*The upright line through the middle.*'

Now that I have drawn the height, what shall I want to know next? '*The width.*'

Where is the leaf widest? '*At the bottom.*'

Compare *AB* (fig. 203) with the height. After eliciting a number of answers, let the pupils measure *AB* with their pencils and verify their answers by stepping the distance up the height line. It will be found to go three times and a little over. Now require the answer to be given in this form : '*AB is a little less than one-third of the height.*' Divide your line into three equal parts as previously shown, and mark the first division, *a*, fig. 204. Now, if we make *bc* and *bd* a little less than *ab*, the

Standard III

correct width of the copy will be ascertained. Join *e* with *d* and *c*, keeping the lines very light.

I would point out here the extreme undesirability of cutting up the height line into halves, quarters, &c., and constructing a framework from these parts. In actual drawings the proportions are very rarely exact parts of the upright line. These divisions should only be used, as in this case, as guides.

Now draw the stalk, and lines *ad* and *ac*, thus producing a general resemblance to the leaf.

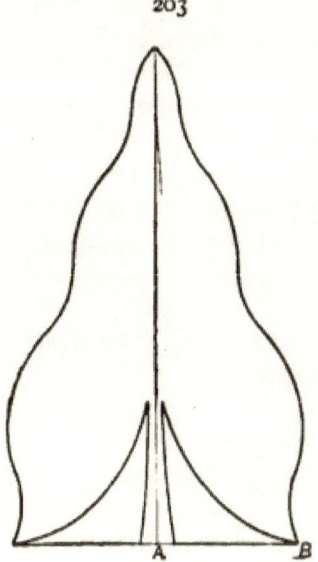
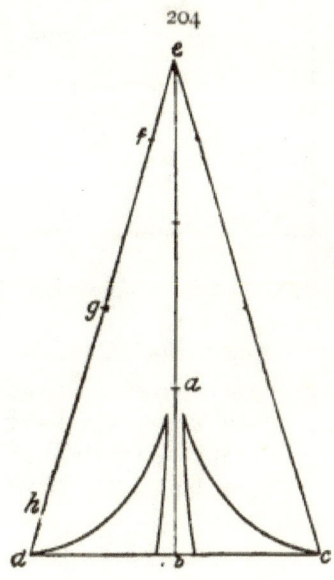

The remainder of the copy is very difficult. The attention of the pupils should be directed to the following points. Notice the number of bends in the side of the leaf, and place a light mark to show where they come, as at points *f*, *g*, *h*. If the pencil be held in a line with *e* and *d*, it will be apparent as to how much of the copy projects outside of the triangle. Also notice that the bottom curves are slightly larger than the others. The left side should then be very lightly indicated, and examined carefully before drawing in firmly, the other side drawn to correspond, and the copy afterwards cleaned and lined in

The advantage of proceeding in this manner is that the pupil is drawing with the head as well as with the hand. It will be noticed that nothing has been told, every step being obtained from the pupils. A copy taught thus takes considerable time at first, but the time will have been well spent, and the teacher will be amply repaid for the trouble taken. A few copies thoroughly taught in this fashion will be found to be of more value than weeks of unintelligent mechanical copying. This example forms a capital test for memory drawing.

Figs. 205-209 are examples of lines springing from a central stem. The dotted lines show the method of construction, and the figures denote the order in which the lines should be drawn. Very great care should be bestowed upon the junctions of the side lines with the stem: they should run into the main line easily, gradually forming part of it. This will need constant illustration on the blackboard.

Fig. 205.—First find the position of a and b, and draw lines starting from the centre line as shown at the side (A). This will prevent the joining line from showing a tendency to run *through*, instead of *into*, the main line as shown in (B). Draw a line to get the level of the two bottom curves. Ascertain the width of bc as shown in the foregoing lesson, and draw the *left hand curve first*. Now balance this with the corresponding curve on the right. *On no account must one half of the copy be drawn first*: this is a most mischievous plan and should never be allowed. Now mark point e and draw a line through it. Fix the position of f and g, and draw the top curves.

Fig. 206 shows an example of alternate radiation. Mark the points a, b, c, d first, and draw the curves as in the last example, commencing with number 1. Notice that each curve bends down more as the bottom is approached, somewhat similar to the branches of a tree.

In all cases always work from the copy placed before the class, so that the pupils may see and understand the reasons for the processes carried on.

In **Figs. 219-231** the necessary construction lines are indi-

Standard III

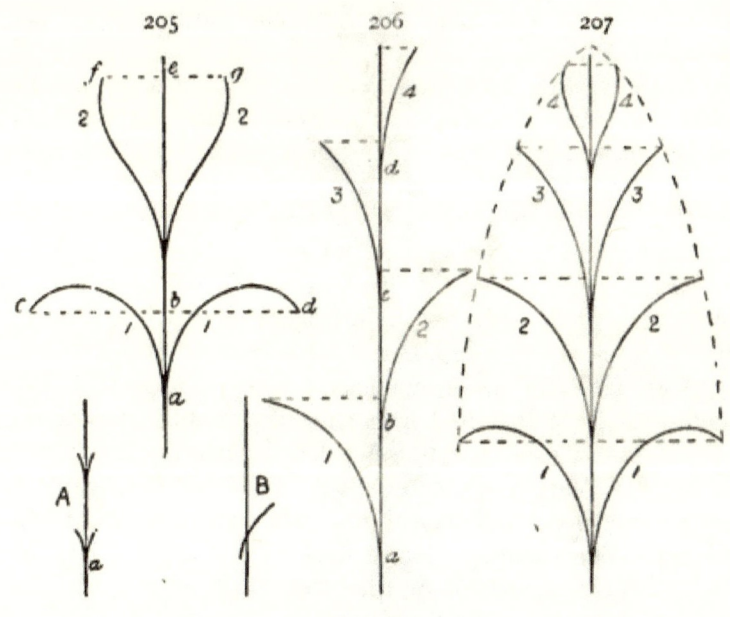
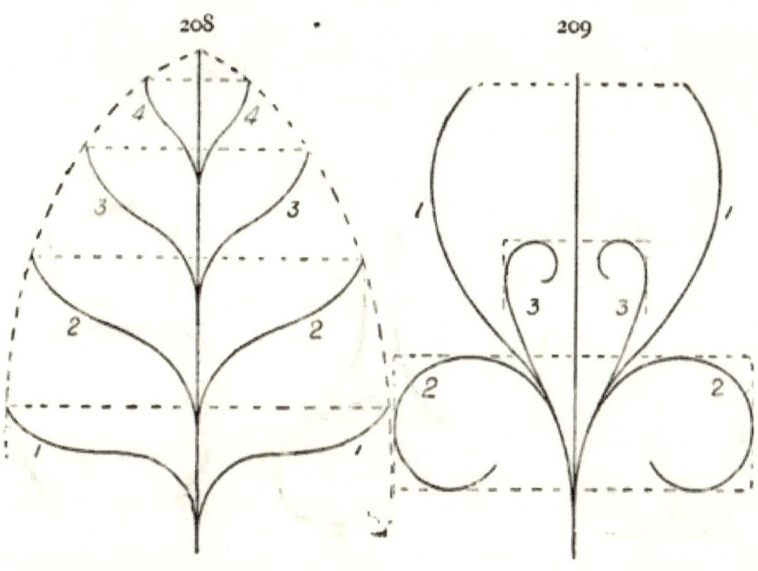

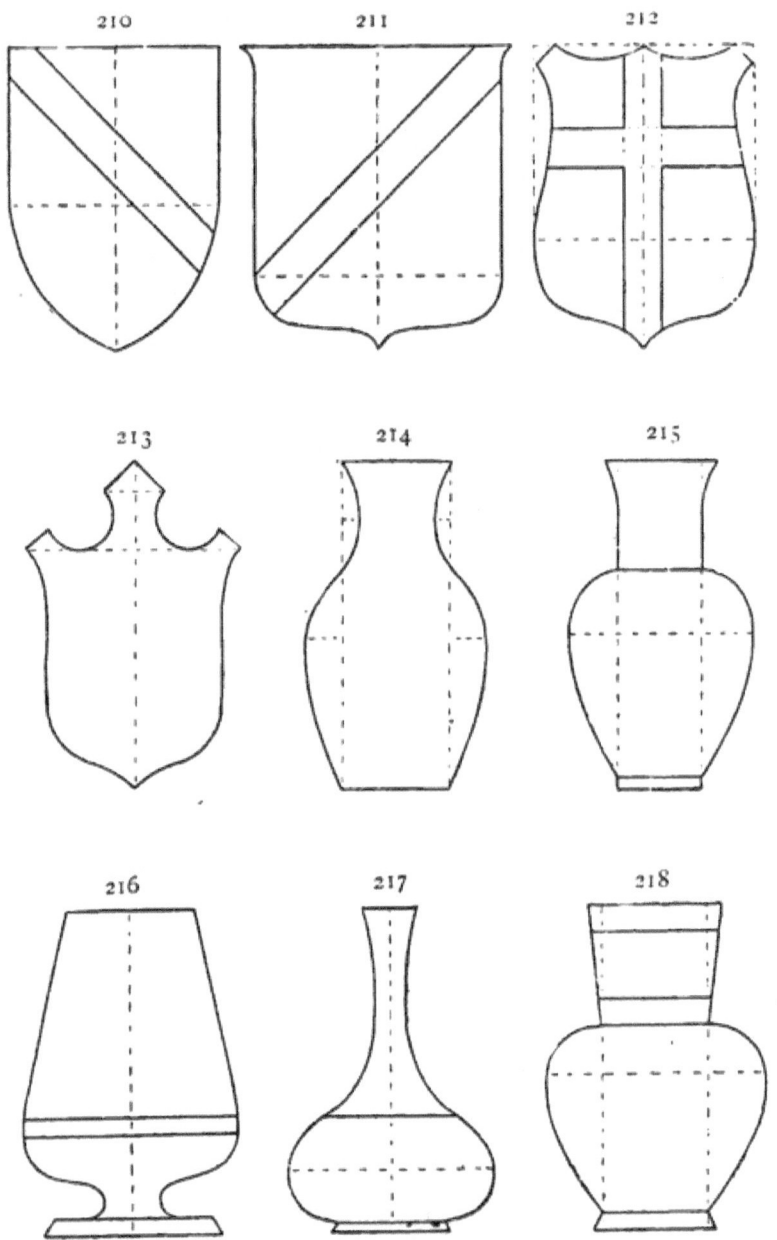

cated by the dotted lines, and those figures which are more difficult are shown in their various stages. At each of these steps the drawings should be carefully examined, the method given in the sample lesson being followed out in all cases. If thought desirable some of these copies may be left at any of the stages shown, as they are rather more difficult than is usually expected from this Standard, although they are given in the syllabus, and form excellent examples to teach from. **Figs. 229-231** are also suitable for the earlier stages of Standard IV freehand.

The work of the lower standards is very rarely tested by cards instead of by the large sheets. If, however, this be done, the general rule is to make the drawing as large as the paper will allow, taking care to leave a fair margin, as this adds to the appearance of the drawing.

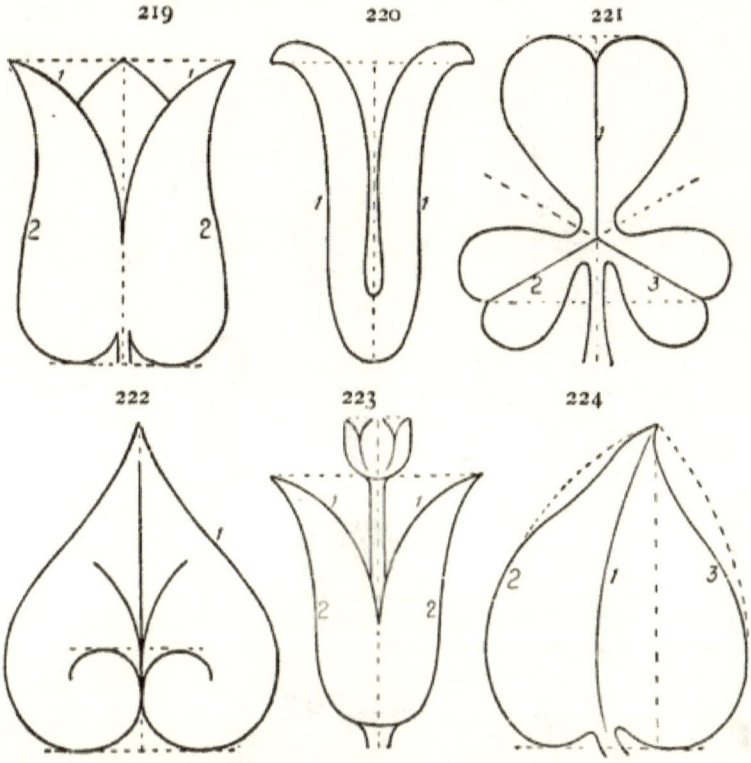

64   *The Teaching of Drawing*

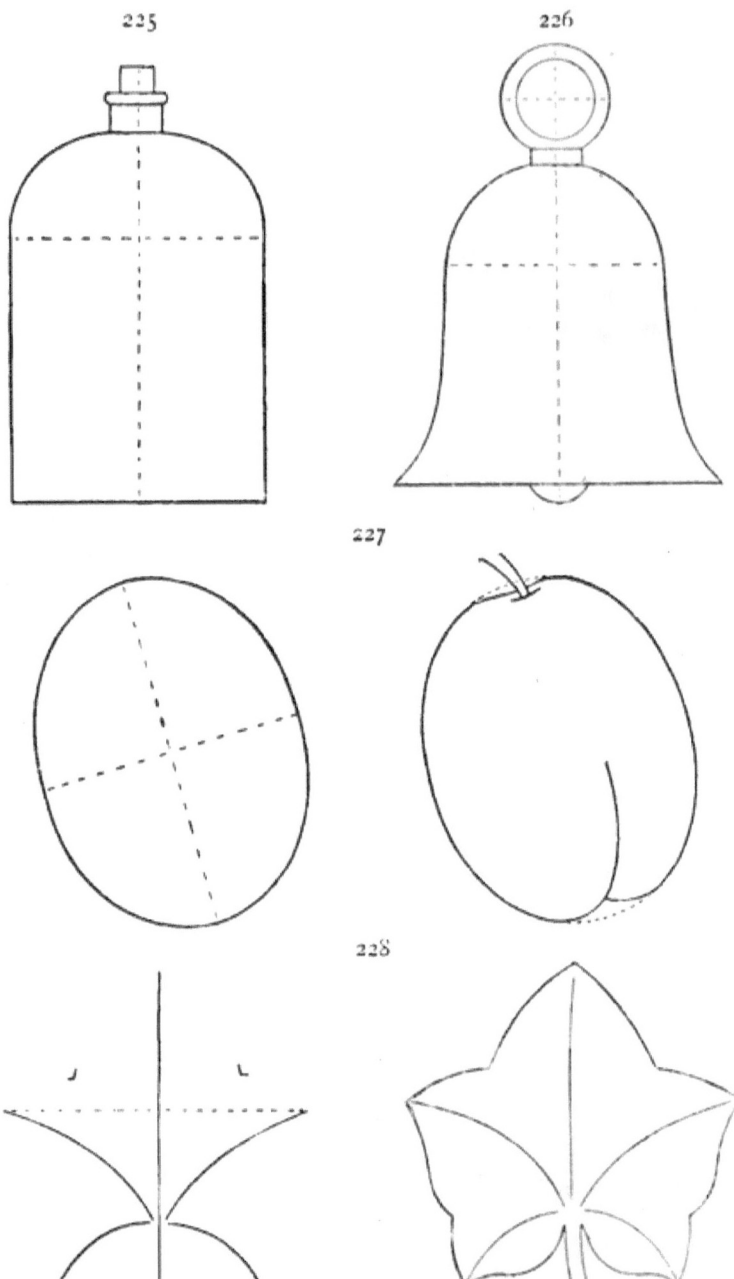

Standard III 65

229

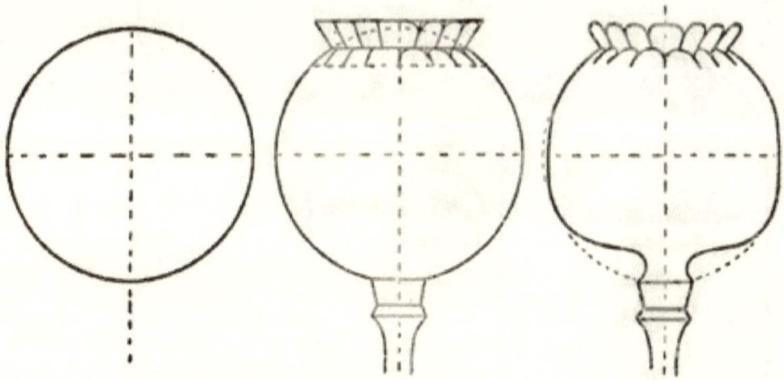

230

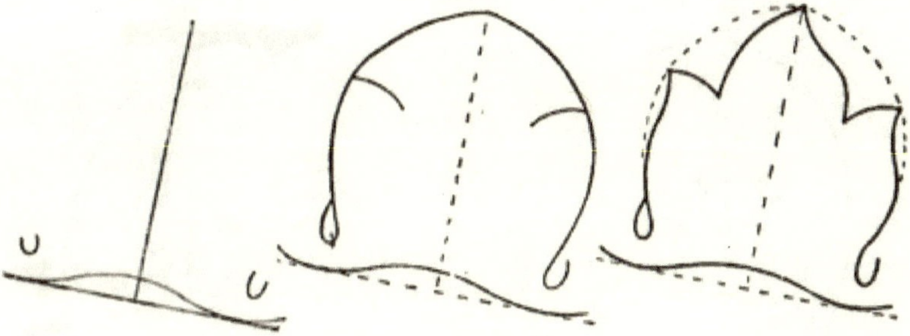

231

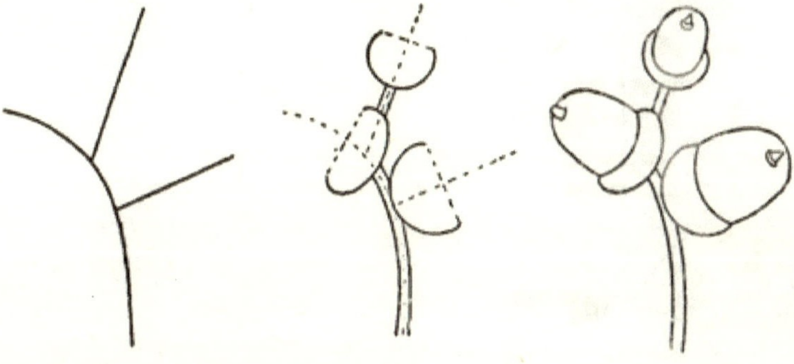

II. FREEHAND DRAWING OF RIGHT-LINED FORMS

This is a continuation of the freehand work of Standard II, and is not very difficult when the children have learned how to estimate the relative lengths of the lines of the figures. The knowledge of proportion which they have already obtained is now especially useful. In the following examples the pupils must be able to see the proper direction of lines which are partly hidden, and also the proper method of drawing the figures.

Figs. 232, 233, 234, 240, and 242 are all examples of one figure overlapping a portion of another. The hidden parts of the lines marked *a* are shown by dots.

Figs. 235 and 237.—Draw the base. Find the position of *b*, by comparing *bc* with *bd*. Draw the altitude, compare it with the base, and complete the triangle. The other vertical lines are drawn from the middle points of the sides.

Fig. 236.—Draw the square first, after comparing its height with the height of the triangle, so that the figure may be properly placed on the paper. Draw *ef* and obtain the equilateral triangle *fgh*. Draw the sides *fg* and *fh* to meet the base of the square produced.

Fig. 238.—Draw the square and produce its base. Compare *np* with the base of the square, and draw *pr*. Compare *lm* with *np*, and draw the other side of the triangle.

Fig. 241.—Begin with lines *ab* and *cd*.

Fig. 242.—Draw the rectangle *bcde*. Find points *f, g, h, l*, and through them draw the lines for the other rectangle.

Fig. 243.—Draw *ab* and find the position of *c*. Draw *ed* and *fg*, comparing *ce* and *bf* with *ac*, and complete the figure.

Proceed similarly with the other figures, in all cases insisting upon a careful study and testing of the figure by measuring with both eye and pencil. Many of the examples for ruler drawing will furnish other suitable exercises.

Standard III

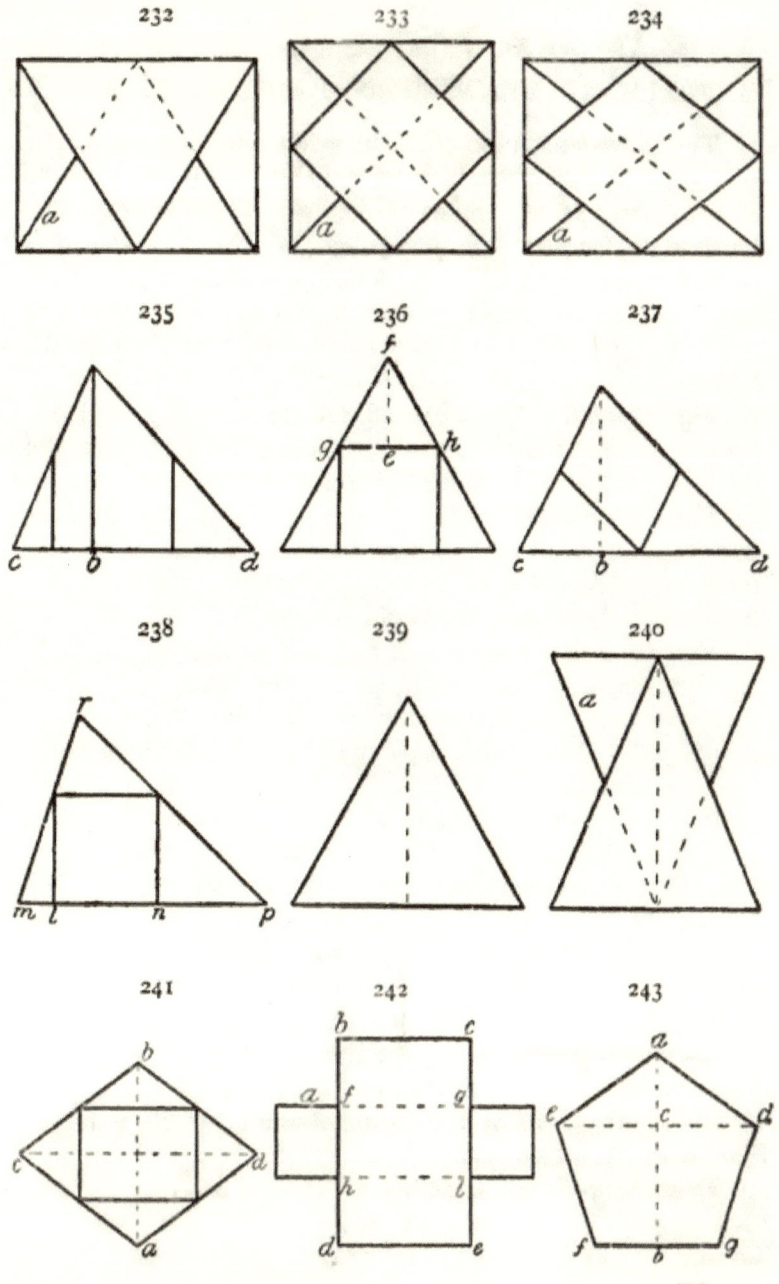

III. DRAWING OF GEOMETRICAL FIGURES WITH RULERS

This is generally the most attractive part of the work of this Standard, and forms an excellent preparation for the geometrical work of the higher standards, as a high degree of neatness and accuracy is demanded. A knowledge of the methods of constructing the triangle, square, rectangle, rhombus, pentagon, hexagon, octagon, and figures based upon them, together with simple bordering patterns, such as frets, &c., is necessary.

It is most important that the pupil should be acquainted with the proper method of drawing these figures, and the plan given in the following lesson should be rigidly adhered to. If this course be adopted the pupils will soon be able to measure up a copy for themselves, and decide upon the size and construction necessary.

The cards given at the examination usually contain two figures which have to be drawn larger. This prevents unintelligent copying, and requires the pupil to possess a knowledge of the construction necessary to draw the example. The paper should be divided into two parts as in fig. 245, and one figure placed in each half.

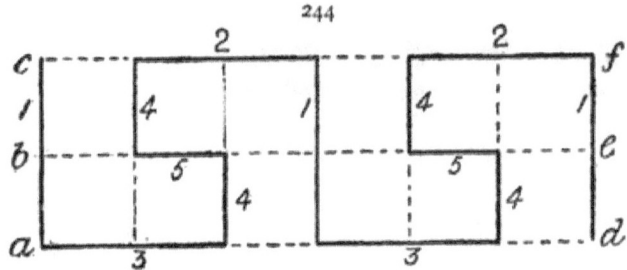

The following lesson will best illustrate the way in which the figures should be taught.

Apparatus.—The board should be placed as in fig. 245, and divided into two equal portions by a line *ab*. It will then correspond with the paper upon which the pupils are drawing. A

Standard III

copy of the figure *without construction lines* should be placed before the class. This will correspond with the card which the pupil will be required to work from at the examination. It will be sufficient for the present if the teacher dictates the sizes of the lines to be drawn. Both teacher and pupils will also need rulers and set-squares.

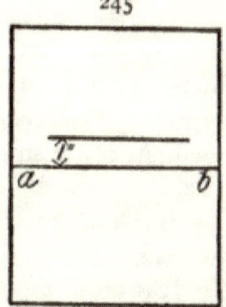

The teacher will explain that he is going to make his drawing a little larger than the copy, and that it must be placed in the top half of the board.

1. Place the ruler on the copy and rule the continuous lines as shown by the dots on fig. 244. The pupils will then see that the copy is constructed upon three parallel horizontal lines, intersected by vertical parallels forming a number of squares.

2. Measure *ab*. Suppose it to measure half an inch; then, if the copy has to be enlarged, *ab* on the pupil's drawing might be made three-quarters of an inch.

Note.—The teacher should have his ruler marked so that four inches on his ruler represent one inch on the pupil's ruler.

3. Draw a *very faint line* of indefinite length about one inch from *ab* (fig. 245), and set off on it as many spaces of three-quarters of an inch each as there are squares required (in this case six). Fix the position of the first point *a* (fig. 244) carefully, so that the copy may be well placed on the paper. About one inch from the margin will do in this case.

4. Set off very carefully at each end of the line two spaces of three-quarters of an inch each, giving the points, *b*, *c*, *e*, and *f*; using the ruler as shown in fig. 91. Rule *be* and *cf* very *lightly*.

5. Place the ruler on *ad*, and with the set-square draw the vertical lines forming two rows of squares.

Note.—The pupils should follow the teacher step by step.

6. Now thicken in the pattern with a good firm line, ruling the lines as directed. First the lines marked 1, then 2, next 3,

then 4, and complete by ruling 5. It is very important to insist upon the ruling being done in this manner, as it secures rapidity and uniformity, and the pattern will always be symmetrical at each stage of the copy.

7. The pupils should now be shown that the pattern may be continued to any length, and illustrations of its application in the decoration of oilcloths, papers, carpets, stonework, &c., given. The bottom half of the paper should now be filled with the same pattern drawn to a different scale.

Notes.— 1. Many teachers prefer to rule the construction lines in dotted line. This gives a very good appearance if the line is carefully ruled with light and even strokes, as the pattern stands out well from the construction. A *very faint* line is much quicker, and can probably be done better by the class as a whole.

2. No construction lines are to be removed, as the line of the copy will be spoiled, and it is essential that the method of obtaining the figure should be apparent. It is not advisable to give out indiarubbers, except towards the end of the course, and then only for the purpose of trimming up the copy if necessary.

3. The squares as a rule should not be of less than three-quarter inch sides.

Figs. 246-259.—These are all based upon two lines of squares.

The dotted lines show the necessary constructions, which should be worked out in a similar manner to fig. 244. The figures indicate the order of thickening in the pattern.

Figs. 260-270.—These figures are constructed upon three, four, and five lines of squares, and can be easily followed from the construction lines.

Figs. 271-281 are based on the square, rectangle, &c. The dotted lines indicate the method of construction. Various exercises of a similar character may easily be devised by the teacher.

The copy without the construction lines should in all cases be placed before the class, and the method of construction elicited before beginning. The pupils should be taught to measure up the copy, and as far as possible to enlarge the various parts proportionately. For example, suppose it were

Standard III

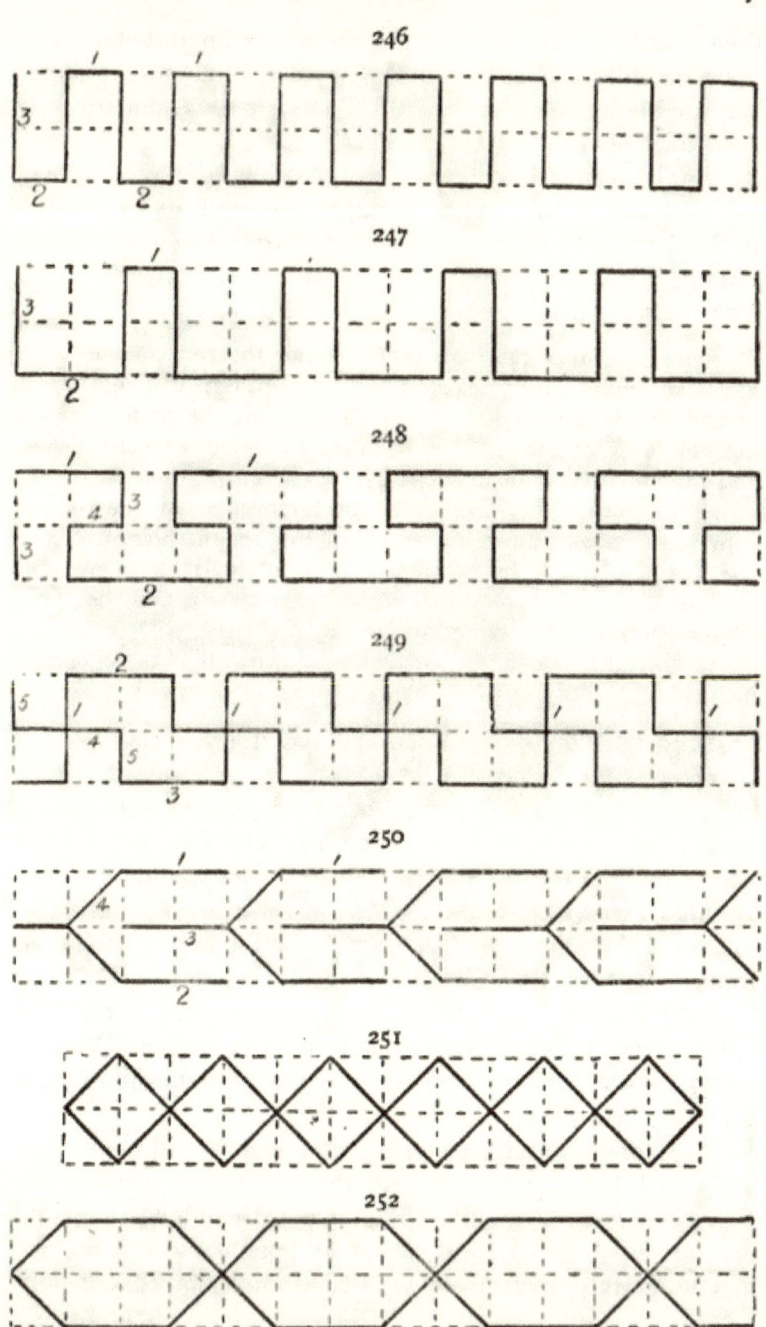

72 The Teaching of Drawing

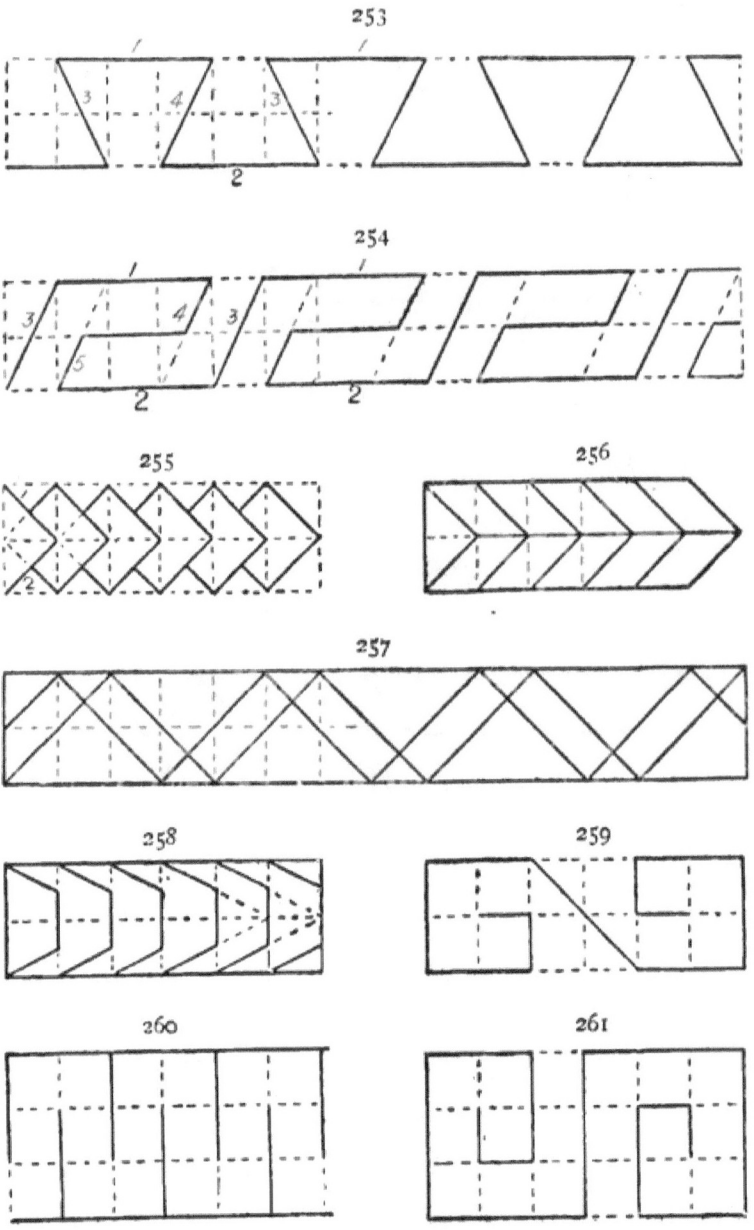

Standard III

73

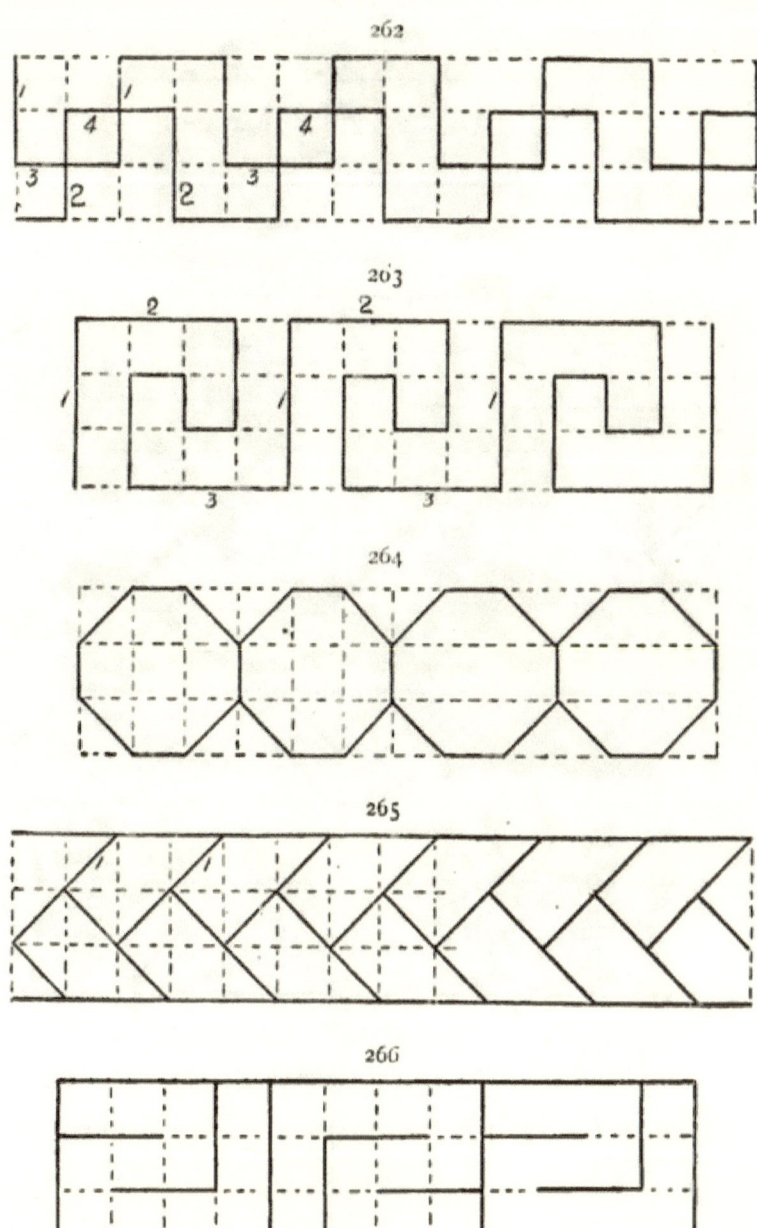

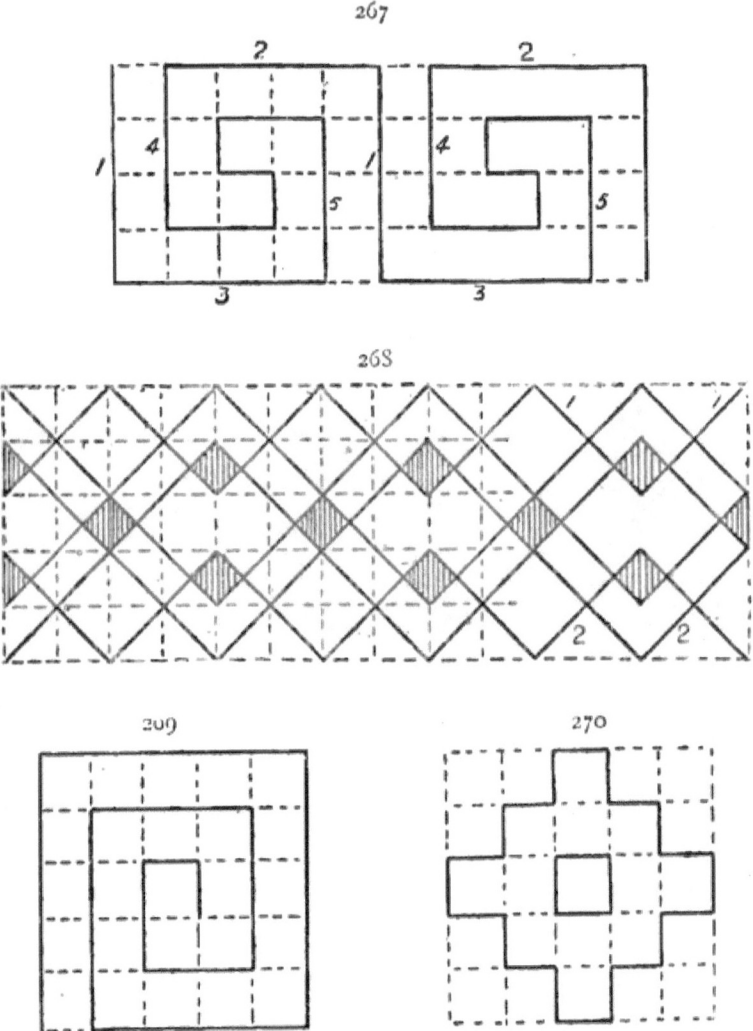

required to make fig. 275 half as large again; then, if $cd = 2$ inches and $ab =$ half an inch, the pupil would make the dimensions three inches and three-quarters of an inch respectively.

Figs. 271-276.—First draw the squares shown in dotted line. Set off the distances marked ab from each angle. Rule in the pattern with a good firm line.

Standard III

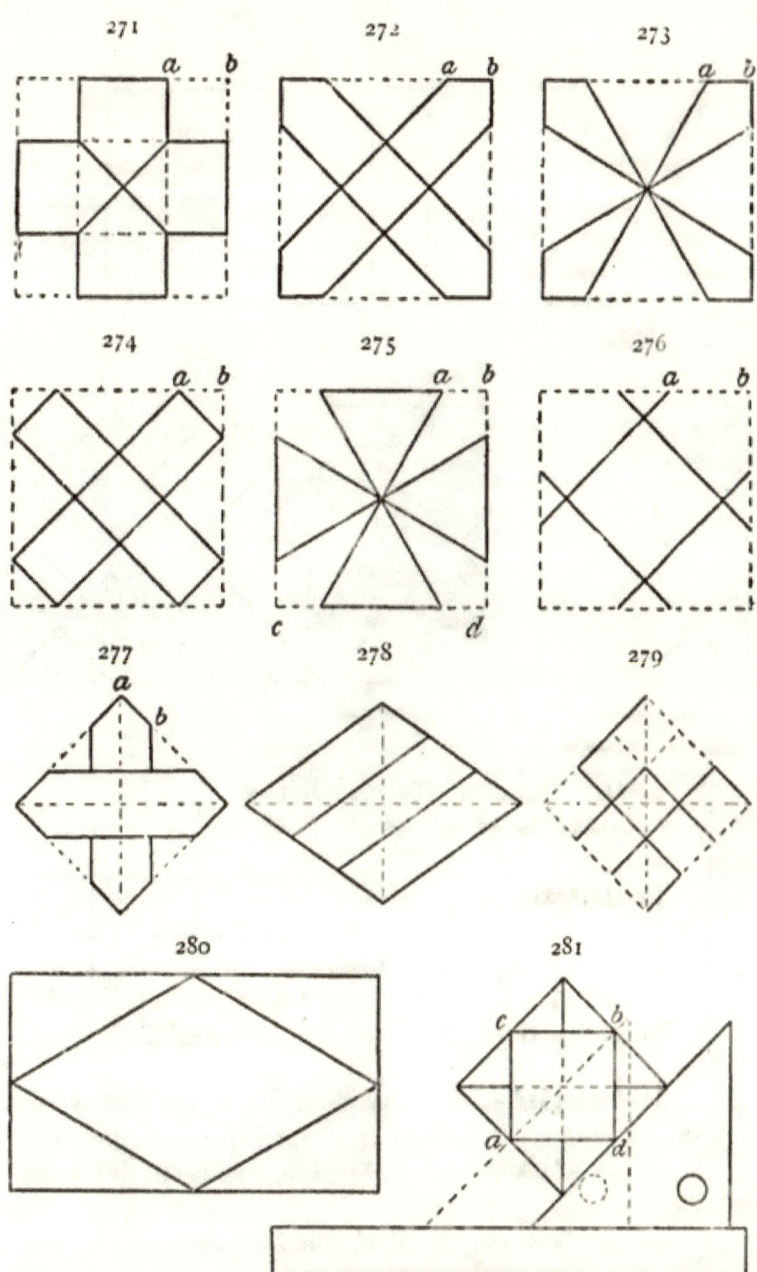

Note.—In figs. 273 and 275 care must be taken to see that the lines pass exactly through the centre.

Fig. 277.—Draw the diagonals and complete the square, and then set off the distance *ab* from each angle.

Fig. 279.—This is rather difficult for children to see at first, but if the teacher places the ruler on the copy and marks in the dotted lines, they will at once perceive that the copy is obtained by dividing each side of a square into three equal parts and emphasizing portions of the lines.

Fig. 281.—Draw the diagonals and obtain the square as in fig. 277. To obtain the middle points of each side of the square, place the 45° set-square with its longest edge on the side of the figure, as shown. Keep the ruler firmly in position, and slip the set-square into the position shown by the dotted lines, so that its longest edge is now on the centre of the square, and mark in the points *a* and *b*. Reverse the set-square, still keeping the ruler in its place, and obtain *c* and *d*.

Note.—This is a very important method, as when the square is constructed from the diagonal the side cannot be bisected easily, as its length is not known. It has also the advantage of being quickly performed, and gives the pupils increased power in the use of the set-square.

Triangles.—These are classified in two ways, either according to their sides or to their angles. When named from their **sides** they are called :—

1. **Equilateral.**—Three equal sides.
2. **Isosceles.**—Two equal sides.
3. **Scalene.**—All the sides unequal.

When named according to their **angles** they are called :—

1. **Right-angled.**—When one of the angles is a right angle.
2. **Acute-angled.**—When each angle is less than a right angle.
3. **Obtuse-angled.**—When one angle is greater than a right angle.

Notes.—1. These two ways of denoting triangles should be frequently explained and defined.

2. It will be quite sufficient for the pupils to test the size of the angle with the set-square in determining whether it be a right angle or not.

The terms **base** and **apex** or **vertex** should be explained.

The equilateral triangle, fig. 282.—Draw *ab* the required size. Place the 60° set-square on the ruler with the angle of 60° at *a*, as shown by the light line, and draw *ac*. Keep the ruler in position, reverse the set-square, and draw *bc*. This is much more expeditious and accurate than bisecting *ab*, drawing a perpendicular, and cutting it with a distance equal to *ab* to obtain the point *c*.

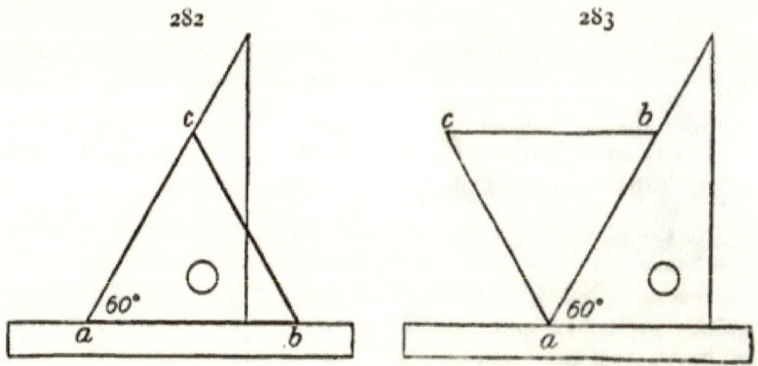

If the figure stands upon its angle, as in **fig. 283**, then place the ruler and set-square as shown, and draw *ab* and *ac* as before. Make *ab* and *ac* the required length, and join *b* with *c*.

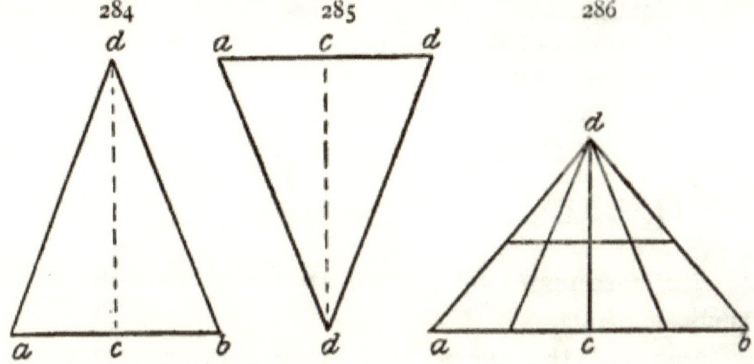

The isosceles triangle, figs. 284, 285, 286.—Draw the base *ab* and obtain the centre *c*. Set up the altitude to the required height, and draw the sides.

The **right-angled triangle** will need no comment. It might be pointed out that it may also be isosceles like the 45° set-square.

Zigzags.—Fig. 287 forms a good exercise on the equilateral triangle. Draw two parallel lines a little wider apart than the

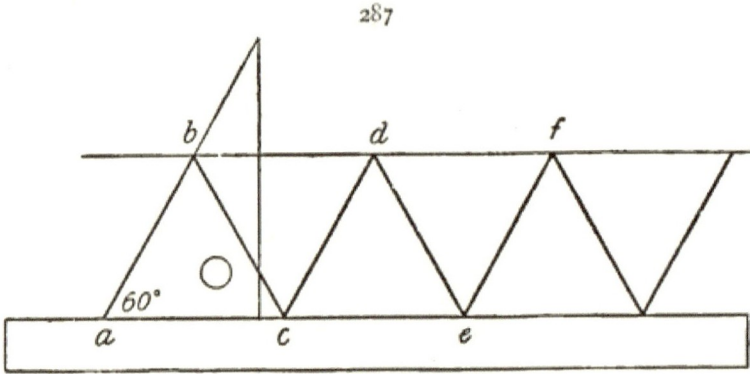

given copy. Mark point *a*. Place the ruler on *ac*, and with the 60° set-square draw *ab*. Reverse the set-square and draw *bc*, then *cd*, *de*, *ef*, &c., reversing the set-square for each line.

Fig. 288.—This is another example of the same character. Draw two parallels as before and obtain the single zigzag *abcdef*

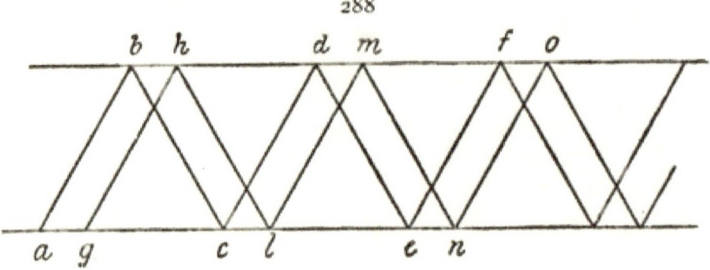

as in the last figure. Now fix the position of *g*, making *ag* slightly larger than the copy. Draw *gh* with the set-square in the same manner as *ab*, and complete the zigzag *ghlmno* as before.

The previous examples are based upon the equilateral triangle. If, however, the lines are not drawn at an angle of 60°, then vertical lines should be drawn as in **fig. 289**, and the zigzag completed by drawing a series of alternate diagonals.

The Hexagon.—This is a very important and interesting figure, as so many pretty and useful exercises may be based on it. It affords excellent practice with the set-square, and will do more to accustom the pupil to ready manipulation of this useful instrument than any other exercise.

I. **Standing on its base, fig. 290.**—Draw ab, say one and a-half inches in length. Adjust the set-square as shown in position A, and draw bc. Place the set-square as in B and draw af. Make bc and af both equal to ab. With the ruler on ab slip the set-square from A to point f as shown by the dotted line, and

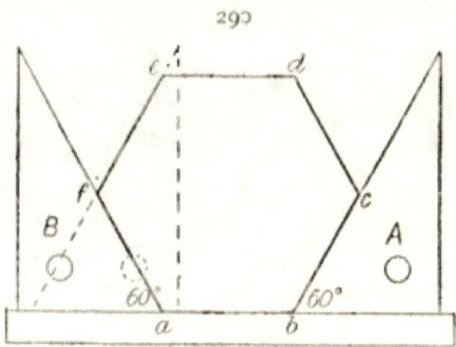

draw fe. Reverse the set-square and obtain cd. Make fe and cd equal to ab. Join d and e. Now let the pupils draw hexagons of various sizes until the figures can be quickly and deftly constructed. If the required hexagon be a large one, then place the ruler on af and obtain fe in the same manner that af was obtained from ab, &c. In all cases it will be necessary for the class to draw the figure line by line with the teacher, and a strict watch must be kept to see that each child always places his set-square *on the ruler*.

Various diagonals, &c., may be drawn across the figure, forming fresh exercises, as in figs. 291-293.

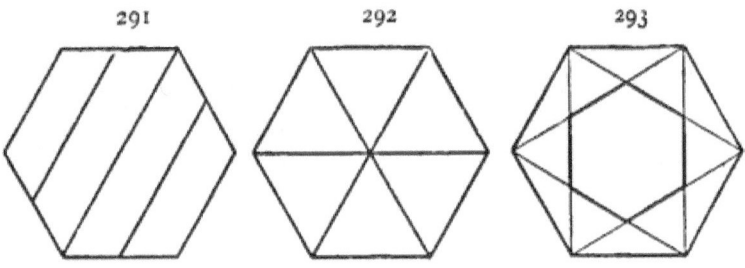

As an exercise in ingenuity the pupil may now be shown how to complete the hexagon without measuring the sides, as in **fig. 294**.

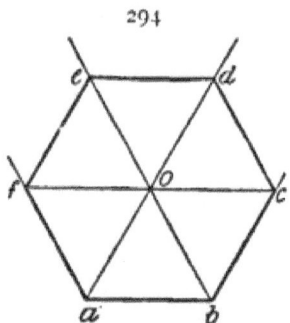

Draw *ab* of the required length. Obtain *bc* and *ad* with the set-square. Reverse the set-square and draw *af* and *be*. Place one edge of the set-square on *ab* and draw a line through *o* parallel to *ab*, cutting off the sides *af* and *bc* equal to *ab*. From *f* and *c* draw *fe* and *cd* parallel to *ad* and *be* respectively, and cutting the lines *be* and *ad* in *e* and *d*. Join *e* with *d*.

II. **When standing on an angle, fig. 295.**—Mark the point *a* and rule a faint line *xy* through it. With the ruler on the line, and the set-square with its angle of 30° placed as shown, draw *ab* and *af* the required length. Keep the ruler in its position and draw *bc* and *fe* at right angles to *xy* and equal to *ab*. Draw *ed* and *cd* parallel to *ab* and *af* respectively by slipping the set-square from its first position across to point *e*. If the set-square be not large enough, then place the ruler on *ec*.

Fig. 296.—This is a common test, and if worked as shown, from the hexagon, presents no difficulty whatever.

Standard III

295

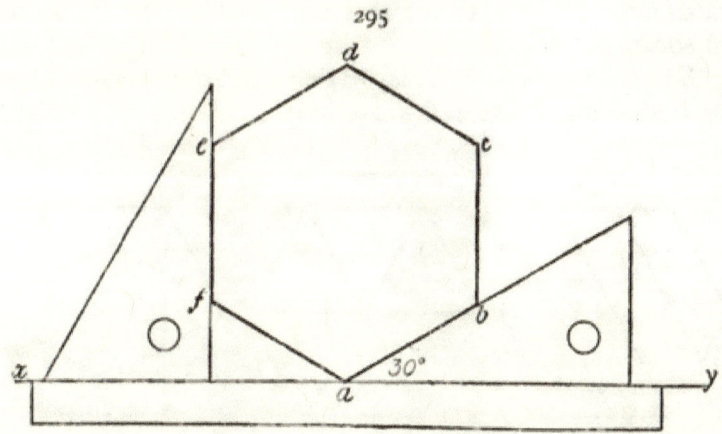

The **lesson** should be given somewhat after the following manner.

A drawing of the figure without any construction lines should be placed before the class. If the pupils be each provided with a copy it will be advantageous.

1. How many points has the figure? '*Six.*'

If I join them, how many sides will the figure have?

What do we call a figure with six sides? '*A hexagon.*'

Elicit illustrations, such as nuts in machinery, bees'-cells, patterns, &c.

2. Draw a hexagon roughly on the board, and join the alternate corners.

What figure is formed? '*An equilateral triangle.*'

Why is it called equilateral?

296

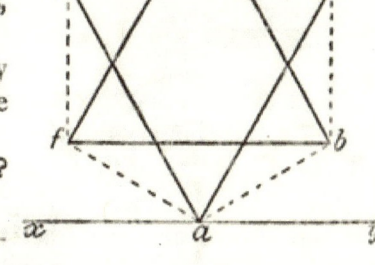

Join the remaining corners. The pupils will now see that the figure formed is the drawing required.

3. Measure the distance between *a* and *b* on the given copy, and explain that as the drawing has to be a little larger each side

G

of the hexagon must be enlarged. For example, if *ab* be one and a-half inches on the copy, then on the drawing it should be made about one and three-quarters of an inch or two inches in length.

4. Draw *xy* and mark a point *a* in the centre.

Which angle of the set-square must be used? ' *The smallest.*'

Now, step by step, obtain the hexagon as in fig. 295, eliciting the reason for each step. Join the alternate angles *f, b, d*, giving the equilateral triangle *fbd*. Complete the figure by drawing the intersecting triangle *ace*.

Notes.—1. Be careful to draw the hexagon either very faintly or in dotted line.

2. Let the pupils draw exercises of different sizes until the method is well understood.

The Octagon.—This forms an exercise in the use of the 45° set-square.

Draw *ab* one inch long. Arrange the set-square as shown (A) : draw *bc* and *ah*, making each line one inch in length. Keep

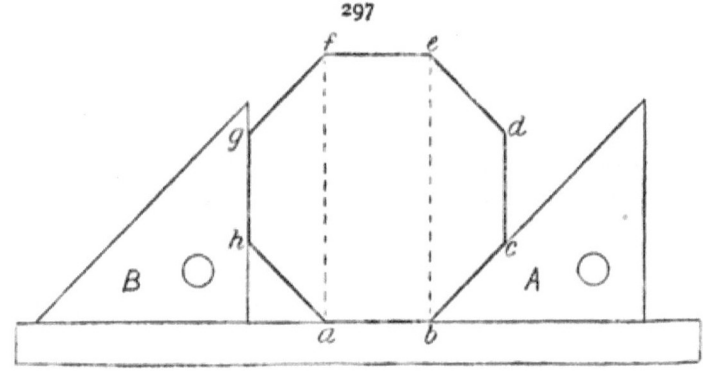

297

the ruler in position, and with the vertical edge of the set-square draw *cd* and *hg* (B). Keep the ruler still on the base, and with the sloping edge of the set-square draw *gf* and *de*. If the set-square be not large enough, place the ruler on *gd*. Vertical lines from *a* and *b* will determine the points *f* and *e*. Join *f* with *e*.

Join the alternate corners as in fig. 298, and two intersecting squares will be produced.

The intersecting squares may, however, be more easily obtained by the method shown in fig. 299.

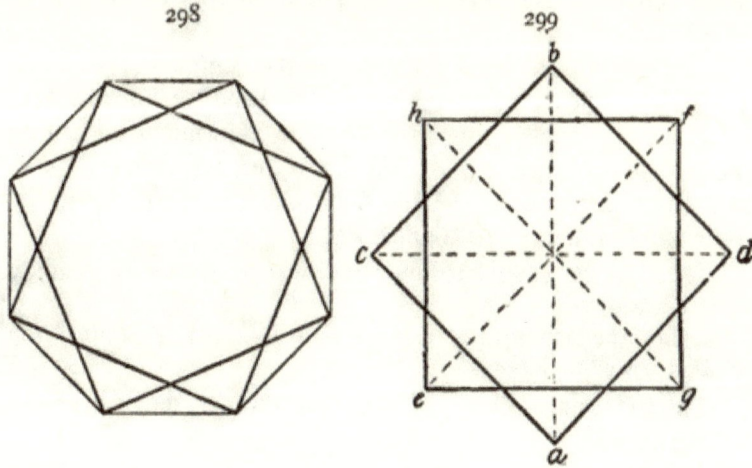

1. Measure the diagonal *ab* on the copy, and decide upon the size to which it should be enlarged. For example, if the diagonal measured two inches, then three inches would be a suitable size for the enlargement.

2. Draw the diagonals *ab* and *cd*, and complete the square *adbc*.

3. Place the set-square on *ad* and draw *ef* parallel to it. Obtain *gh* in a similar manner. Make *ef* and *gh* equal to *ab*, and draw the square *egfh*.

The Pentagon.—This figure cannot be drawn accurately without the use of the compass or the protractor, and should really not be set as a geometrical figure for this Standard, as it cannot be correctly drawn with the ruler only. Various mechanical devices have been given, none of which are very satisfactory, as they are after all only approximations.

The most accurate device is to use the protractor, but as this may not be readily obtainable the teacher can easily cut out in paper angles of 108°, and use these to draw the angles of the figure. The paper angle must be placed so that its edge is exactly on the base *ab* with the angle of 108° at *b* (fig. 300). Place a little tick *c* to mark where the line has to be drawn.

Remove the paper and rule the line. Make the side equal to *ab*. Place the paper at *a* and draw *ae*, then at *e* and draw *ed*. Join *d* with *c*.

The proportions given on **fig. 301** will give a sufficiently accurate pentagon of a convenient size. Let $ab = 2$ in. Draw

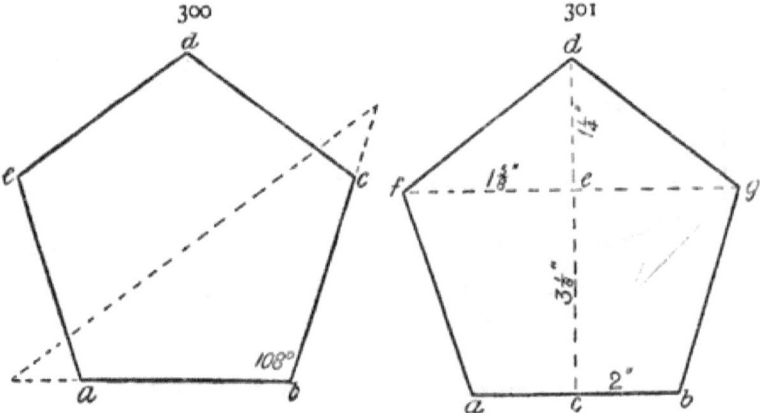

cd perpendicular to *ab* from the middle point *c*, and make it $3\frac{1}{8}$ inch long. Set off *de* = $1\frac{1}{4}$ inch. Draw *fg* parallel to *ab*, and make *ef* and *eg* each = $1\frac{5}{8}$ inch. Draw *af*, *bg*, *fd*, and *gd*.

Note.—In this case the pupils must have the proportions given them.

CHAPTER VI

FREEHAND DRAWING. STANDARDS IV, V, VI, AND VII

IF the methods of obtaining the proportions of the different parts of the copy, and the drawing of the leading and the containing lines have been well taught in Standard III on the methods shown in figs. 203-231, the freehand drawing of the higher standards becomes an easy and pleasant task. The main points that will now require attention are :—

(1) Greater degree of difficulty in the examples.
(2) Increased power in analysing and blocking in the copy.
(3) More skill and finish in the lining in of the drawing. And here I would again point out the necessity of strict attention being paid to the *lining in*. On no account must the pupil be allowed to hurriedly blacken over the lines of the drawing. A careful, clean sketch shows much better and more artistic work than a carelessly lined in drawing. The primary object of lining in is to improve the shape, and to give finish to the work.

It has been thought desirable to take the whole subject of Freehand in one chapter, as it is quite impossible to divide the subject into standards by any arbitrary rule. A selection of suitable copies—including those given in the 'Illustrated Syllabus,' and many that have been set as examination tests—are appended for the teacher's guidance.

Sample lessons are also given, and those copies which illustrate important principles, or present special difficulties, are shown in various stages to indicate the methods by which they should be taught. In some cases the dotted lines are sufficient to indicate the construction. The figures in all cases indicate the order of drawing the lines.

The following arrangement of the examples given is suggested :—

Standard IV.—Figs. 302–329.
Standard V.—Figs. 330–356.
Standard VI.—Figs. 357–376.
Standard VII.—Figs. 377–383.

Standards VI and VII are frequently examined from **cards** instead of large copies placed before the class, and practice must therefore be given in both methods of testing. The pupils when drawing from cards must never be allowed to draw the example the same size as the copy. It should always be either enlarged or reduced; generally the instruction is to make the copy fairly fill the paper.

The time taken for the drawing must be borne in mind, especially towards the examination; fairly rapid work should be encouraged, but on no account must the pupils be allowed to finish their drawings to time at the sacrifice of accuracy in the shape. A portion well drawn and correctly planned is far more valuable than an incorrectly finished exercise.

The following **lesson** indicates the way in which the examples should be taught :—

(1) Place a drawing of the figure before the class, and proceed to question generally as to what it is called, what grows like it, and ask for illustrations of its application in metal scroll work of various kinds. Explain that the drawing is obtained by selecting the important lines only of the object from which the idea is taken; the details and little irregularities are rejected, not being suitable for the required purpose.

(2) Commence with the upright line and mark in the middle point, as the half is very useful for purposes of comparison, even though no line may pass through it.

(3) Mark the point *a* where the bottom curve commences, judging the distance with the eye. Find point *b* by measuring with the eye and pencil.

Where is it? '*A little above the half of the line.*'

What do we want to know next? '*The position of point c.*'

Find the width of the curve on the right and mark point *d*.
Is point *e* as far from the centre line as point *d*?

(4) After marking in point *e* proceed to draw the bottom spiral, taking care to keep the curve continuous throughout. The first time of drawing a spiral the pupils may, if thought well, draw the dotted lines shown on **fig. 303** as guides for the curves. They should, however, be discarded afterwards, as

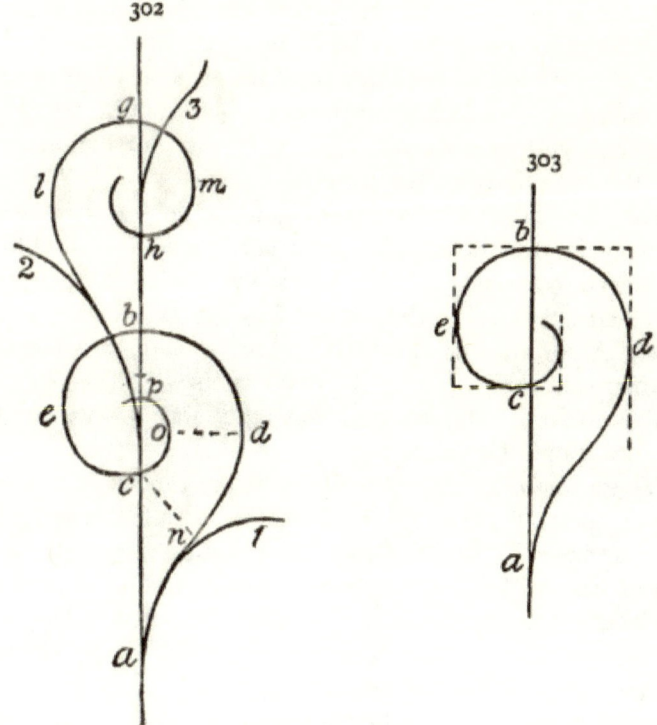

all aids of this character tend more or less to limit the pupil's confidence and freedom in drawing bold curves.

(5) Draw the top spiral in a similar manner, first marking in points *g*, *h*, *l*, *m*.

(6) Now show how the parts 1, 2, and 3 branch off from the other lines. Notice that they form a continuous line with the previous part of the curve as in *A*, not as in *B* (fig. 304).

Attention must also be directed to the fact that the spiral gradually decreases towards its centre, *od* is slightly less than

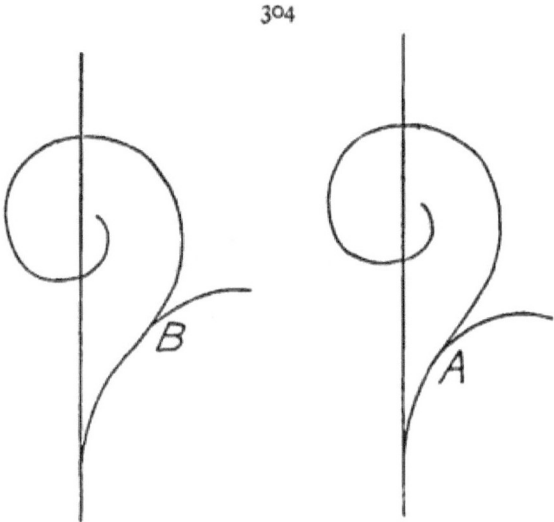

304

cn, and *bp* less than *od* (fig. 302). This point may be easily illustrated by rolling a piece of paper so as to form a spiral.

Standard IV

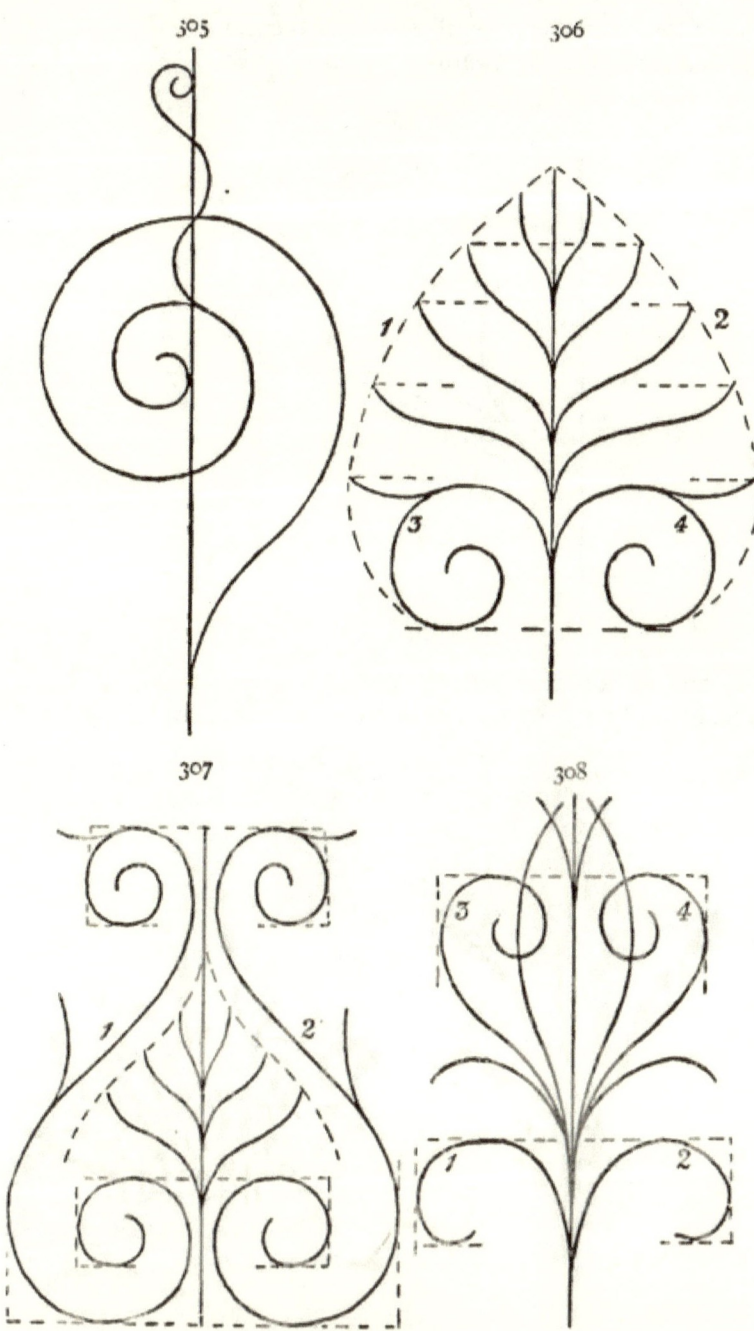

309

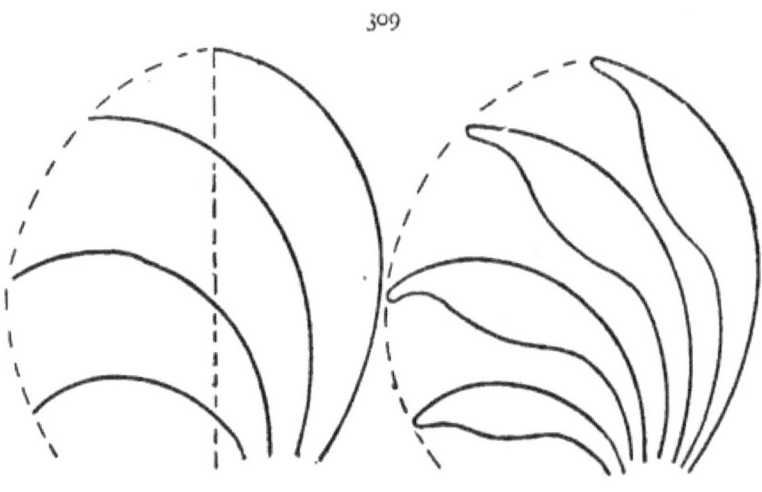

310

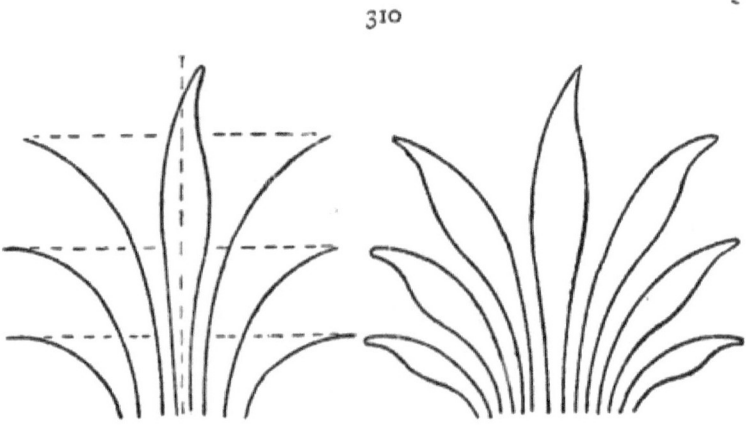

Standard IV

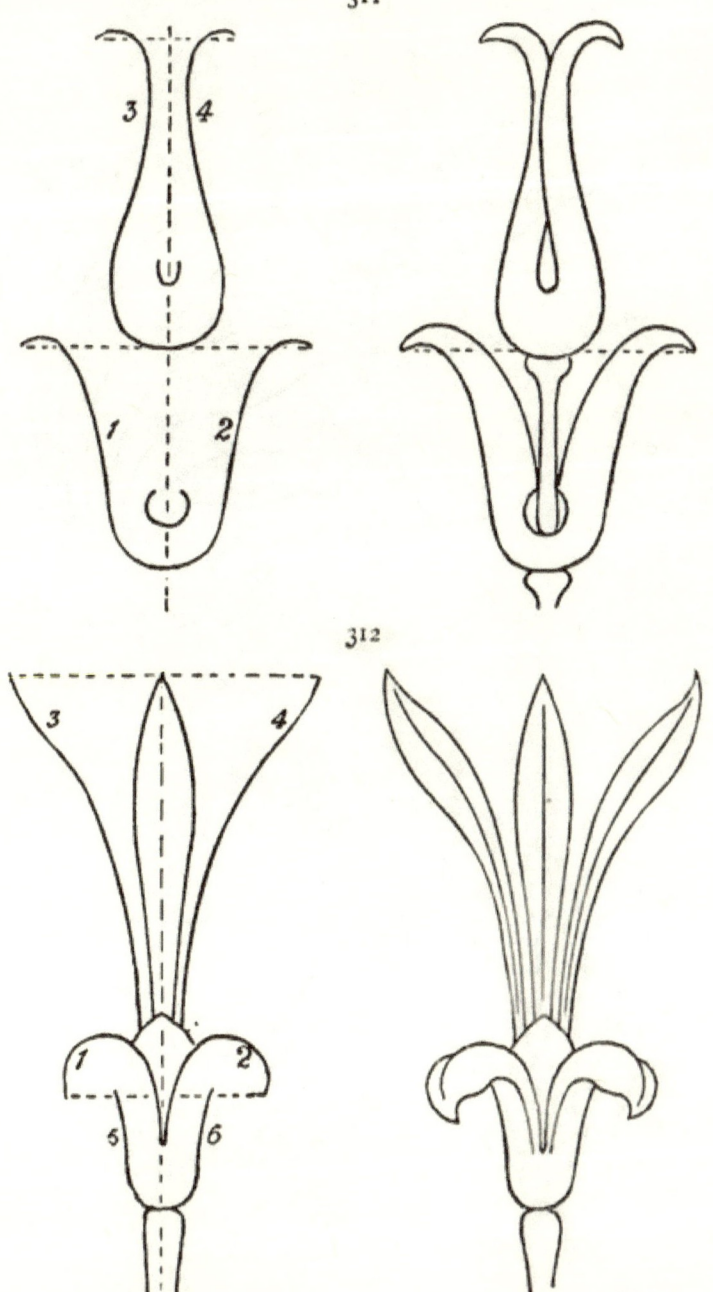

311

312

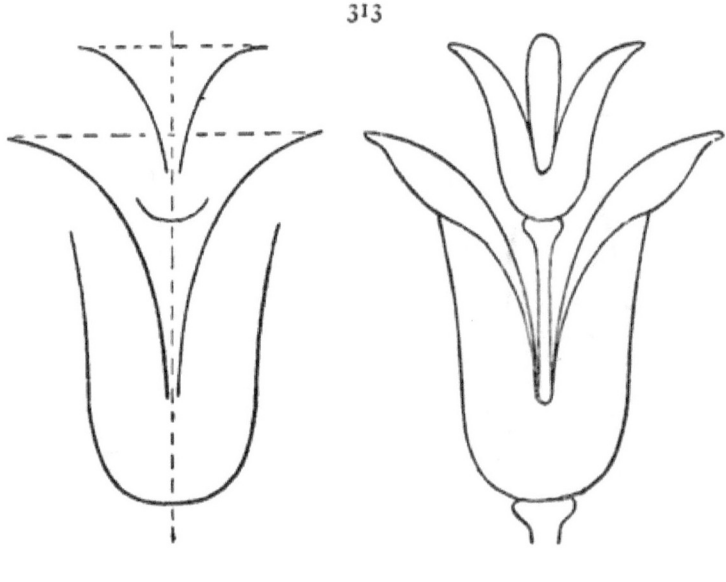

313

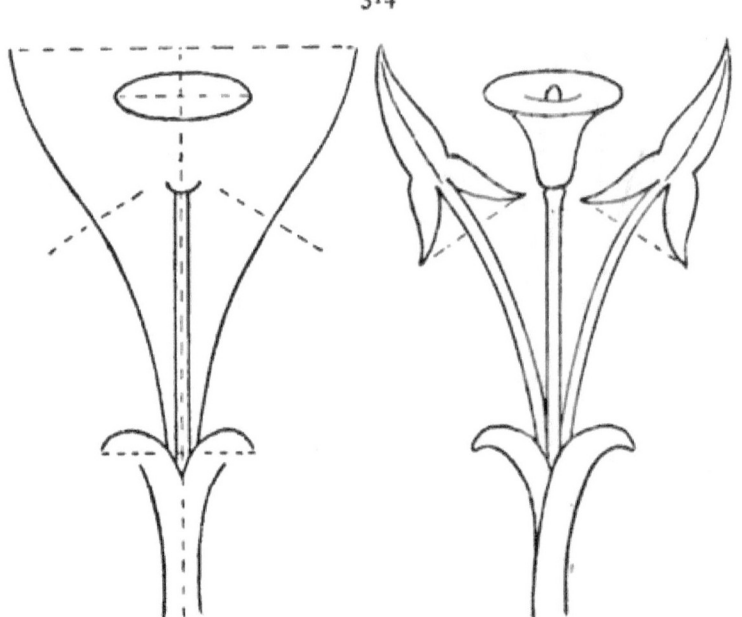

314

Standard IV

315

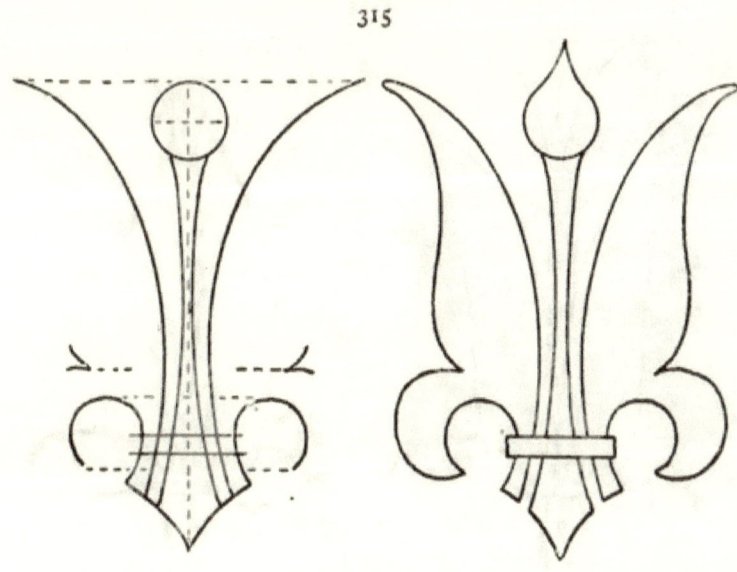

316

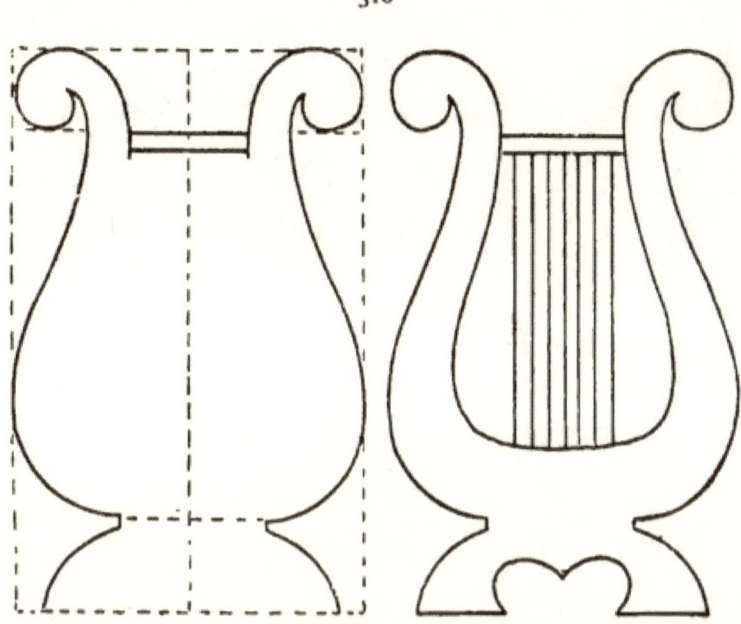

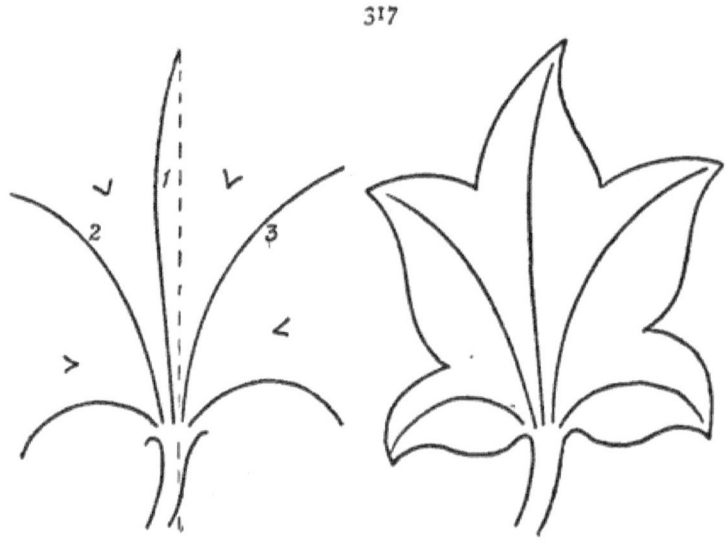

317

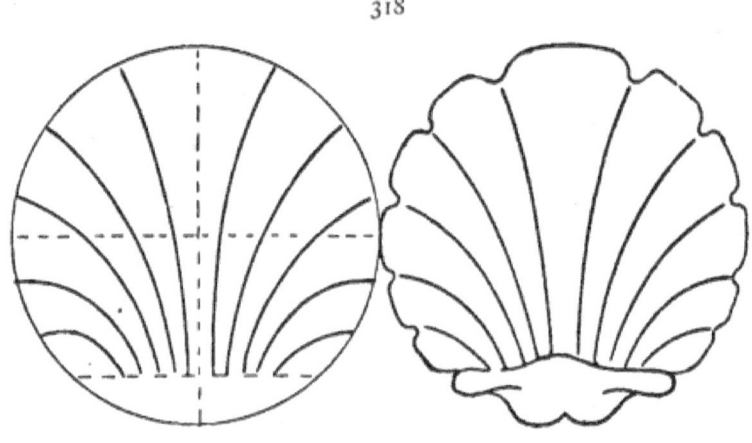

318

319

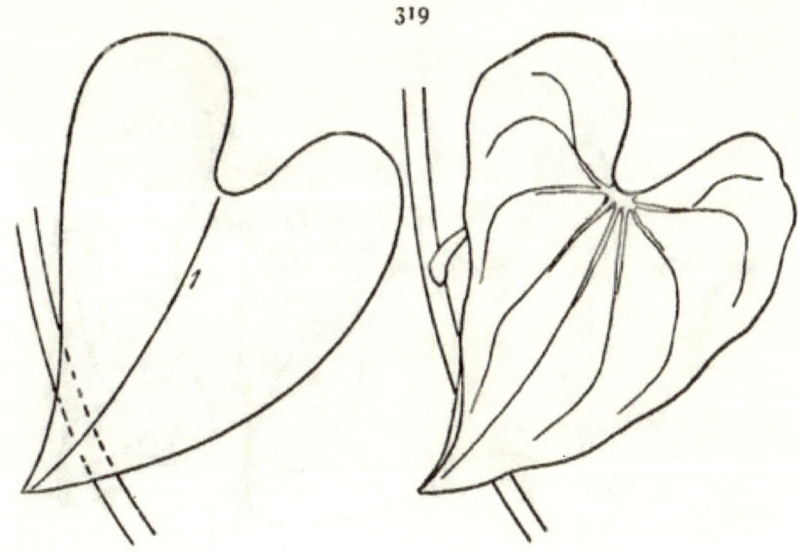

320

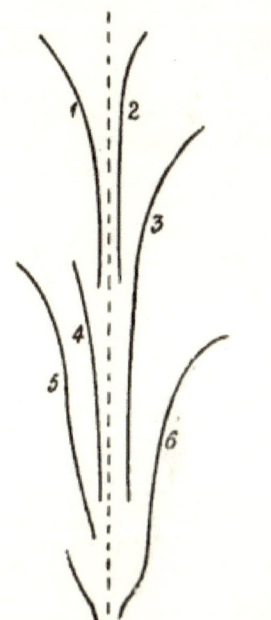 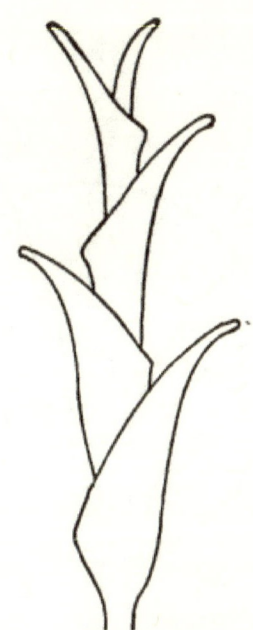

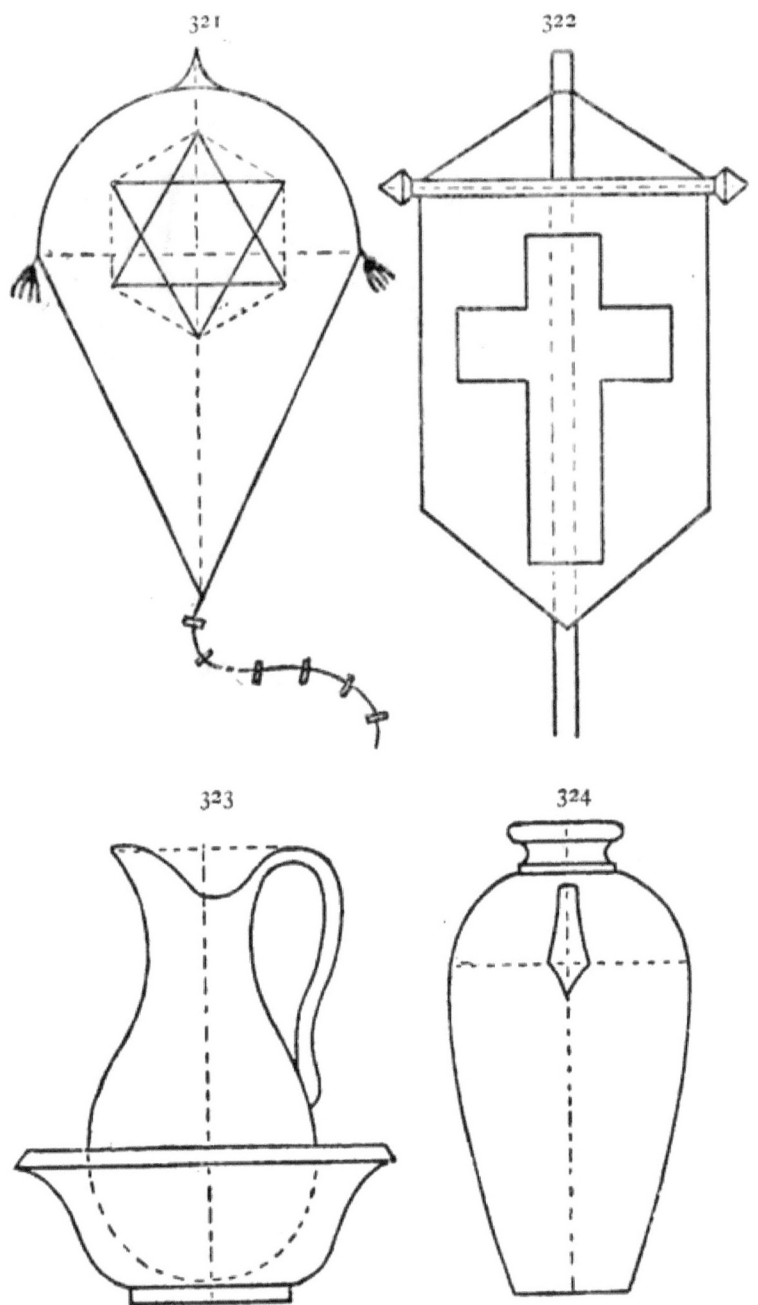

Standard IV

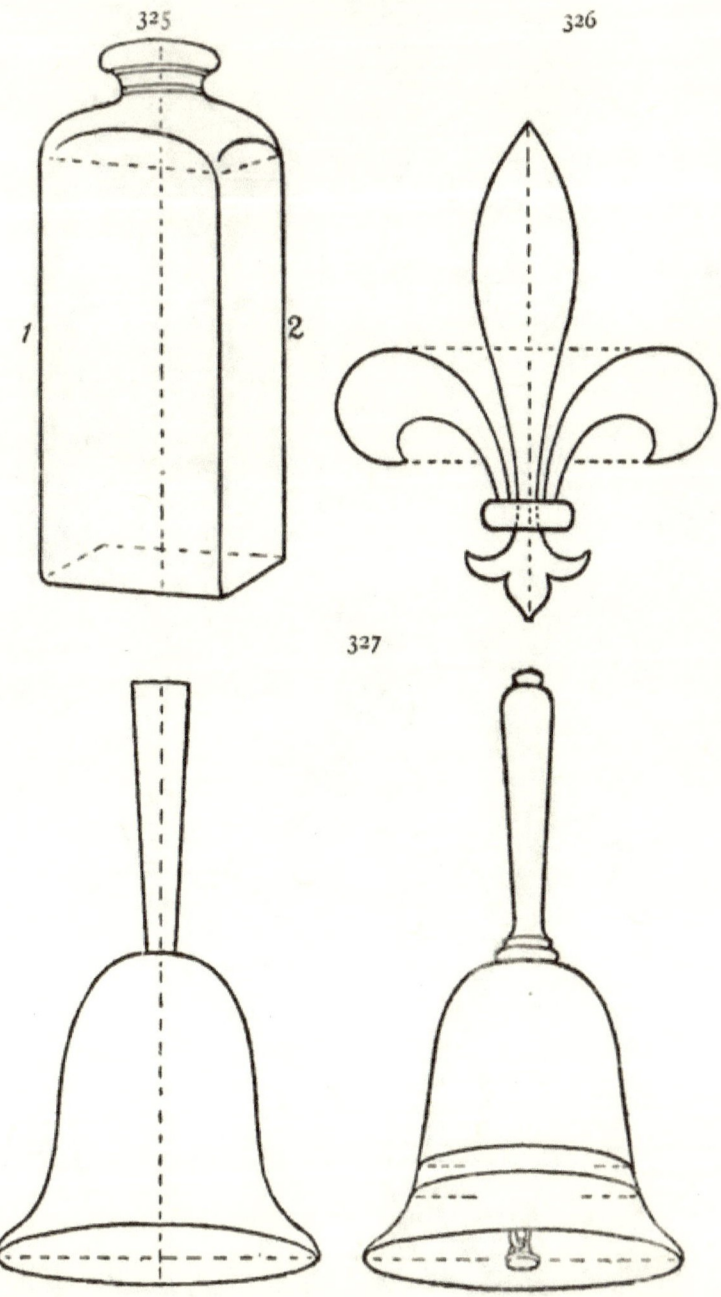

98 The Teaching of Drawing

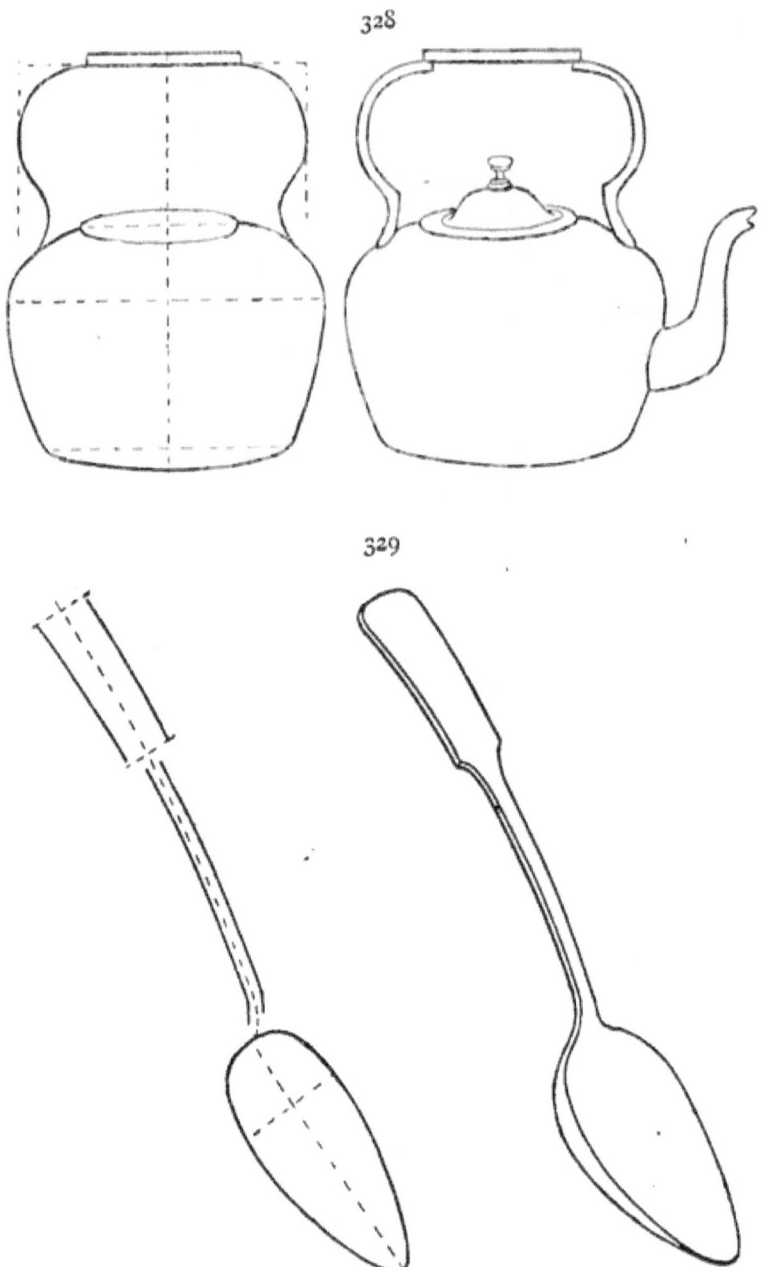

STANDARD V

The figures suggested for this Standard are arranged more with reference to their form and the principles which they illustrate, than to the order in which it may be most desirable to teach them. It will probably be found more interesting to intermix the vases shown in figs. 332-338 with the other copies, than to draw them in the order in which they are given. These vases are typical shapes, possessing great beauty of contour, and are those which are most commonly used in model drawing. They afford excellent practice in the drawing of bold, symmetrical curves. As vases when placed in a vertical position present a somewhat similar appearance to all the class, it will be found to be of considerable assistance to the model drawing if the pupils have previously practised the vases as freehand exercises ; the same method of working being followed out in both model and freehand.

Attention should be directed to the fact that all the vases given are based on the oval—that is, one end of the body is larger than the other, like an egg. This form gives a much more elegant shape than either the circle or the ellipse would do.

The method of drawing is shown in stages and by the aid of dotted lines. The following steps refer particularly to **fig. 334,** but are also generally applicable to most vases.

1. Draw the centre line, *ab*.
2. Find the position *c* of the widest part of the vase.
3. Compare the greatest width with the height, and set it out, *de*.
4. Draw the diameters of the mouth and foot of the vase, *fg* and *hk*, comparing them with the greatest width, *de*.
5. Carefully sketch in the oval for the body, afterwards removing the parts which are not needed.
6. Draw the ellipses for the mouth and foot.
7. Mark the narrowest part of the neck, *lm*.
8. Draw the curve uniting the mouth with the body.
9. Suggest the thickness as shown in fig. 330. It will be necessary to make enlarged drawings on the board of the details

connected with the mouths and feet of vases. For example, the mouth of fig. 334 is suggested in the following manner. The edge being rounded off, the thickness is only visible at each side.

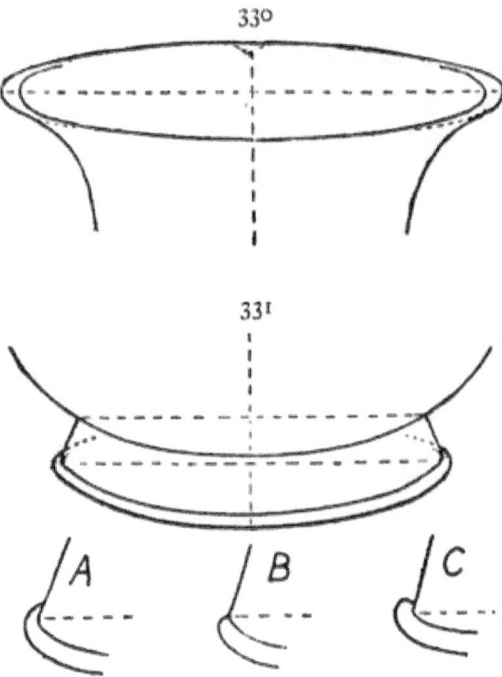

The foot of fig. 338 should be drawn as in **fig. 331**. The outer ellipse should be shown going behind the inner ellipse, as in A, not like B or C.

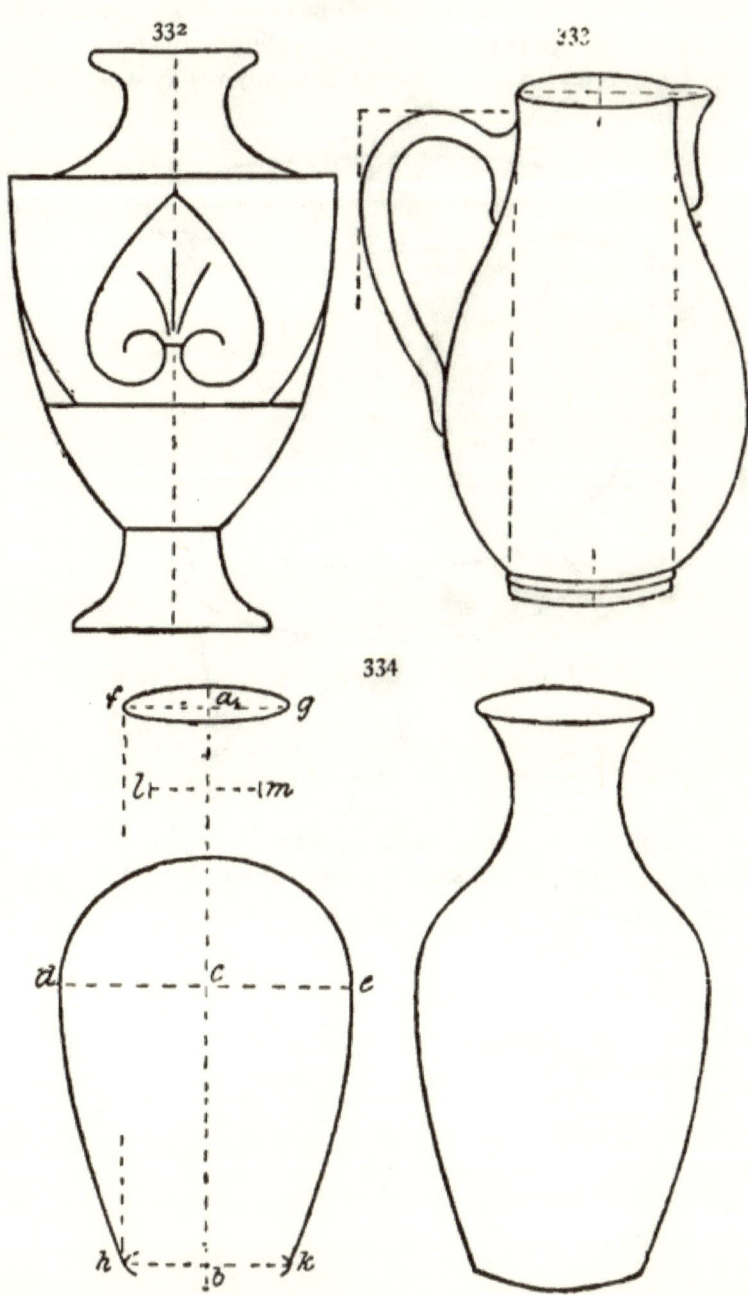

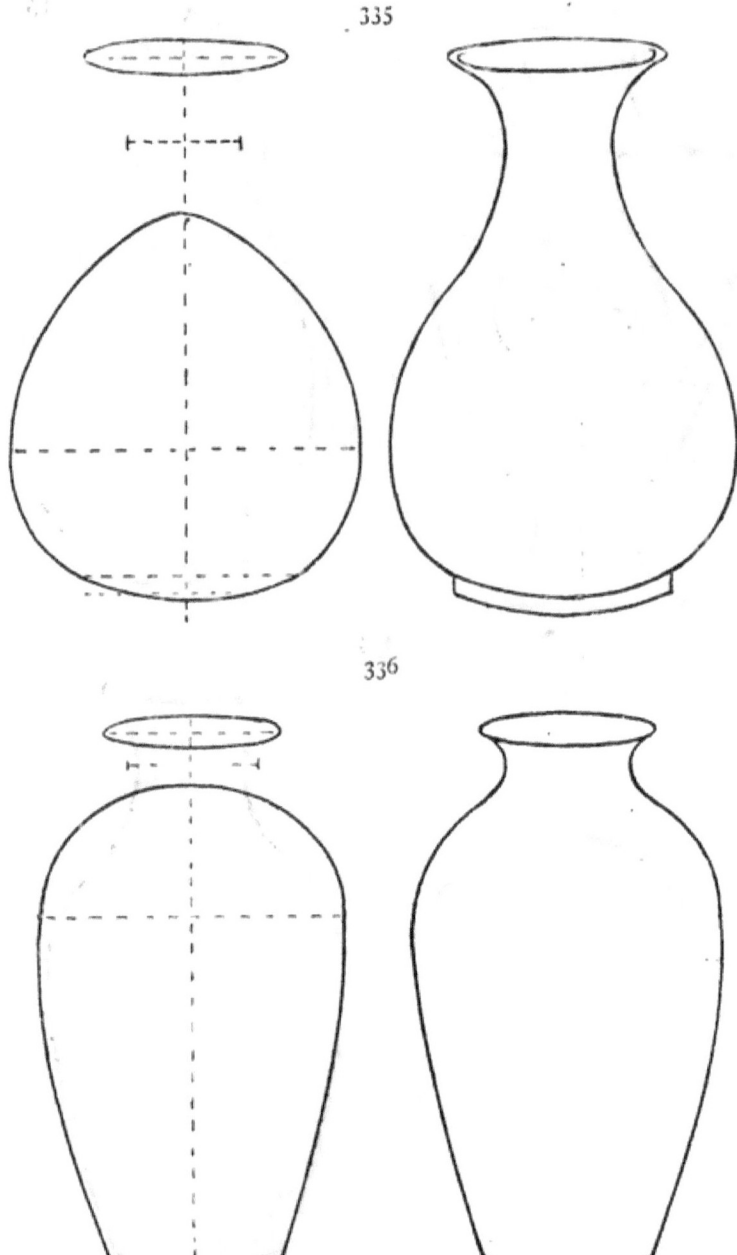

Standard V

337

338

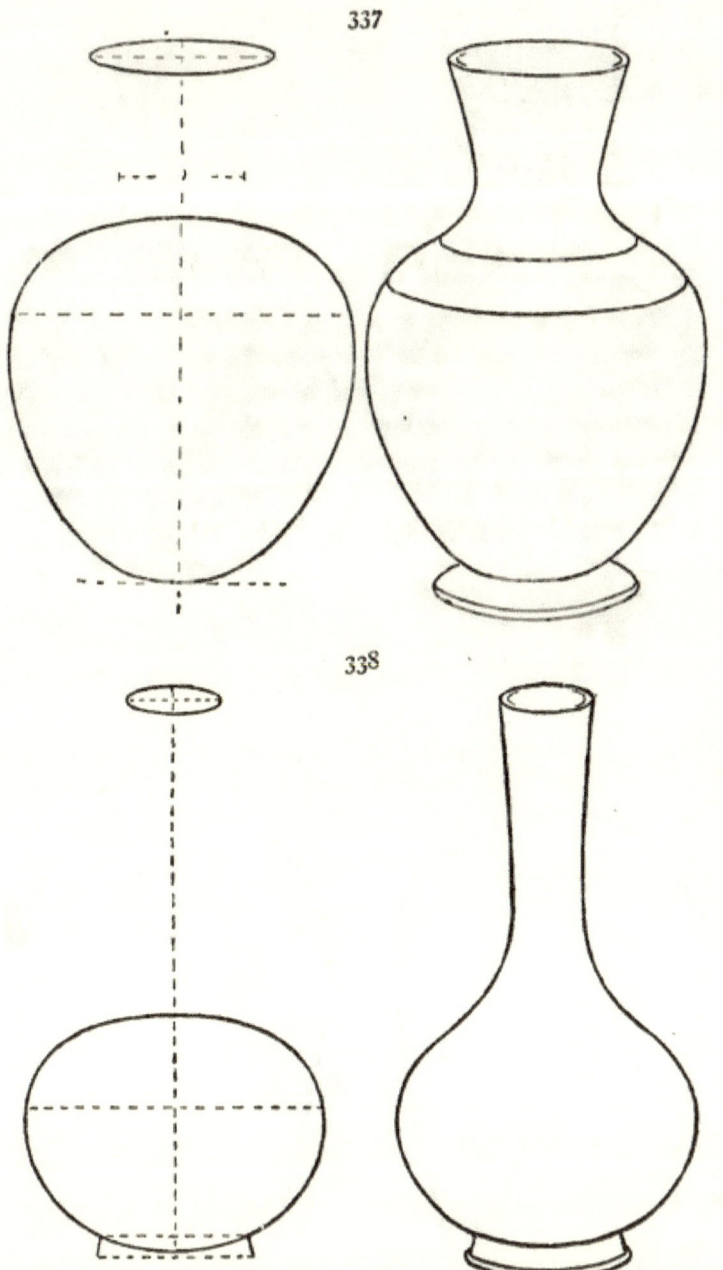

Fig. 339 is an excellent example for teaching from, as it affords practice in analysing and blocking in a copy. It is shown in three stages of development, and should be taught in the following manner :—

1. Draw an upright line, *ab*.
2. Draw *cd* just below the point *a*.
3. Compare *ed* with *ab*.
4. After marking the position of *c* and *d*, fix the points *f* and *g*, and draw the curves *cf* and *dg*.
5. Find the position of *h* and draw a line through it.
6. Mark the points *l* and *m*, comparing *hl* with *ec*.
7. Draw the curves from *l* and *m*, taking care to let them run into *cf* and *dg*, so as to form a continuous curve from *f* to *l* and from *g* to *m*.

The leading lines of the figure are now obtained, and the drawings should be carefully examined before proceeding any further. When this stage has been correctly drawn the pupils may go to the stage marked *B*.

8. Mark the width of the middle leaf at its widest part, *no*.
9. Draw the middle vein, noticing that the point of the leaf bends over to the right.
10. Draw the sides of the leaf, taking care to let the lines run into *cf* and *dg* gradually.
11. Mark the width at *p* and *q*, and draw the curve.
12. Draw the lines *rs* and *tu* at right angles to *cf* and *dg*, and put in the top curves of the flower.
13. Unite *l* and *m* with the bottom curve as is shown on the left hand side of fig. *B*. This is rather a difficult curve, and requires great care.
14. The leading lines and masses of the figure being now completed, the drawings should again be carefully examined, after which the figure may be finished as in *C*.
15. Mark the position of *v* and *w*, and draw the short curve first.
16. Draw the bottom curve of the flower as shown on the left side of *C*.
17. Put in the stems and complete the figure.

339

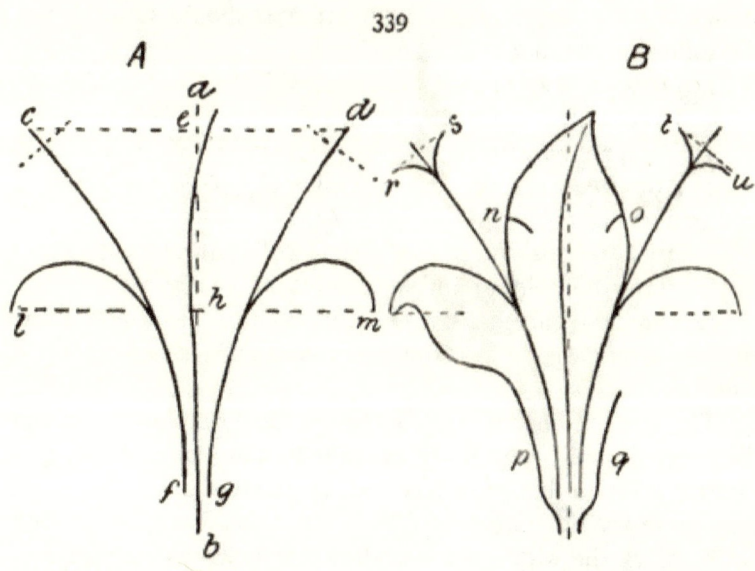

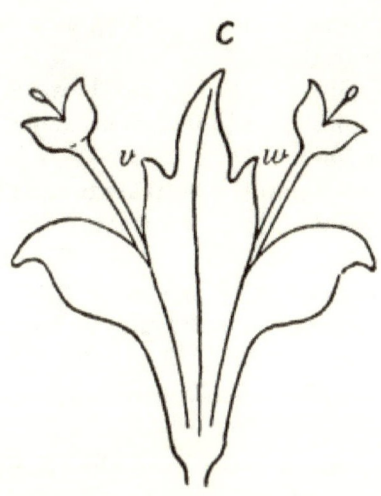

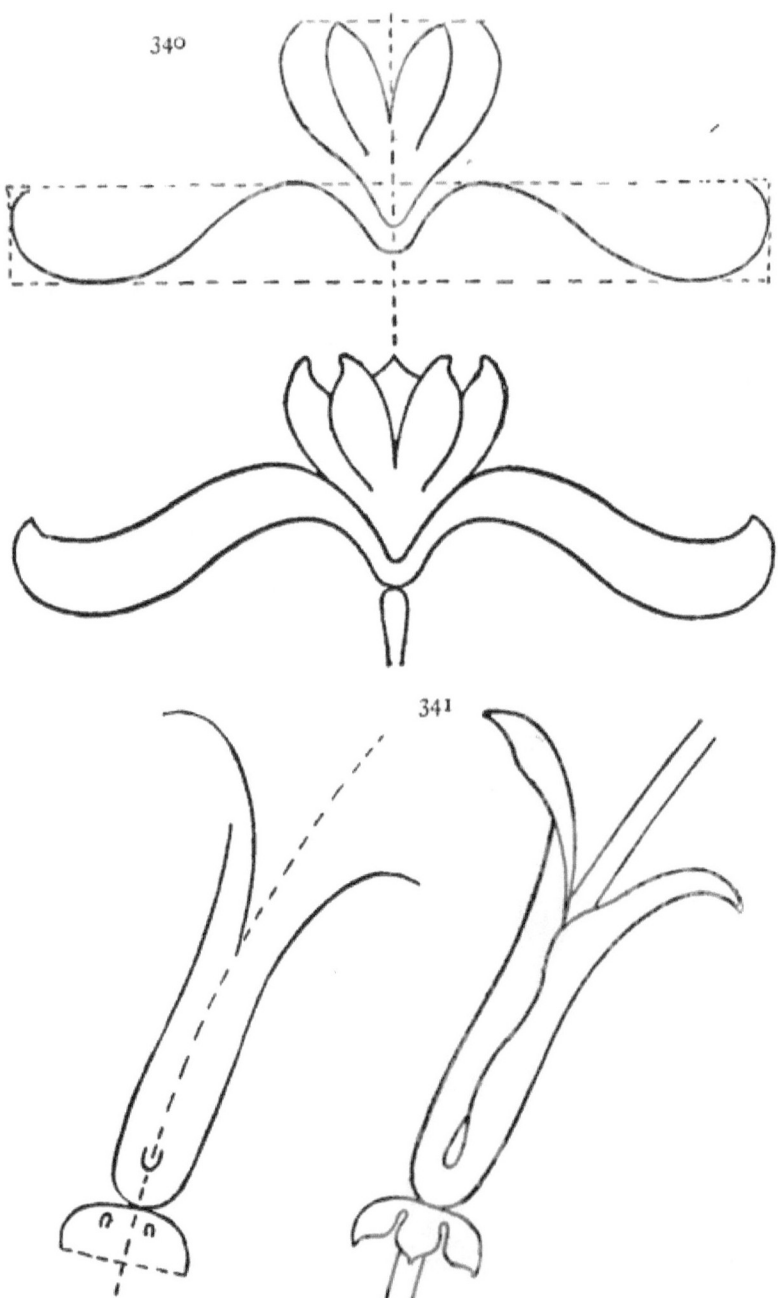

Standard V

342

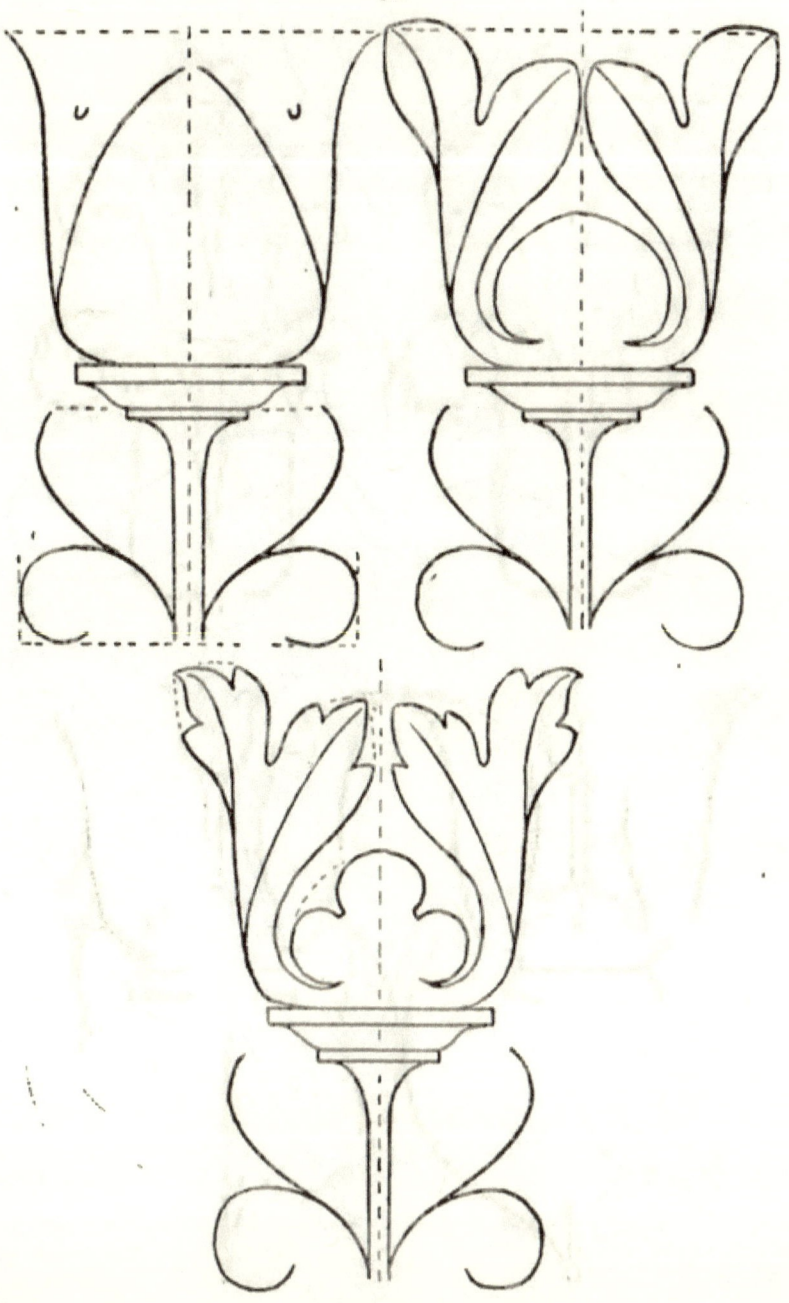

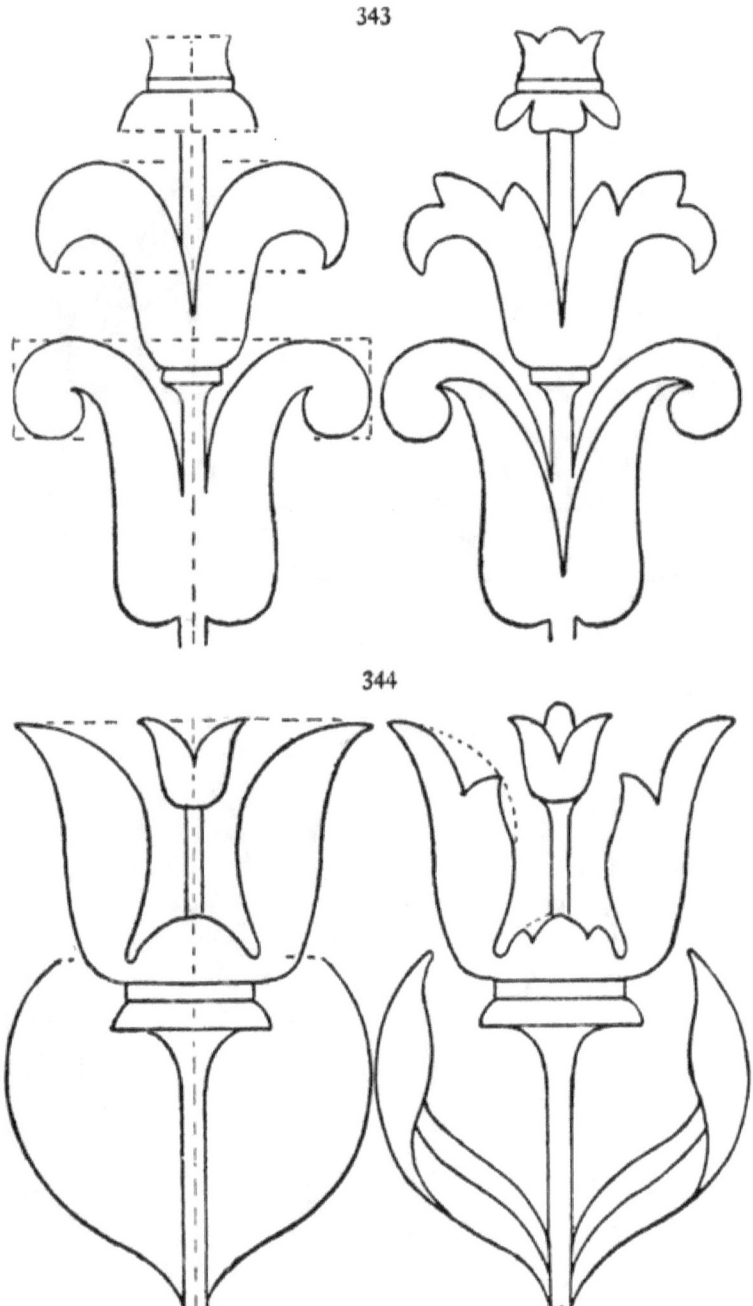

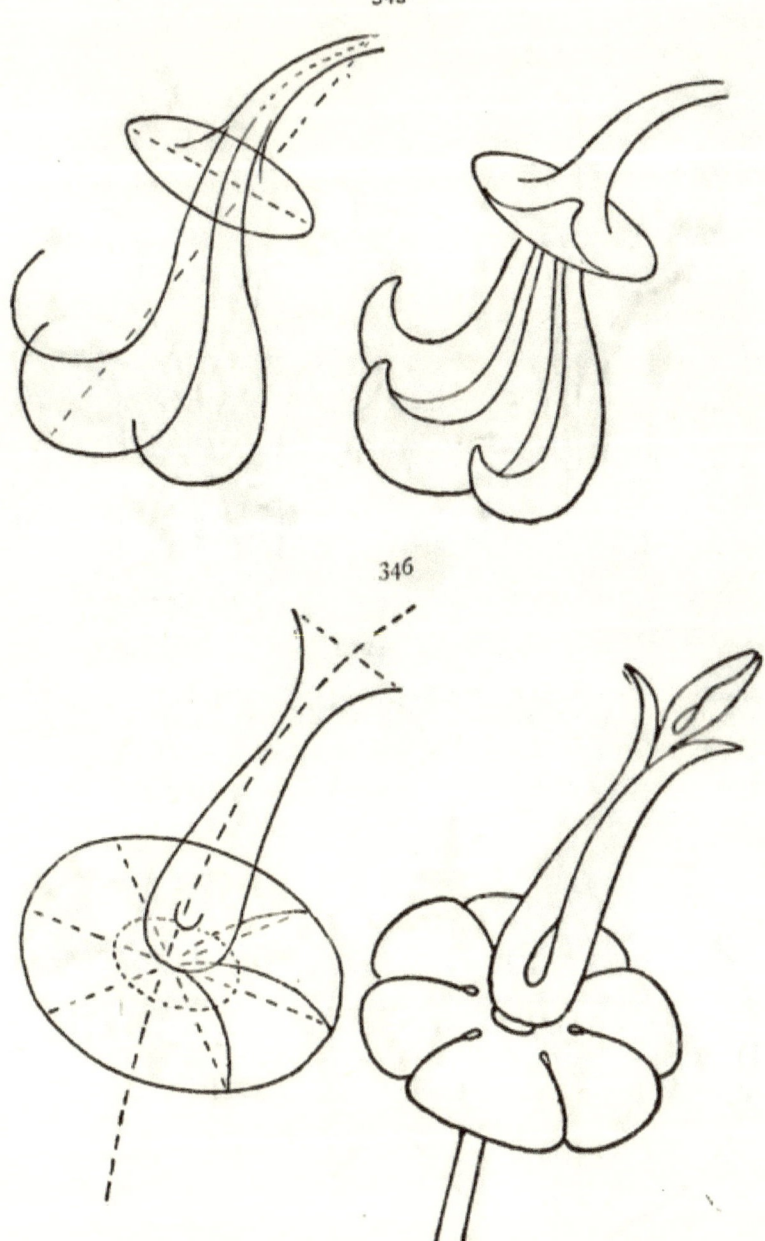

345

346

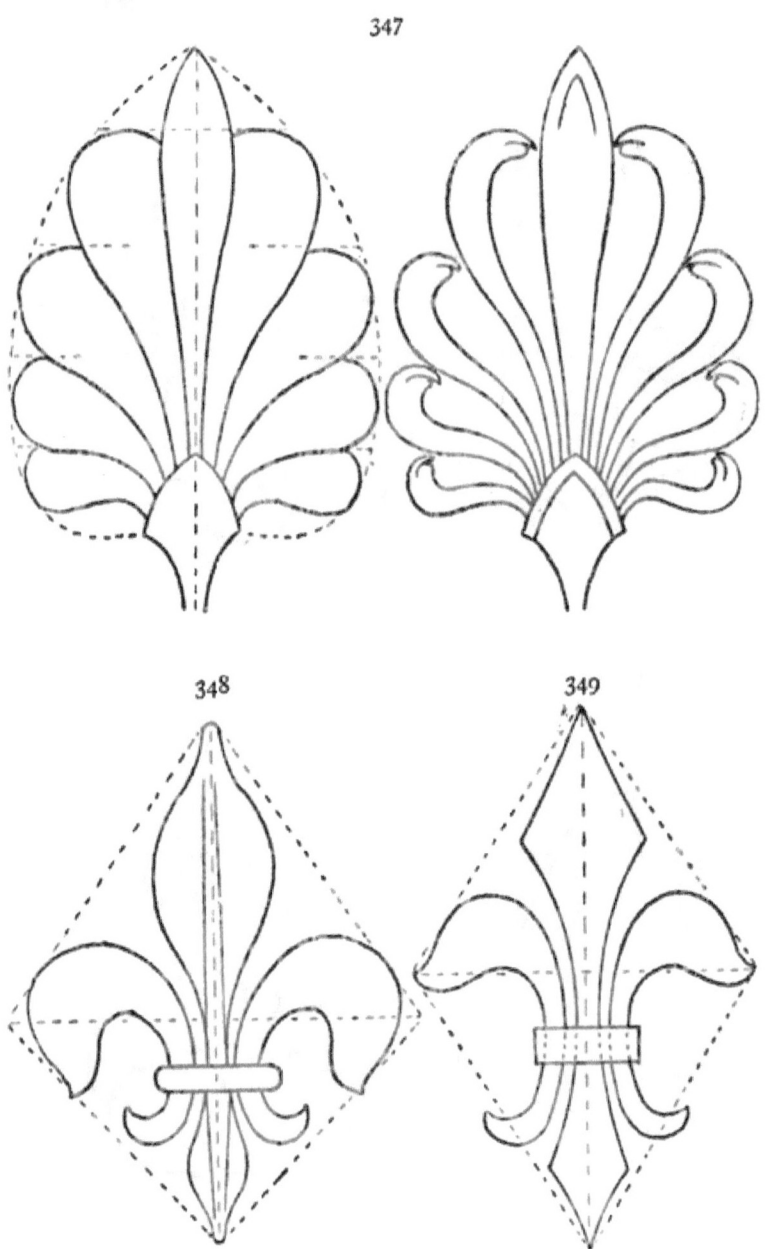

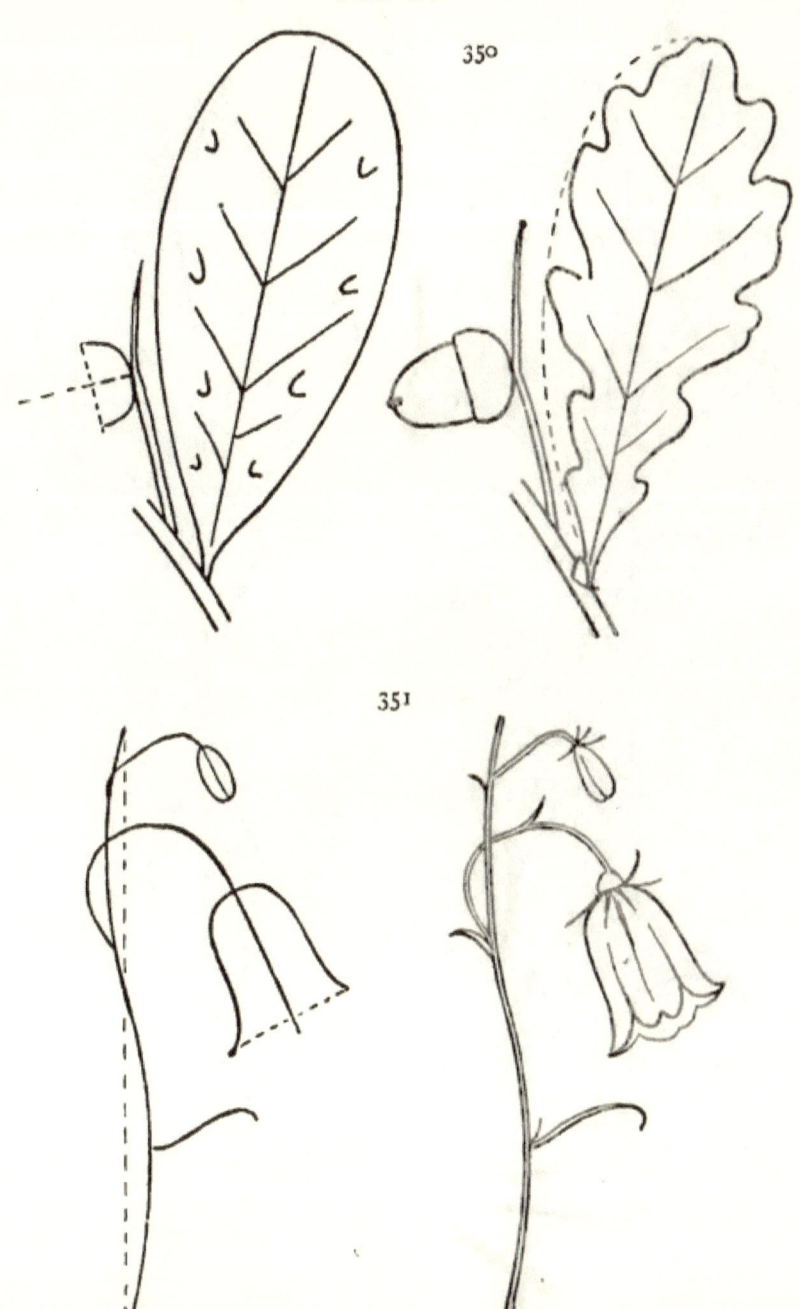

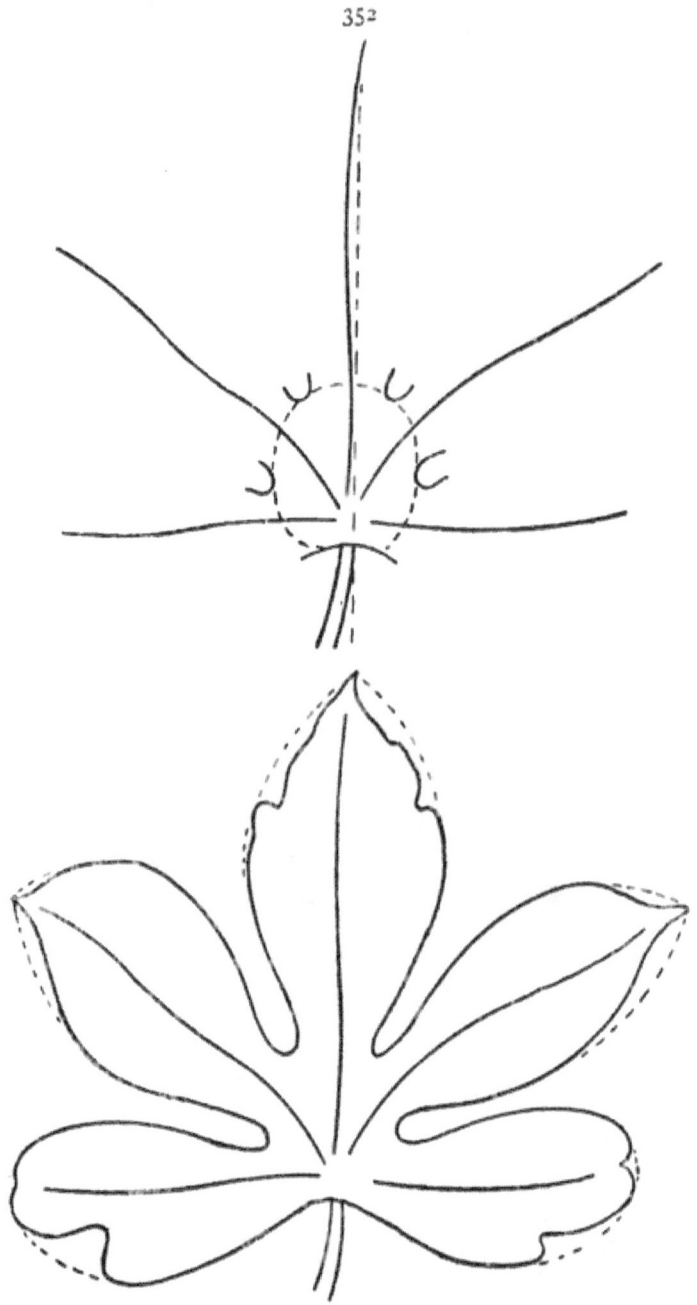

Standard V

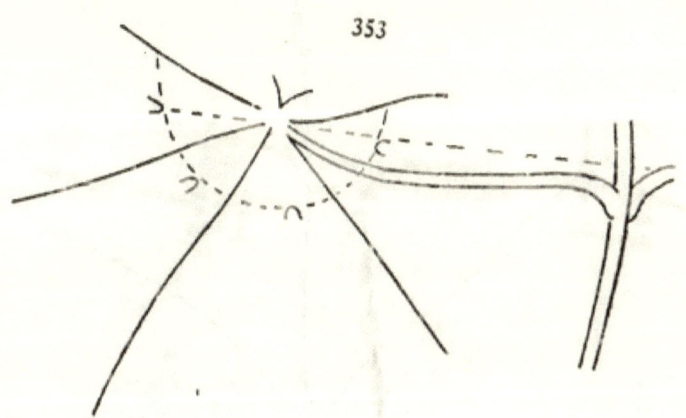

353

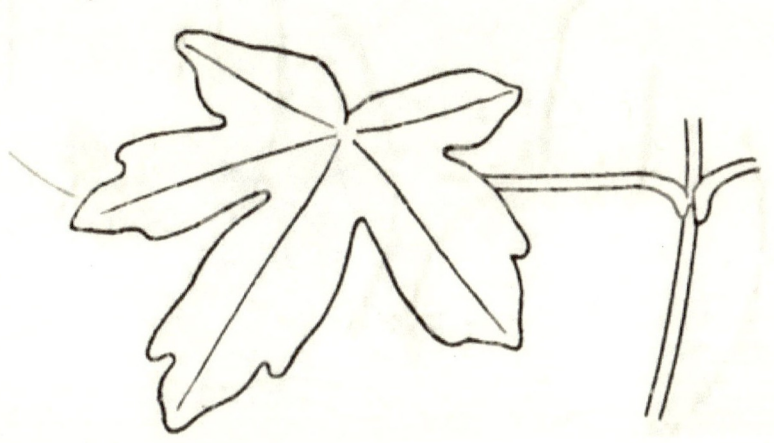

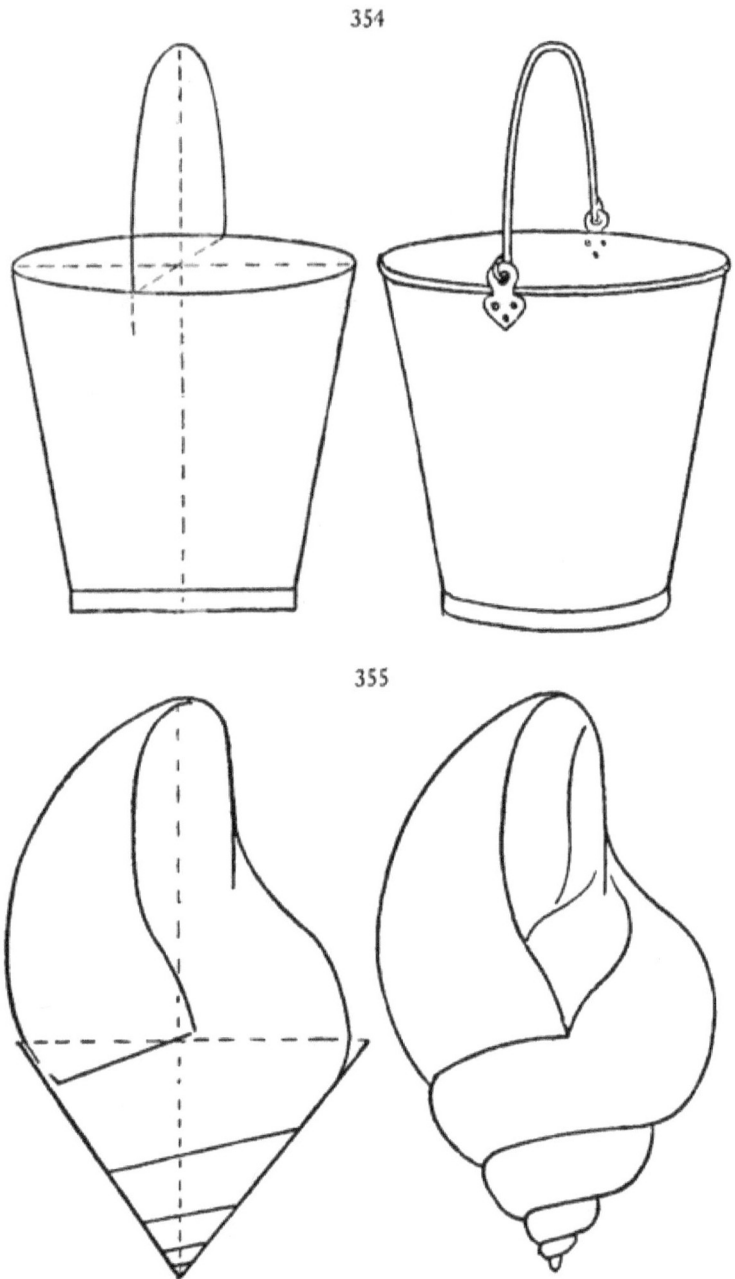

354

355

Standard V

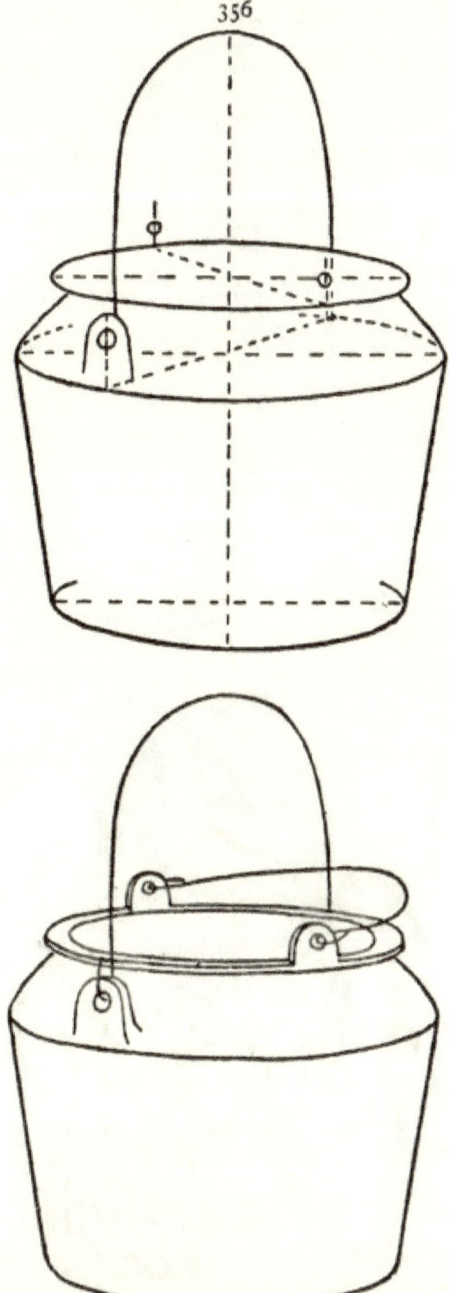

356

STANDARD VI

Increased attention must be paid to the finish of the drawing, as in this and the next Standard the work leads up to the work required for the Elementary Drawing Certificate. If the pupils have been well grounded through the previous standards, they will now find no special difficulties here.

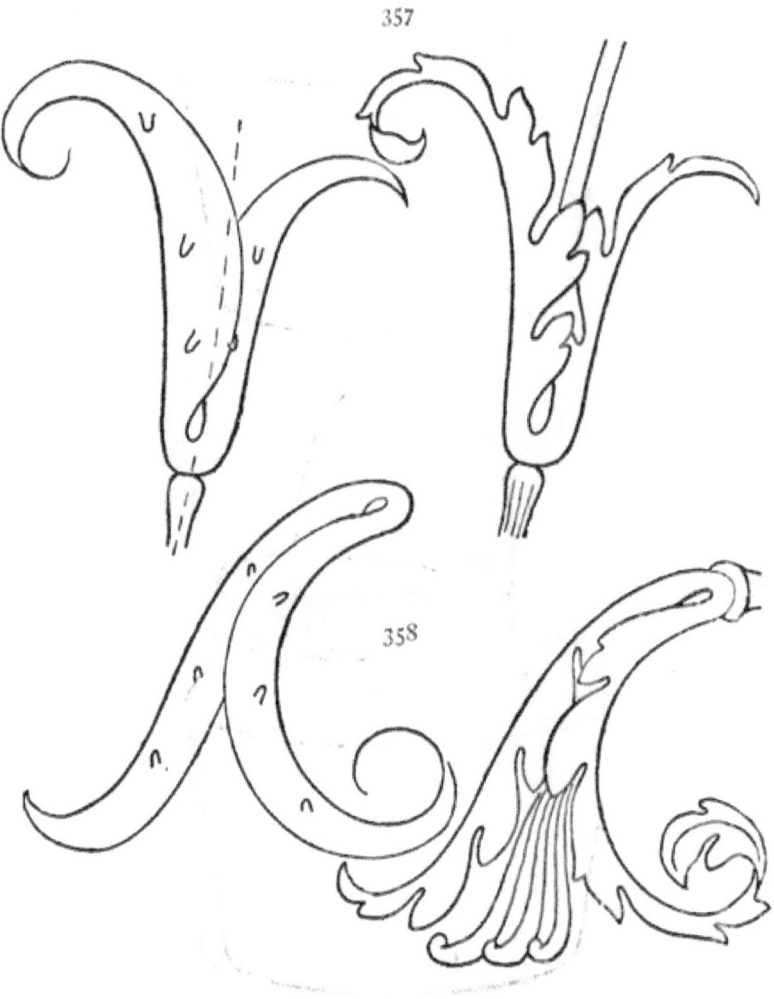

357

358

Standard VI

359

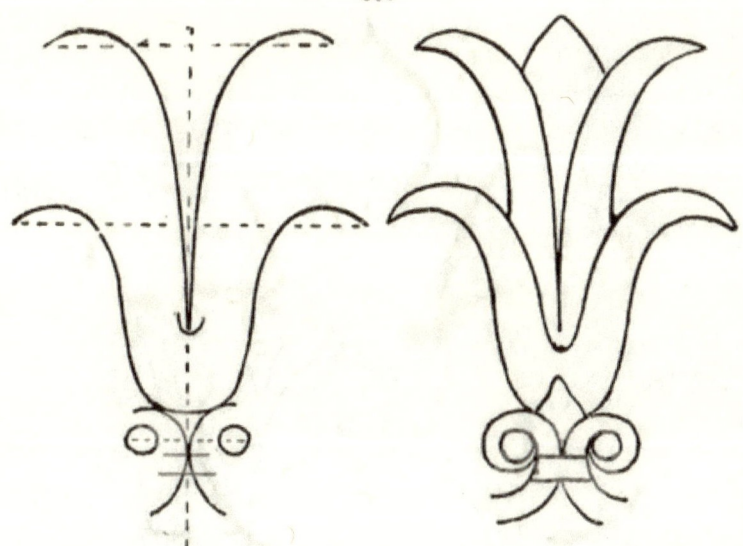

360

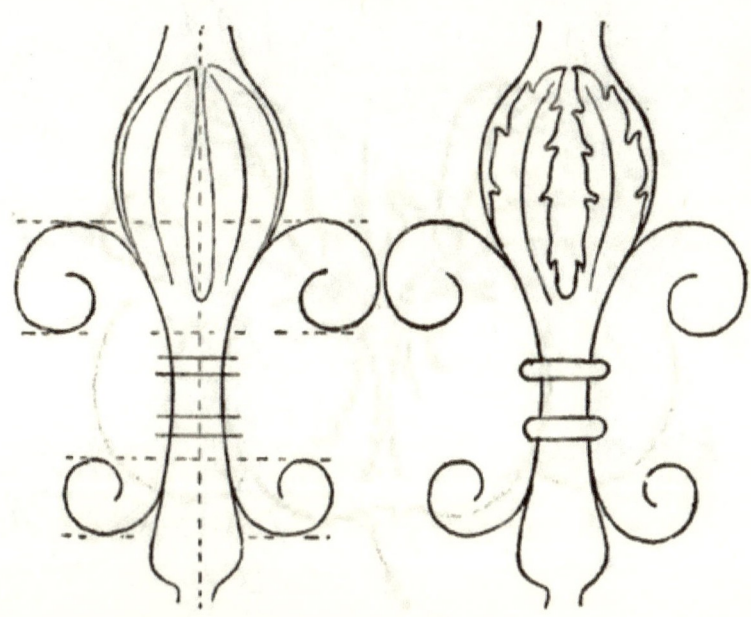

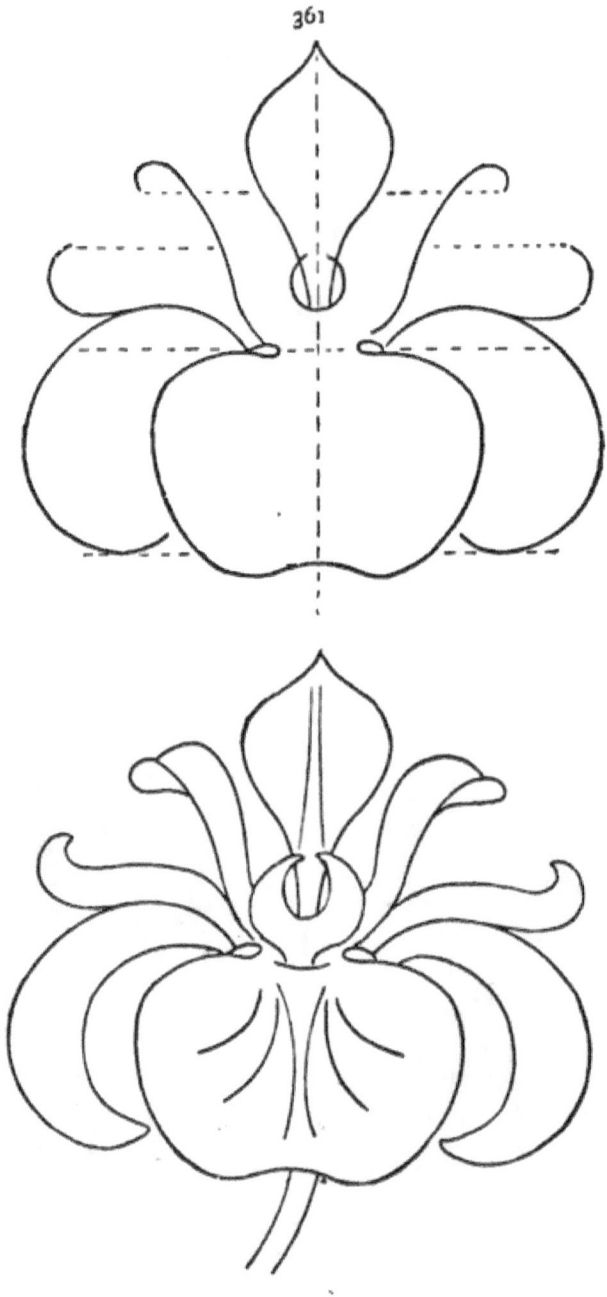

361

Standard VI

362

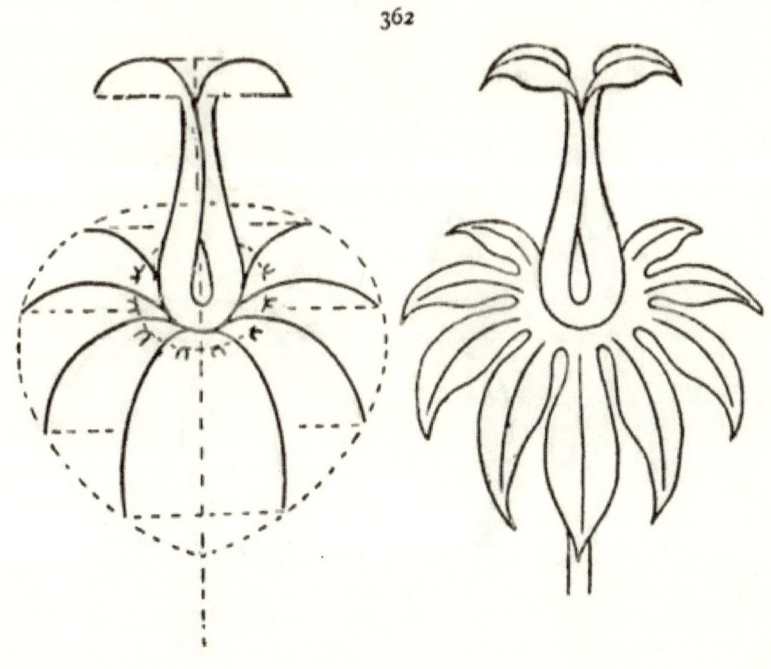

363

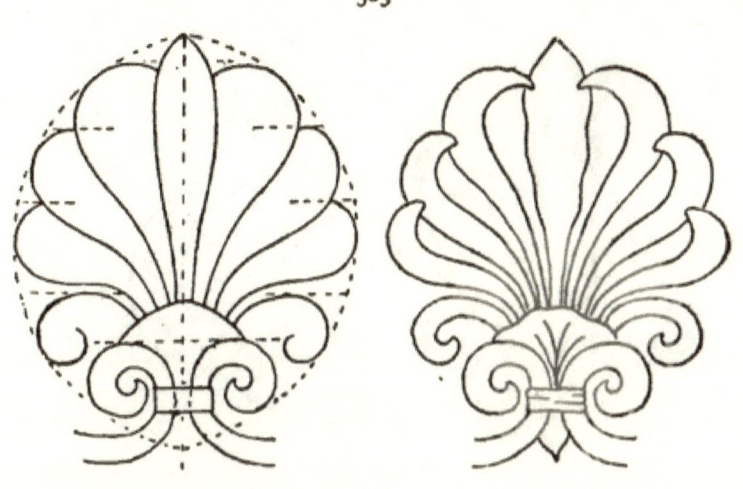

364

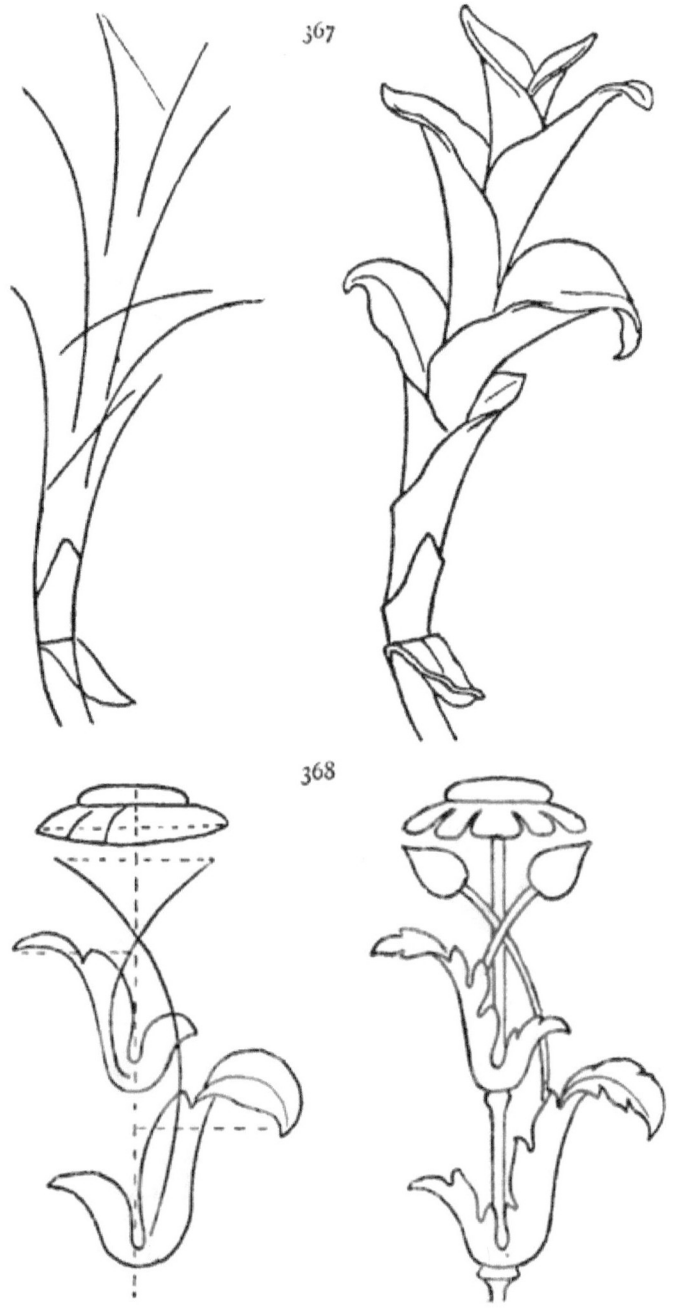

Standard VI

369

370

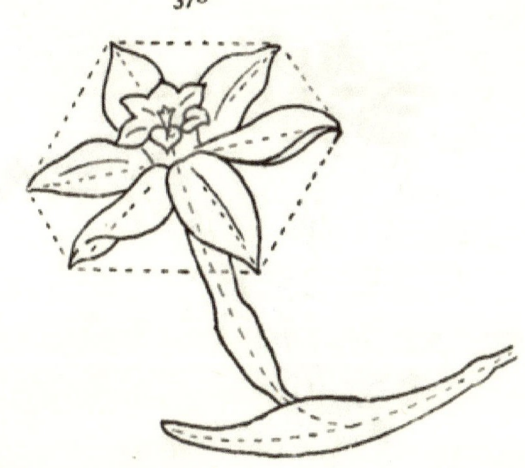

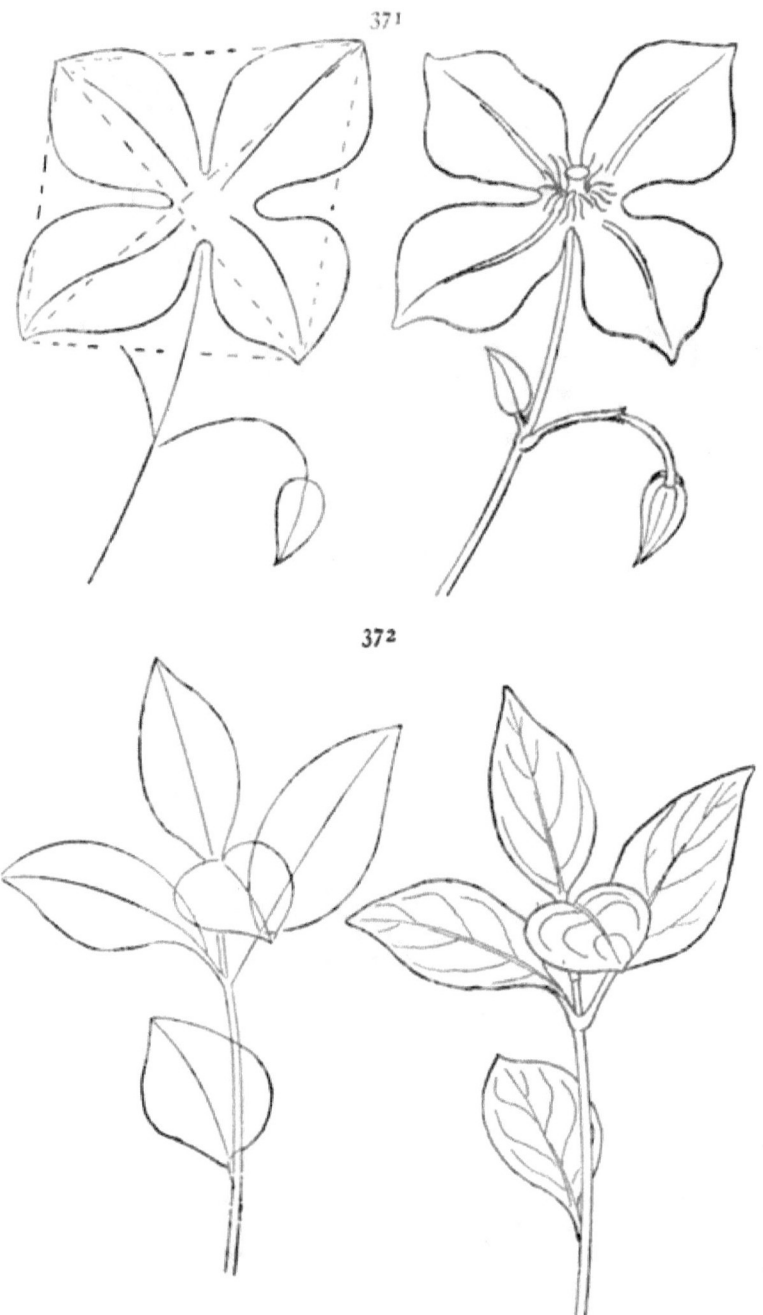

Standard VI

373

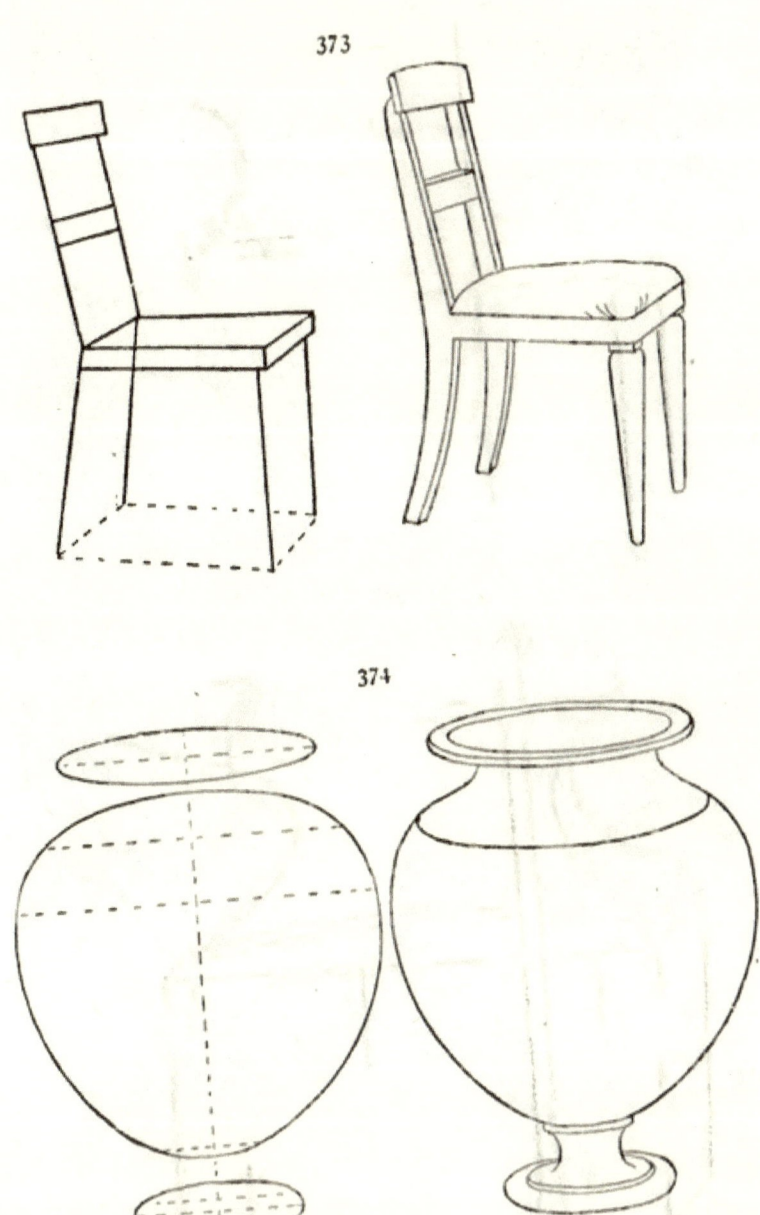

374

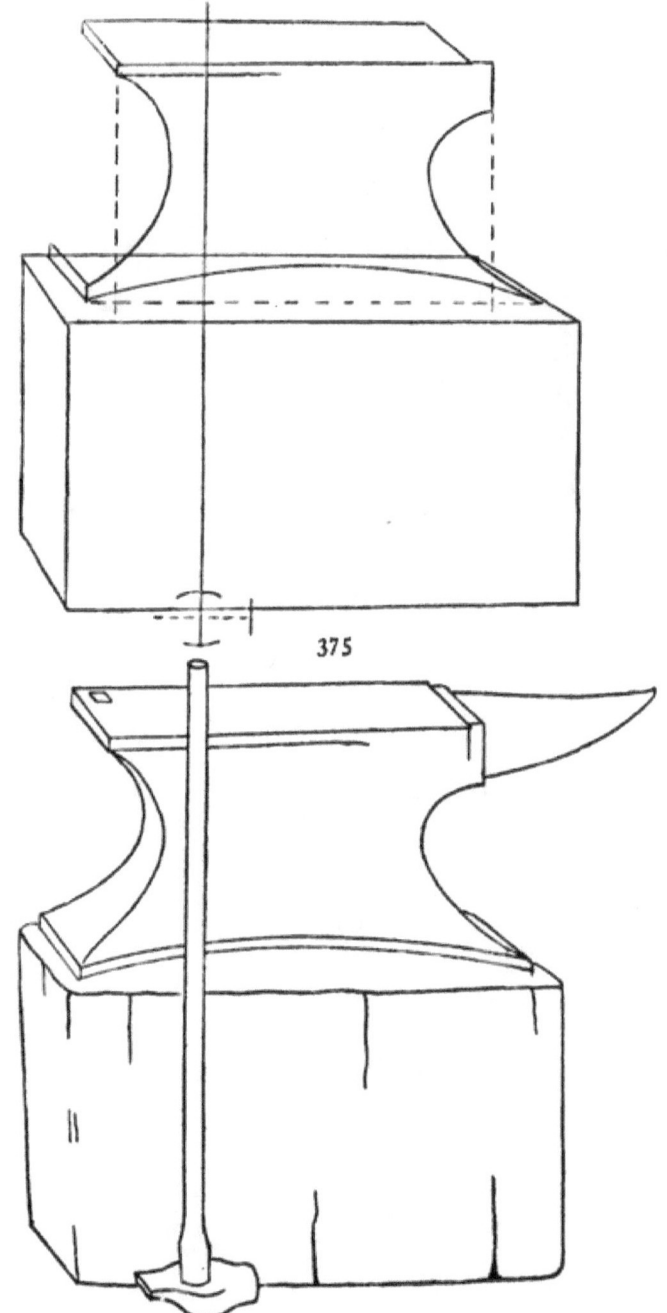

375

Standard VI

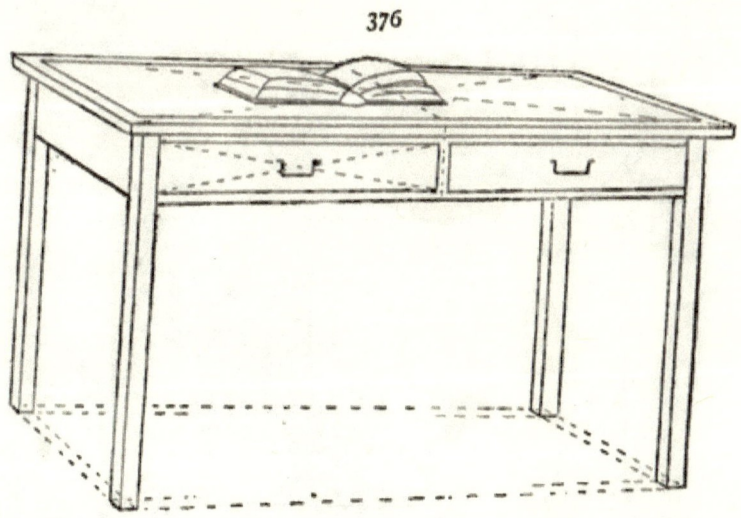

376

STANDARD VII

.The pupils should now have reached a stage of proficiency requiring much less help from the teacher, and should themselves be able to apply the principles taught in the previous standards. A few examples are given as an indication of the character of the tests. Accuracy and finish should receive great attention. Second Grade cards form very suitable examples for the work of this Standard.

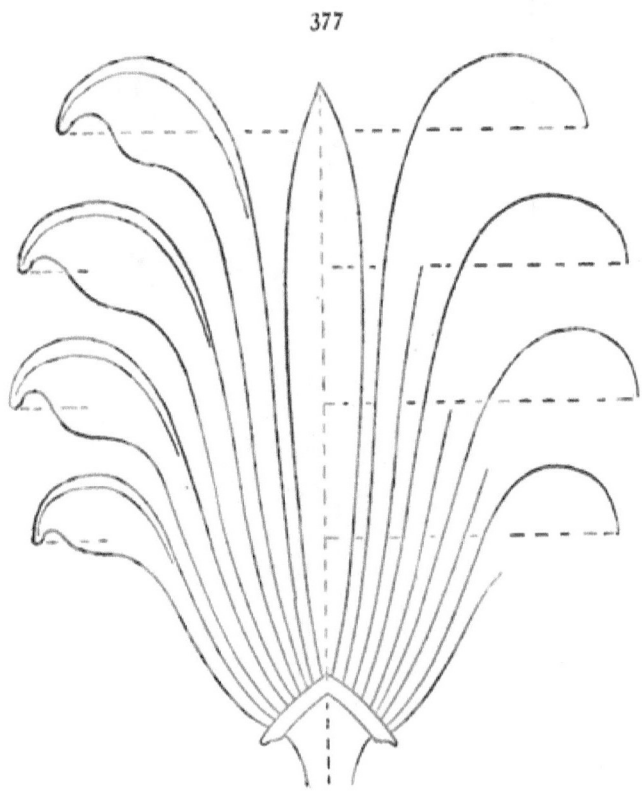

377

Standard VII

378

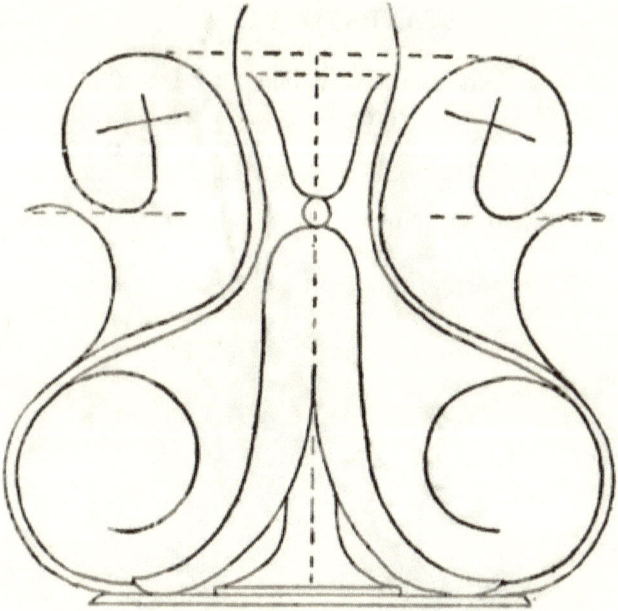

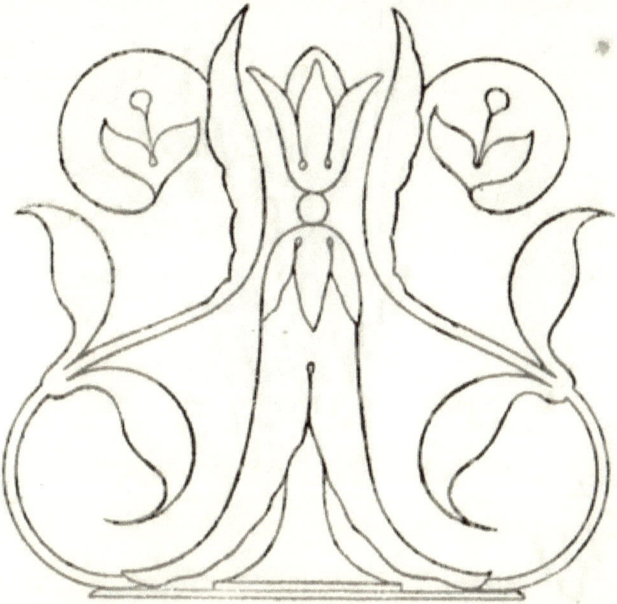

K

379

Standard VII

380

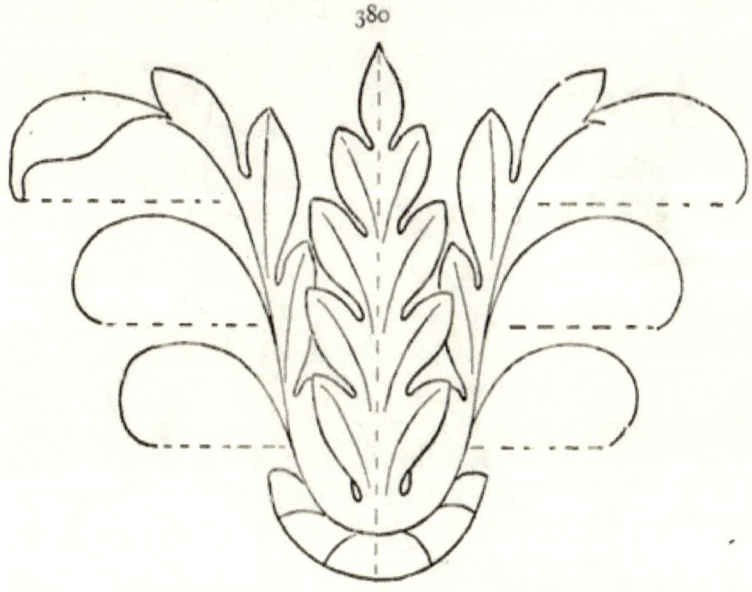

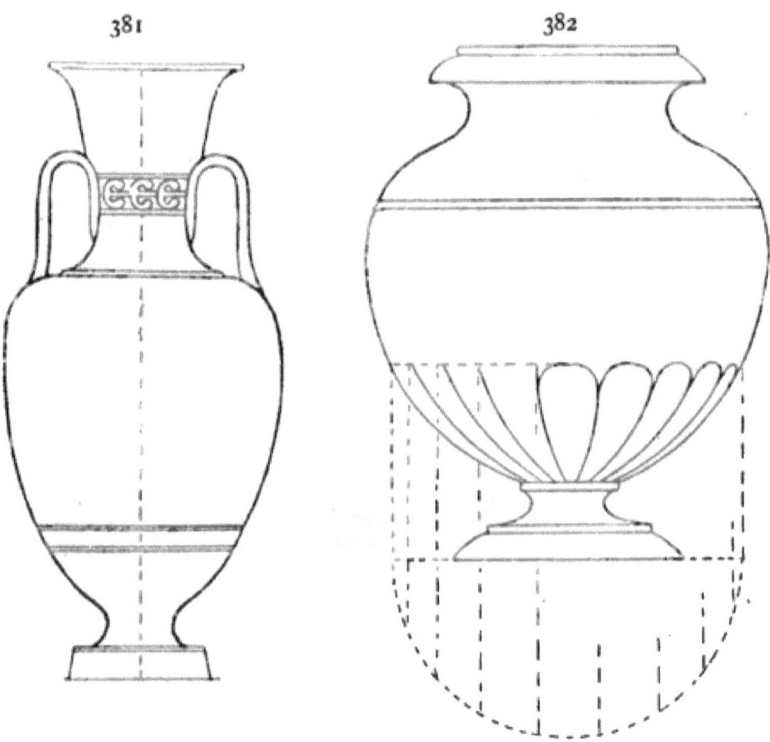

Fig. 382.—Attention is here directed to the method of obtaining the flutes on curved surfaces. As the pupils will have done some solid geometry, they will easily understand the way in which this common form of decoration is obtained. The semicircle shows half the plan of the vase at the top of the fluted part. If the semicircle be divided into as many equal portions as there are flutes required, and projectors drawn as shown, the correct widths for the flutes will be obtained. The left hand side shows the necessary construction.

Figs. 383 and 372 show a small piece of foliage, and indicate the way in which the plant should be drawn from nature. The method of obtaining the serrated edges is shown on the bottom leaf of the laurel in fig. 383, half being left plain to show the way in which the leaves should be sketched. The veins should be kept light and delicate, gradually dying away as they approach the edge of the leaf.

Standard VII

383

CHAPTER VII

SCALE DRAWING. STANDARD IV

Syllabus.—*Simple scales and drawing to scale.*
Drawing to scale will be limited to the following subjects:—
To draw and take dimensions from a scale of feet and inches.

To draw a plan or other figure on squared paper from a sketch having dimensions marked on it.

To enlarge or reduce plane figures to scale.

These requirements may be conveniently divided into four parts.

1. The measurement and drawing of lines, and the construction and use of scales.

2. The drawing of objects to various given scales on plain paper.

3. The drawing of objects on squared paper.

4. The enlarging and reducing of given drawings.

The **apparatus** necessary for the **teacher** will be: large set-squares 45° and 60°, a 3 ft. slip or T-square marked in inches as in Standards I and II, and a blackboard squared on one side with red lines one inch apart.

The **pupils** will require plain drawing books or paper 11 by 7¼ inches, set-squares, indiarubber, &c., as in the previous standards, and in addition **squared paper** ruled very faintly with lines one-eighth of an inch apart. If every fifth line be ruled heavier it is of considerable assistance in counting.

An **H pencil**.

A **9-inch ruler** marked with twelfths and eighths.

Scale Drawing. Standard IV

The following diagram represents a convenient scale ruler for this subject. Ordinary rulers, such as are used for arithmetic, &c., are not very suitable, as the edges get notched and the divisions obscured by ink. Good hard-wood scales may now be obtained very cheaply. The teacher will find it better to keep a set purposely for scale work. It is not advisable to procure any scales that are not properly figured. The first unit on the

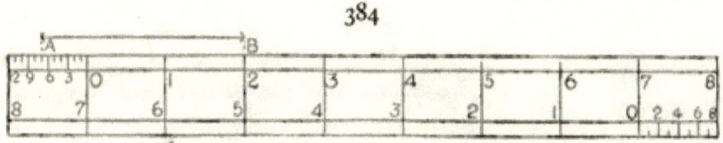

384

scale ought always to be marked zero (o), as distances can then be measured from it without fear of mistake. Suppose, for example, the distance of 2 ft. 7 in. is required to be set off to a scale of one inch to a foot, then the space marked AB (from the 2 to the 7), fig. 384, will be the required distance. In the same manner other distances may be marked off directly; 5 ft. 9 in. would be represented by the distance between 5 and 9 on the scale. On an ordinary ruler the pupil would have to calculate the distance by counting up the inches and parts.

Compasses.—If thought desirable, a pair of compasses or dividers may be used. They are not, however, necessary for this Standard, as all the dimensions can be more accurately taken by the pupils from the scale ruler.

In giving a lesson the teacher should in all cases have either the object to be drawn or a drawing of it before the class. This subject is a valuable means of stimulating general intelligence, and is always popular with children, as its practical application is so apparent to them.

The subject will be treated in the four sections mentioned at the beginning of the chapter, but the construction of plain scales should not be attempted until the pupils have obtained a thorough mastery of their instruments. The easiest plan is to commence with sections two and three—that is, the drawing of objects to scale on plain paper, and the exercises on squared paper—working the two concurrently.

Introductory Lesson.—1. Refer to Standard I geography, where the pupils have already acquired the idea of representing long lines by taking shorter units, when drawing plans of the room, school, &c., and illustrate this by plans, maps, &c., drawn to various scales. Explain that this is 'Drawing to Scale,' and show that it is not only necessary to draw large objects to a smaller scale, but in the case of small objects—such as the parts of a small instrument or the wheels of a watch—it would be necessary to make the drawing to a larger scale.

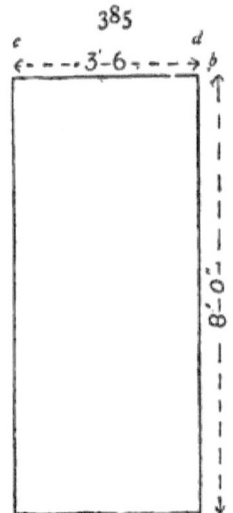

2. Give mental exercises on the representation of lines of various lengths to different scales, such as:—

If the door be eight feet high, how long will the line be to represent it, if one inch stands for one foot?

If half an inch and two inches respectively represent one foot, how long then?

3. Measure up the outline of some simple object, such as a door or window, make a rough dimensioned sketch on a corner of the board, as in figure 385, and from this draw to a scale of 1″ to 1′ 0″.

4. Explain the method of representing the dimensions; that feet are represented by (′), and inches by (″), and that 3′ 6″ reads 3 feet 6 inches. The 8′ 0″ in fig. 385 represents the distance between the arrowheads *a* and *b*, and the 3′ 6″ between the arrowheads *c* and *d*.

5. Commence with the base line.
How long is it? '*Three feet six inches.*'
What distance must be taken to represent it if the scale be one inch to one foot? '*Three inches and six-twelfths.*'
Then set off from your rulers from the three inches to the six-twelfths.
How high is the door?
What distance shall we mark off from the ruler? '*From 0 to 8.*'

Scale Drawing. Standard IV 137

What kind of an angle do the sides make with the **bottom** of the door? '*A right angle.*'

How, then, must the sides be drawn? '*With the set-square.*'

6. After the outline of the door is completed, draw it again to a scale of two inches to one foot, and if time permits to a scale of half an inch to one foot.

Show that the three drawings represent **the** same object, **and that** the **relative proportions** of the parts **are** maintained in each.

This should be followed by the measuring **up** and drawing of a **window or** some such object in **a similar** manner to the previous one.

The pupils will then have **a** clear understanding of **what** drawing to scale really means, and will readily comprehend the reasons for the various processes which follow.

Note.—The teacher will **mark** arbitrary divisions on his ruler **to** represent inches, such as 4 **in.** to stand for 1 in. It is a very useful plan to mark the ruler so as to correspond with the pupil's ruler ; each line **that** the teacher measures will then correspond exactly with that measured by the pupils.

As this book is intended for the teacher's **use,** the section dealing with the construction and use of scales, although the most difficult, is taken first, as it is essential that the teacher should thoroughly understand the principles upon which scales are constructed and **the method of** using **them** before teaching the subject.

SECTION I

The construction of simple scales.—The scales required in this Standard are what are known as **plain scales**—that is, scales showing **equal** divisions—and **from them** we get two dimensions such as feet and inches, or miles **and** furlongs, &c.

Before constructing any scales, explain that *the scale is used to measure distances* on the drawing, and illustrate this by measuring on plans and maps from the scales given on them. As scales **are perfectly** useless **unless accurate,** very great care should be taken in their construction; a sharp pencil should be used, and the divisions marked off with exactness. This is about the most difficult operation that has to be done in this Standard.

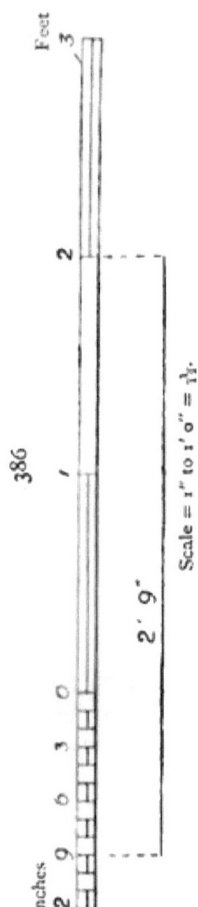

The method to be adopted will be best seen from the following example:—

Construct a scale of 1 inch to 1 foot, showing feet and inches, long enough to measure 4 feet. *From this scale draw a line 2 ft. 9 in. long.*

1. Ascertain how long the line must be that will represent 4 feet.

2. Draw a line 4 inches long, and mark the inch divisions on it from the ruler.

3. Rule the parallel line above it and about one-twelfth of an inch from it, and very carefully mark in the short vertical lines showing the divisions.

4. Figure the scale as shown, and be careful to insist upon the first division being marked zero (o).

5. Explain that we have now marked the *units*. (If 1 inch represents 1 foot, then the inch is the unit.) The sub-divisions of the unit will be shown on the left hand side of the (o).

6. Now if 1 inch represents 1 foot, what distance will represent 1 inch? 'One-twelfth.'

Take the end of the ruler which is divided into twelfths, place it carefully on the first division, and mark in first the half-inch, then the quarters, and afterwards the twelfths.

Note.—Be careful to insist upon the vertical lines being ruled. This may be done with the set-square if thought desirable. For the first exercise it will probably be sufficient to mark in the quarters only.

7. Figure the sub-divisions 3, 6, 9, 12, and print *feet* at the right and *inches* at the left.

8. Write under the drawing '*Scale = 1" to 1' 0".*'

9. Explain and show the advantage of figuring the first division (o) by the second part of the question, viz :—'*to draw a line 2 ft. 9 in. long.*' The pupils will see that from the 2 to the 9 is the distance required, and that when the scale is correctly numbered, the figures will always indicate the distance. Let the pupils come out to the board and show other distances thus :—3 ft 7 in., the right-hand forefinger on the 3 and the left-hand finger on the 7, &c.

10. Thicken in the bottom line and every alternate division for the sake of clearness.

The representative fraction should be explained, as it helps to a better understanding of the subject.

If 1 inch stands for 1 foot how much smaller is the line drawn than its actual size? '*One-twelfth of the real size.*'

Then $\frac{1}{12}$ is the representative fraction, and shows that the real object is twelve times larger than the drawing of it.

If half an inch represents 1 foot what is the representative fraction? $\frac{\frac{1}{2} \text{ inch}}{1 \text{ foot}} = \frac{\frac{1}{2} \text{ inch}}{12 \text{ inches}} = \frac{1}{24}.$

If 1 inch stands for 1 yard, what is the fraction? $\frac{1 \text{ inch}}{36 \text{ inches}} = \frac{1}{36}.$

Other similar questions will easily make this point clear.

Scales of two inches, half an inch, and one and a-half inches to the foot should now be drawn, as shown in figs. 387, 388, 389.

Note.—The eighths of an inch will give the twelve sub-divisions for the scale of 1½" to 1' 0."

A variety of ways in which these problems may be set are given, and should be frequently and carefully practised.

Fig. 390.—*Construct a scale of three-quarters of an inch to one yard, to show* 5 *yards* 1 *foot.*

What is the unit? '*Three-quarters of an inch.*'

What does it stand for? '*One yard.*'

If the scale is to measure 5 yards 1 foot, how many units must be set off? '*Six.*'

140 The Teaching of Drawing

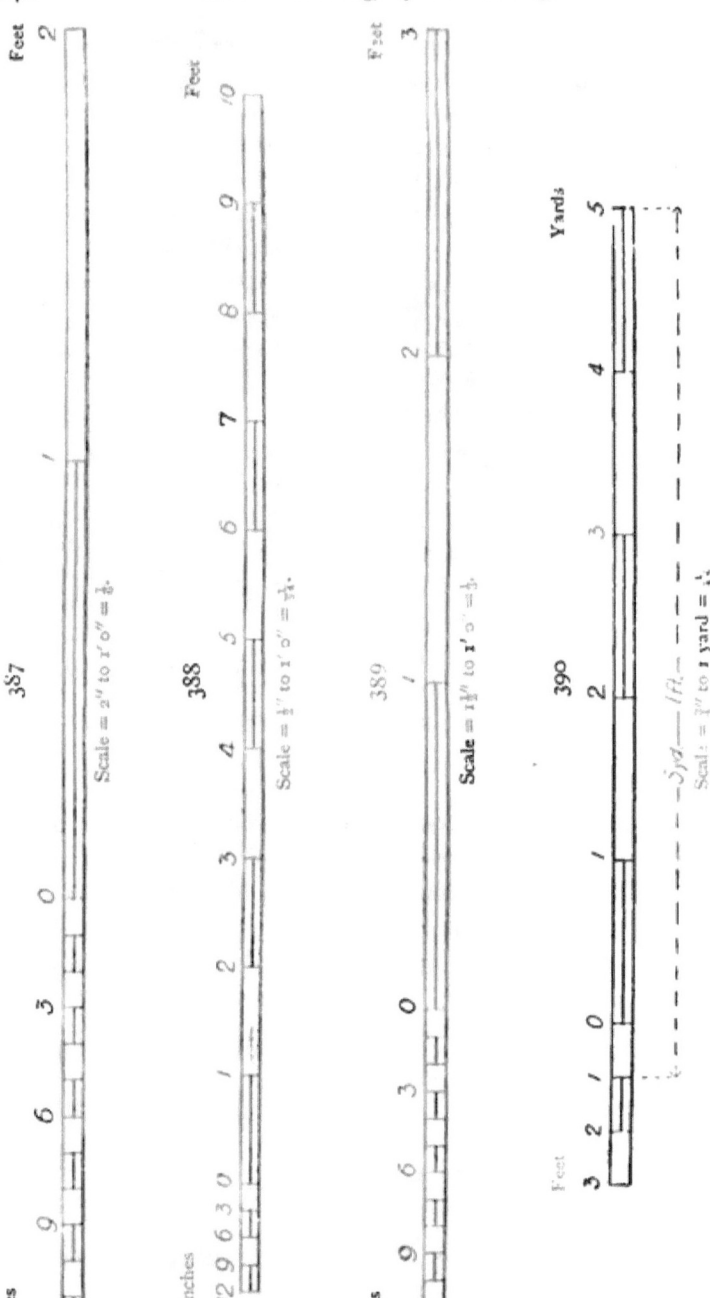

Scale Drawing. Standard IV.

How long will the line be? '6 *inches* × ¾ *inch* = 4½ *inches*.'

Rule a line 4½ inches long, and set off on it six spaces of three-quarters of an inch each.

Note.—These dimensions may, of course, be set off with the dividers, if preferred. Our own experience is that they are not necessary, and that the pupils mark off the divisions more accurately and quickly from their rulers.

Figure the scale and write yards at the right hand.

If three-quarters of an inch represents 1 yard, what will represent 1 foot? '*A quarter of an inch.*'

Mark in and figure the sub-divisions, and complete the scale.

Now indicate the distance required, 5 yards 1 foot, as shown above.

Fig. 391. — *Draw a scale of 5 ft. 7 in. to a scale of* 1″ *to* 1′ 0″.

Fig. 392. — *Draw a scale of* 3′ 6″ *showing inches.* Let 1½ inches stand for 1 foot.

Fig. 393. — *Draw a scale to measure* 5 *miles, showing furlongs.* Let 1 inch *represent* 1 mile.

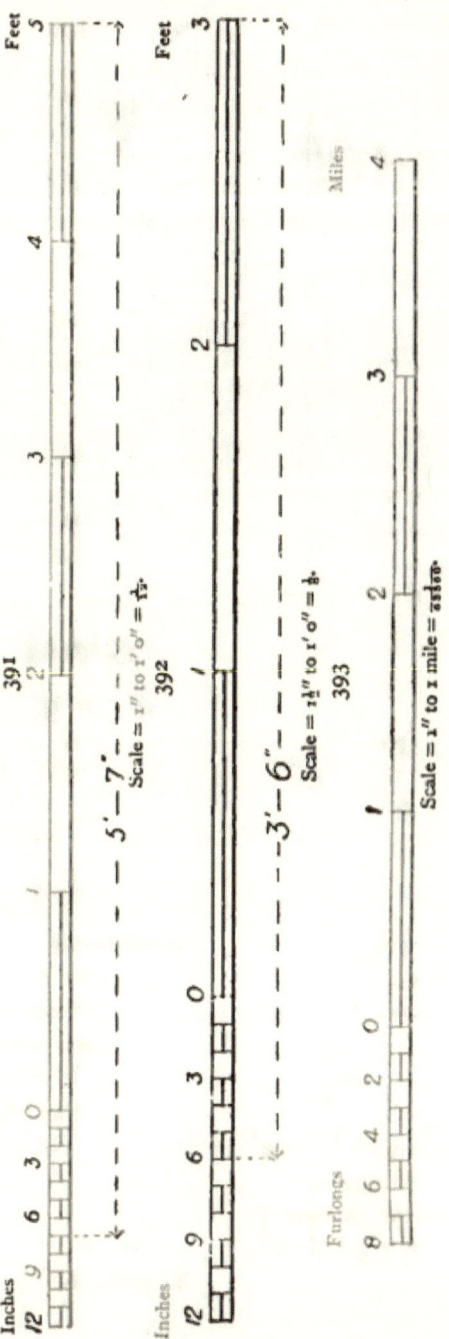

Notice that the end of the ruler marked with eighths will give the furlongs.

The following exercises, most of which have been set for examination, should now be worked.

1. *Draw a scale of 1" to 1' 0" and draw from it a line 3' 4" long.*
2. *Construct a scale of half an inch to one foot, and draw a line from it 3 ft. 6 in. long.*
3. *Draw a scale of one and a-half inches to one foot, and show on it 2 ft. 2 in.*
4. *Draw a scale of 8 ft. 3 in. Let two feet be represented by one inch.*
5. *Draw a scale of two inches to one foot, and mark off a distance showing 2 feet 3 inches.*
6. *If two and a quarter inches represent a longer line on a scale of one inch to one foot, what is the actual length of the line represented?*

SECTION II

The drawing of objects to scale on plain paper.—This naturally follows the construction of scales.

A dimensioned sketch of the object must be placed before the class, as in fig. 394.

Commence with the base line, first ascertaining its length. Complete the rectangle *abcd*. Set off *af* and *de* each four twelfths (0 to 4), and rule the lines *eg* and *fh* with the set-square. This is preferable to setting off the measurement on each side, as time is saved and dexterity in manipulation acquired. *These lines should be either dotted or ruled with a very light line.*

The points *l* and *m* must now be found, *de* + *lm* + *fa* = 1 foot. Then *el* + *mf* = 1 foot 6 inches, and *el* = 9 inches.

Set off *el* and *fm* each nine-twelfths and draw *lo* and *mp* with the set-square as before, making them the required length. Set off *fq* four-twelfths, and complete the figure by carefully thickening in the outline.

All construction lines must be left in to show the method of procedure; hence the necessity for fine lines.

Scale Drawing. Standard IV

The figure when finished should stand out boldly from the construction lines.

Note.—The pupils should be shown how to obtain the dimensions of the parts which are not figured. For instance, in fig. 394, 4 in. is only given once, as it is evident at a glance that the other widths are the same; again, *el* is easily found from the other given dimensions.

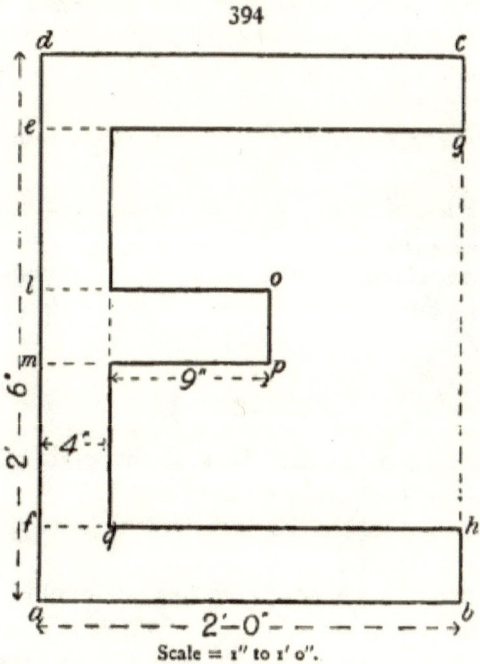

394

Scale = 1" to 1' 0".

A few typical examples are given to illustrate the methods of treating the figures; for additional exercises the ordinary books, such as 'Longman's Drawing to Scale' (2*d*.) will furnish an abundance of suitable examples.

Generally speaking, the bulk of the figures may be solved either by enclosing the figure in a rectangle, as in fig. 394, or working from a centre line. If the sides of the figure are inclined to one another, one of these two plans must be adopted. As a rule, working from a centre line is the neatest and most workmanlike method. In the following examples the construction lines are dotted, and show the method of work. Explanations are also given where thought necessary.

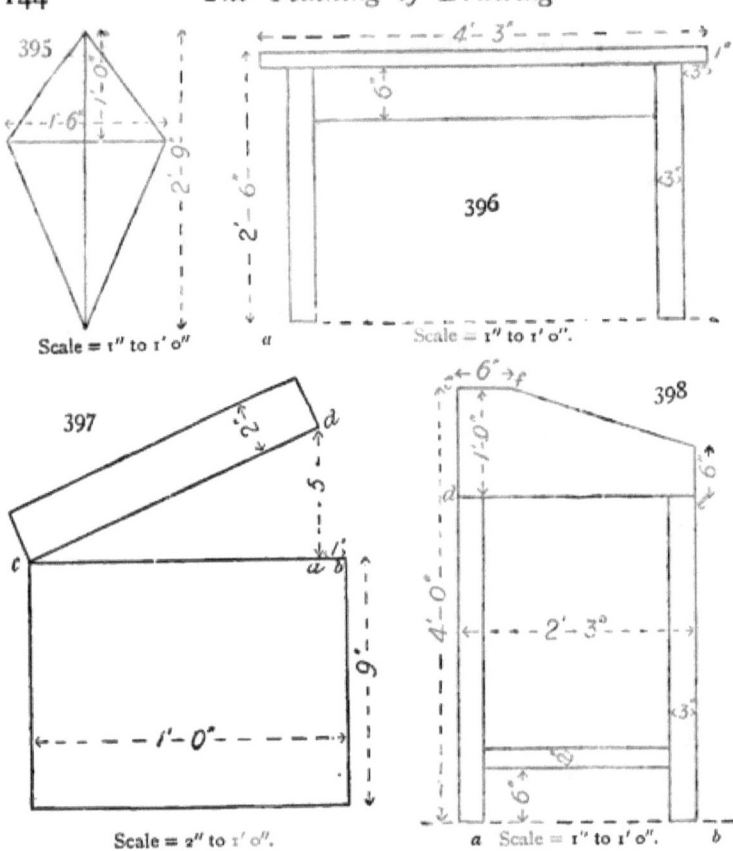

Fig. 395.—Draw the vertical line 2¾ inches long. Set off 1 inch from the top and set out the horizontal line with the set-square. Make each side ₁³⁄₂ inch and complete the figure.

Fig. 396.—Draw the top line. Set off 2½ inches and draw *ab*. Complete the top, set off ₁³⁄₂ inch from each end, and with the set-square **draw the outer** lines of the legs. The completion is now easy.

Fig. 397.—Draw the box first. For the lid set off *ab* and erect a perpendicular. To get the thickness of the lid, place the ruler on *cd* and draw perpendiculars at *c* and *d* with the set-square.

Fig. 398.—Draw *ab* 2¼ inches long. At *a* draw the perpendicular *ac* 4 inches. Set off 1 inch from the top and with the set-square draw *de* parallel to *ab*. At *b* erect a perpendicular. Draw *f* parallel to *de*. The rest of the figure presents no difficulty.

Scale Drawing. Standard IV

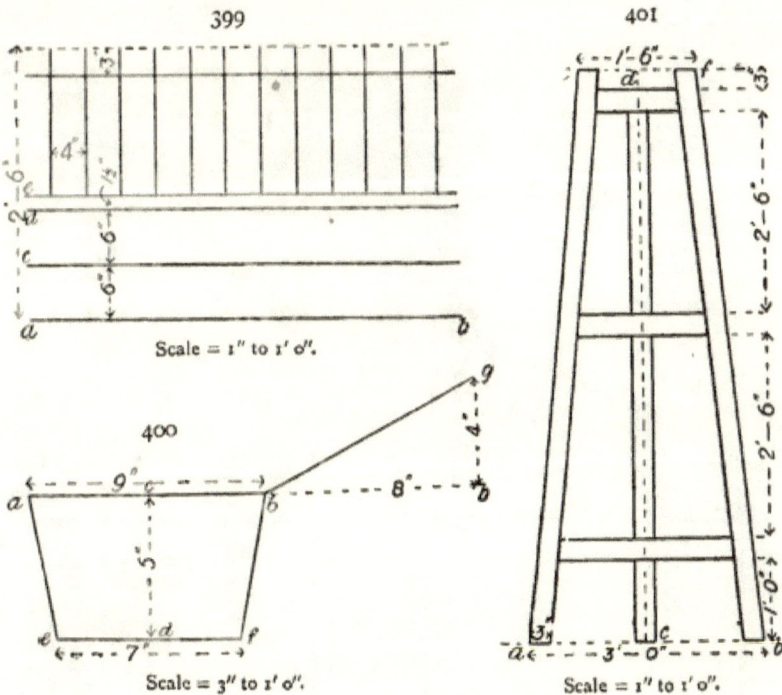

Fig. 399.—Draw *ab*. Set off 2½ inches and draw the dotted line at the top. Set off ½ inch for the lines at *c* and *d*, and draw them parallel to *ab*. For the line at *e* set off ⅛ inch (1½ inches = ⅛ foot). For the palings set off distances of $\tfrac{4}{12}$ inch.

Fig. 400.—Draw *ab* 2¼ inches long. (A scale of 3″ to 1′ 0″ is a scale of ¼, so that each line will be ¼ of its real size.) Find the centre *c*, and draw *cd* 1¼ inches long. Draw *ef* parallel to *ab*, and make *de* and *df* each ¾ inch. Draw *ea* and *fb*. To obtain *bg*, produce *ab* and make the produced part 2 inches long. Draw *hg* perpendicular to *bh*, and complete.

Fig. 401.—Draw *ab* 3 inches long, and at the centre *c* draw the perpendicular *cd* = 7 inches. Through *d* draw *ef*. Draw *ae* and *bf*. The rest of the figure is easily followed. The width of the rails must be set off on the centre line, and not on the oblique sides of the easel.

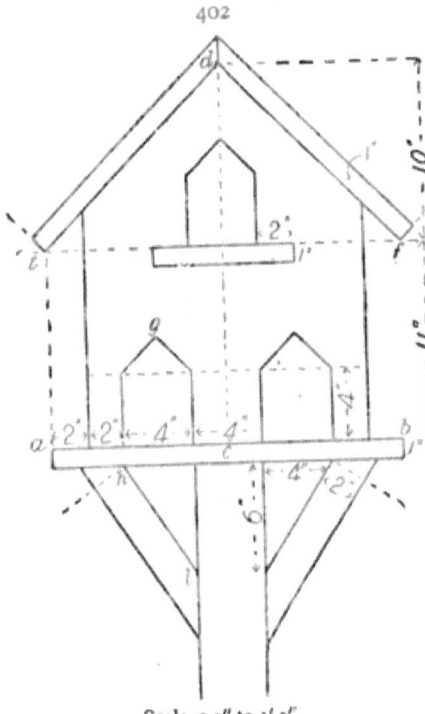
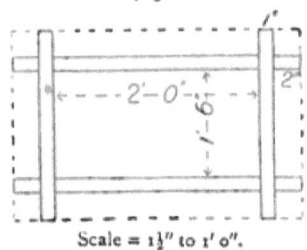

Fig. 402. — This figure requires very careful drawing. Begin with the line *ab* $3\frac{4}{12}$ inches long. Draw the centre line *cd*, on it set off $1\frac{10}{12}$ inches, and draw the line *ef*, parallel to *ab* and equal to it. Set off $1\frac{8}{12}$ inches on the centre line above *ef*, and draw *de* and *df*. Set off $\frac{4}{12}$ inches from *a* and *b*, and rule in the sides. For the holes draw a horizontal line $\frac{8}{12}$ inch above *ab*, set off the width, and draw the vertical lines ; the lines to *g*, &c., are obtained with the 45° set-square. *For the thickness of the roof,* draw lines at *e* and *f* at right angles to *ed* and *df*, on these lines set off the thickness, and rule the lines parallel to *ed* and *df* with the set-square. The width of the struts must be obtained in the same manner. Draw *hl*. At *h* draw a perpendicular, and on this set off $\frac{4}{12}$ inch.

Note.—This is a very important point. The pupils should be shown why the thickness must be set off at right angles to the side, and not on the vertical nor horizontal lines.

Fig. 403.—The sketches given are not always drawn to scale ; the pupil should be taught to draw from the figured dimensions, and must not necessarily expect the drawing to look like the sketch given in the question. In this figure first draw the rectangle shown in dotted lines, and set off the distances from each corner. The length and breadth must first be calculated from the dimensions given.

SECTION III

Drawing on squared paper.—This is the easiest portion of the course, and is on that account frequently taken before the other sections. It only requires accurate counting and care in ruling. The following example will illustrate the proper method of working.

Draw the given figure on squared paper. **Let the side of each square represent half an inch.**

1. First count up the greatest length and breadth of the figure, so that it may be placed to advantage on the squared paper and not crammed into a corner. The given figure is $10\frac{1}{2}$ inches by $8\frac{1}{2}$ inches, and will therefore require 21 squares in one direction and 17 in the other.

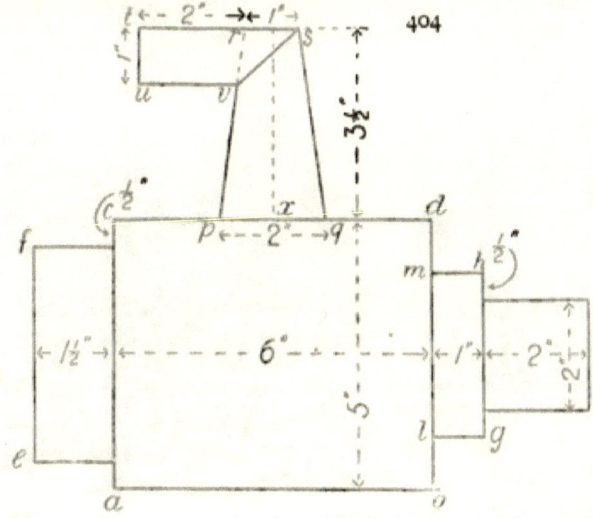

2. Count about 20 or 25 lines from the top of the paper, and mark the points *a* and *b* with small **dots 12 squares apart** and about equidistant from the centre of **the space in which** the drawing is to be placed, as in fig. 405. In the same manner indicate the points *c* and *d*, and rule in the rectangle *abcd* with a *firm bold line*, so that the drawing **stands** out well from the chequered lines.

This is much better than marking the whole figure in **with dots** before ruling, as when **a line is** ruled in, the position of **the lines** adjoining it can be more readily fixed. The dots must on no account be made **large, or** they will show after the lines are ruled.

L 2

3. Obtain *e* and *f*, and rule in.

4. The points *m* and *l* are obtained as follows :—*gh* = 2 inches + ½ inch + ½ inch = 3 inches. Therefore *dm* = 1 inch. Complete the right hand side.

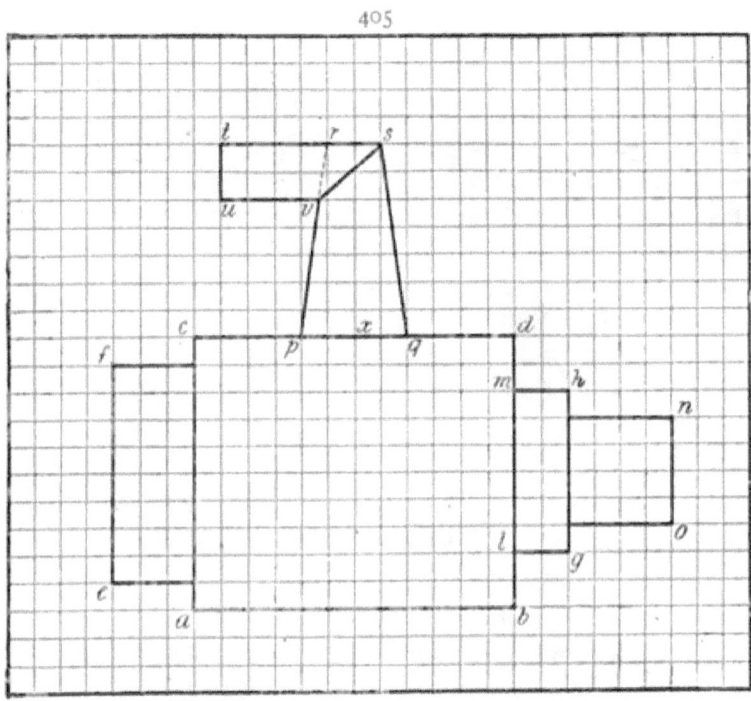

405

5. Find the middle (*x*) of *cd* and mark in *p* and *q*, each two squares from the centre. Count up 7 squares from *x* and mark the points *r* and *s*. Rule in *qs* and *pr*, dotting the upper portion. From *r* count 4 squares and rule in *st*. Mark *u* and rule *uv*. Join *v* with *s*. Notice that *v* is not at the corner of a square. The figure when completed should show a clear bold line of uniform thickness throughout.

The same plan must be followed out with regard to the following examples, always taking care to estimate the size and position of the figure on the paper before starting. India-rubbers should not be used at all.

Note.—The plain paper examples may be used as exercises for the squared paper, and *vice versâ*.

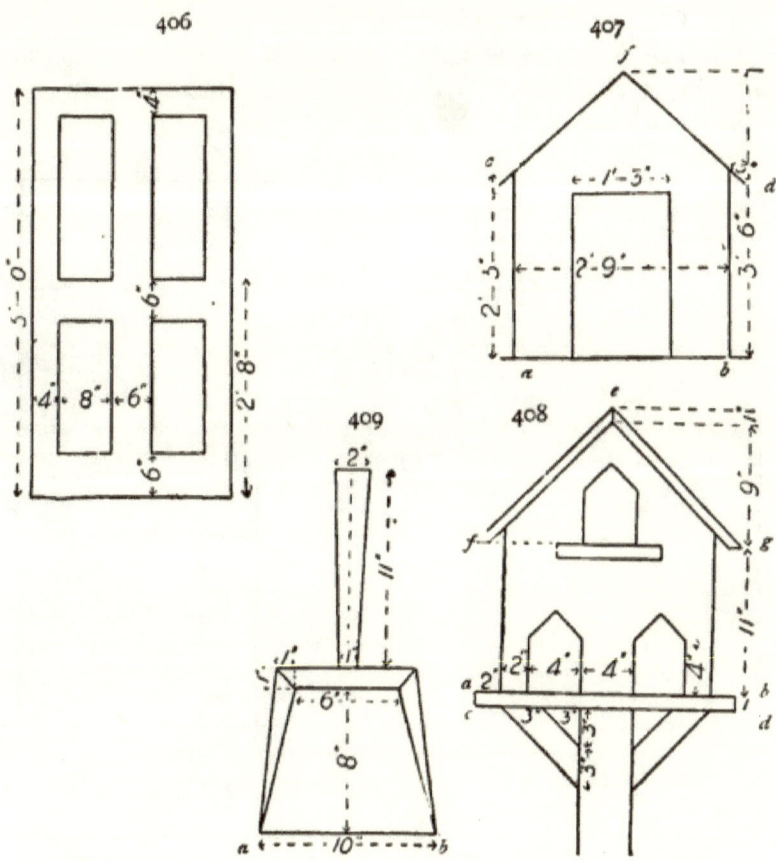

Fig. 406.—Let the side of each square equal 2 inches.

Fig. 407.—Let the side of each square represent 3 inches. First obtain *ab* and the two side lines *ac* and *bd*. From the centre of *ab* count up 14 squares, and mark *f*. This point will fall on the middle of the side of the square, and must be carefully marked. The rest of the figure presents no difficulty.

Fig. 408.—Let the side of each square represent 1 inch. Mark in *abcd*, 20 squares by one square. Find the centre, and mark point *e*, 20 squares above. Mark points *f* and *g* over *a* and *b*.

Fig. 409.—Let the side of each square equal 1 inch. Draw *ab*, and get the centre line. Notice that the bottom of the handle will come to the middle of the side of the square.

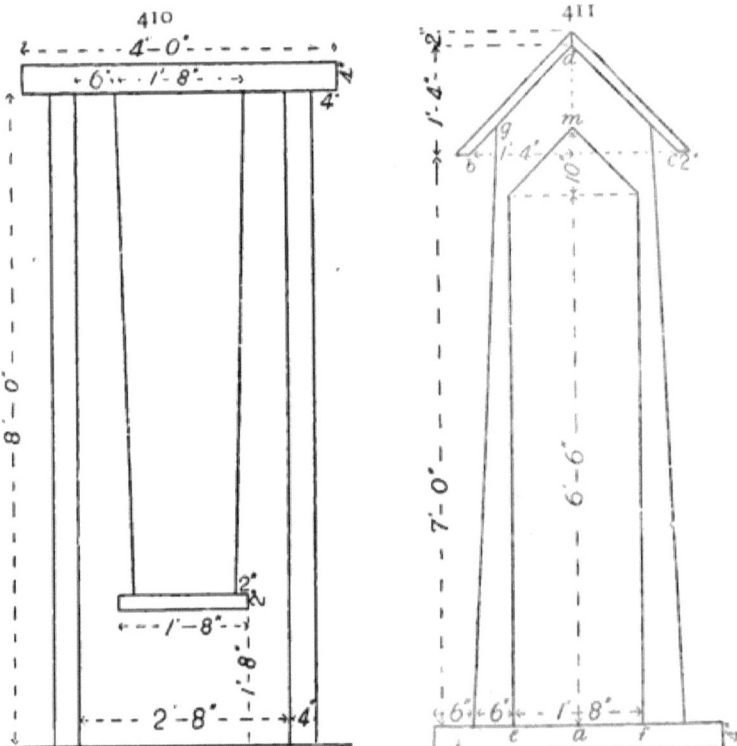

Fig. 410.—Let the side of each square represent 2 inches. Draw the beam at the top 24 squares by 2 squares. Fix the position and width of the posts, count 48 squares down, and rule the ground line and posts. Now mark the position of the ropes at the top. To obtain the seat, count 10 squares up from the ground and 3 squares from each post, and rule in the bottom line. Complete the seat, and mark one square from each end for the position of the ropes. Notice that the ropes are not vertical.

Fig. 411.—Let the side of each square represent 2 inches. Fix the point *a* in the centre of the base, and draw the bottom part of the figure. Count up 42 squares from *a*, and from this point set out 8 squares on each side of the centre line, giving points *b* and *c*. For *d*, count 8 squares above *bc*, rule in *bd* and *cd*, and complete the roof. Mark points *e* and *f*, and complete the opening. For the point *g* set off 6 squares on each side of *m*. Draw the sloping sides.

SECTION IV

Enlarging or reducing **a given figure.**—In enlarging and reducing simple figures it will be found much neater and easier to teach the pupil to measure the lines with the scale, and then calculate the required length, rather than to measure or divide by means of compasses or dividers. Suppose, for example, it is required to draw a rectangle with its sides half as long as those of the given figure. Instead of bisecting, let the pupil measure each of the sides. He will find them $2\frac{1}{4}$ inches and $1\frac{1}{2}$ inches respectively, and will at once know that the required figure will have sides of $1\frac{1}{8}$ inches and $\frac{3}{4}$ inch.

412

As a general rule it will be found that most figures will scale, and their dimensions can be readily calculated. Small dimensions can neither be correctly divided nor accurately set off by children with ordinary compasses.

The following lesson will illustrate the method suggested above :—

Draw the bell tent (fig. 413), making the lines three times as long as those of the given figure.

1. Commence by drawing the base line of indefinite length, and mark in the point *a* and the centre line *am*.

2. Now place the ruler on the base line, and measure *ab*. Suppose it to scale $\frac{3}{4}$ inch, then the pupil will set off $2\frac{1}{4}$ inches on each side of the centre.

Note.—The proper method of doing this must be explained clearly. If the distance be less than 1 inch, then place the o of the scale on *a* and read off to the left. If over 1 inch and less than 2 inches, then place 1 on *a* and read off as before. If over 2 inches and less than 3 inches, place 2 on *a*, &c.

3. Measure *bd*. Suppose it to scale $\frac{x}{12}$ inch, then $3 \times \frac{x}{12}$ inch = 2 inches must be set off. Draw *bd* and *ce* at right angles to *bc*, and complete the rectangle *bced*.

4. Scale *bf*, set off thrice the distance, and draw *fh* and *gl*.

Note.—It is better to scale the longer distance *bf* than the shorter distance *af*, as the measurement is likely to be more accurate.

5. Measure *am*. If it measures 1½ inches, then the pupil will set off 4½ inches. Draw *dm* and *em*.

6. With the set-square draw *hn* and *ln*, parallel to the lines *dm* and *em* respectively.

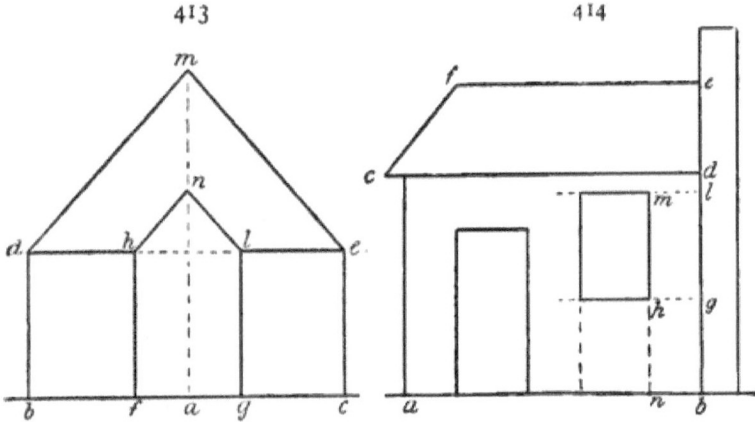

The figure should be carefully thickened in, and all the construction lines left either dotted or very thin. The pupils should be taught to thicken in lines like *bd*, *dm*, *fh*, &c., when first ruled, as it saves time and is likely to produce neater work.

Fig. 414—*Draw the given figure with lines three times the given size.*

Find the dimensions as in the previous figure.

Scale Drawing. Standard IV

1. First draw *abcd*, then the chimney
2. Find position of *e*, and draw *ef* parallel to *cd* with the set-square. Join *fc*.
3. Measure up and draw the door.
4. The window must be obtained as shown by the dotted construction lines. Measure *nh* and set it off at *g*. Now measure *nm*, and set off at *l*. From *g* and *l* draw lines parallel to *ab*. Measure *gh*, set it off, and rule a perpendicular *hm*. Obtain the other side of the window in a similar manner.

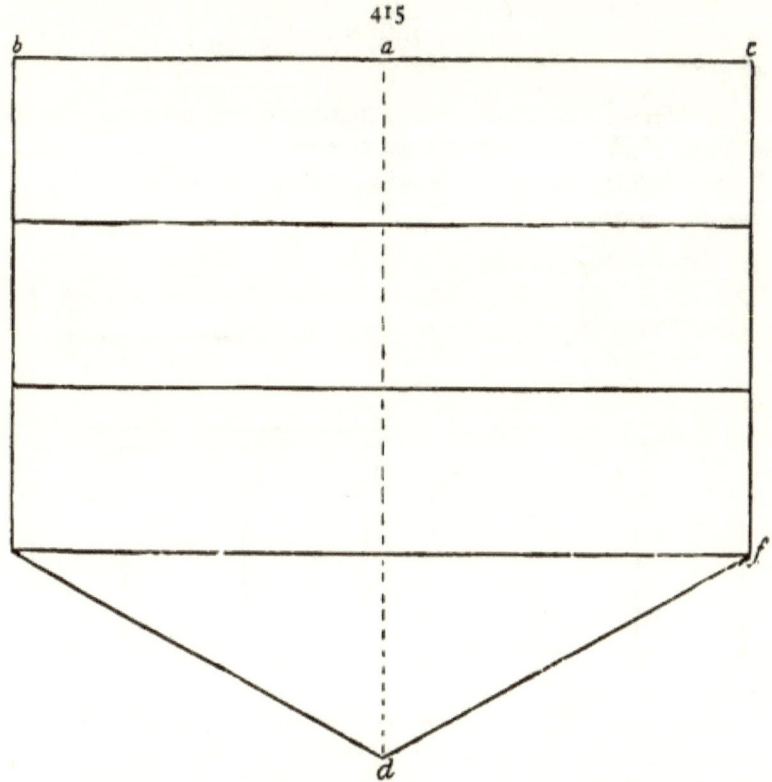

Fig. 415.—*Draw the figure with lines half the size of those given.*

1. Begin with line *bc*, and then rule the centre line *ad*.

2. If *ab* equals 1¾ inches, then the pupil will set off ⅞ inch on each side of *a*.

3. Complete the **rectangle** *bcef*.

4. Measure *ad*, **set off** half the distance, and complete the figure.

Examination Tests

Two papers are given to show the character of the tests the children may expect. There are usually two problems to be drawn, and great **attention** should be given to the proper arrangement of the examples so as to show to advantage on the paper.

Test-paper A *(to be worked on plain paper)*

1. Draw a scale of 1½ inches to 1 foot, and from it draw a line to represent 2 ft. 4 in.

2. Draw figure **416** with lines **twice the length of those** given.

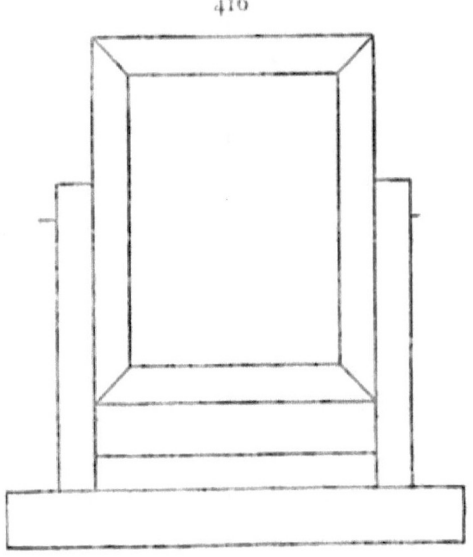

416

Scale Drawing. Standard IV

Test-paper B *(to be worked on squared paper)*

1. Draw fig. 417 from the given dimensions, letting the side of each square equal 1 **inch**.
2. Draw fig. 418 from the given dimensions, letting the side of each square equal 3 **inches**.

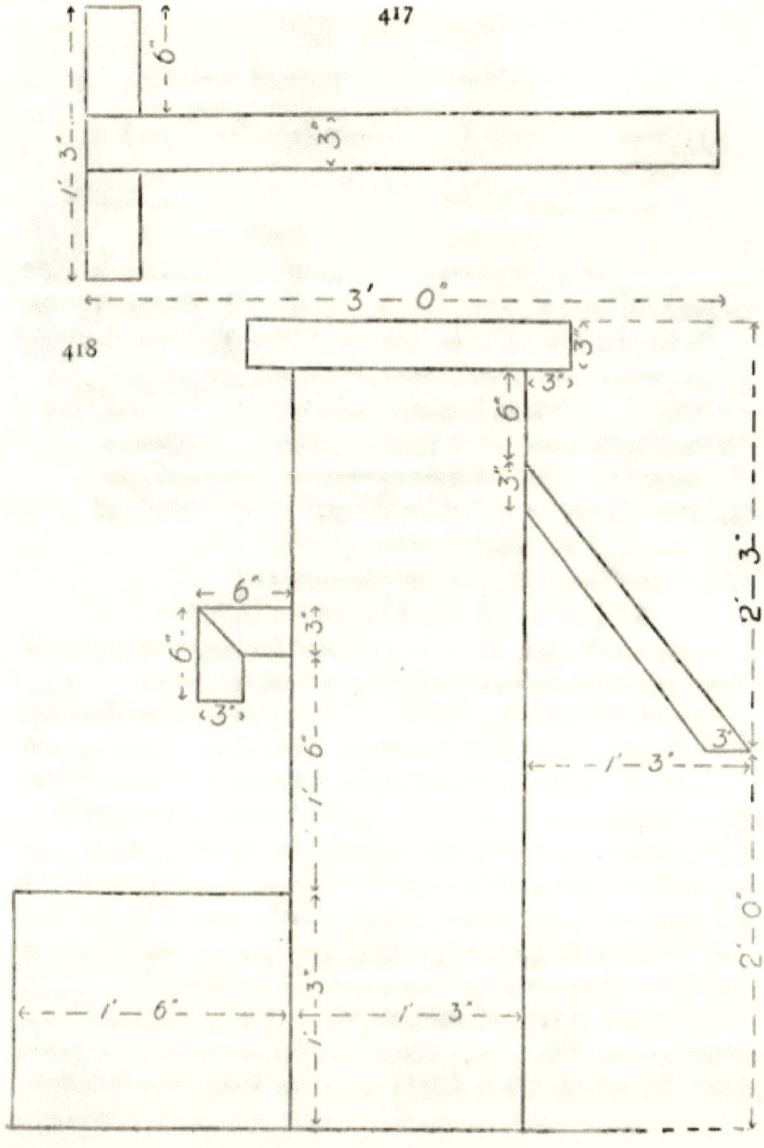

CHAPTER VIII

PLANE GEOMETRY. STANDARDS V AND VII

Syllabus, Standard V.—*Geometrical figures with instruments and to scale.*

This section will include such problems as the division of a given line into a number of equal parts by trial with the dividers, and also by construction ; the drawing of lines parallel and perpendicular to given lines by means of the set-squares, and also by construction ; the construction of an equilateral triangle or a square of a given side ; the construction of an angle equal to a given angle ; the bisection of a given angle ; the construction of a triangle, its sides or its sides and angles being given.

Apparatus.—The **teacher** will require a pair of large chalk compasses about 15 inches in length, in addition to the apparatus necessary for Standard IV.

The **pupils** will require the same material as for Standard IV, with the addition of pencil compasses. Where expense is no object small dividers are very useful for dividing lines and taking off measurements, but they are not essential.

Compasses.—These should be as good as can be obtained, as it is utterly impossible to expect that children can do neat and accurate work with the wretched instruments that are commonly supplied to schools. It is not desirable that very delicate or expensive instruments should be supplied, as they are very liable to be soon damaged. The best cheap compass with which we are acquainted is known as 'Harris's Patent,' fig. 419. It is strongly made, with a good point, and does not get out of order easily, the pencil being held firmly by a screw collar which envelops both jaws. Pencils can be bought to fit the compasses, and should be sharpened so as to form a chisel point, as this lasts longer and gives a much better line.

Plane Geometry. Standard V

The figure to be drawn should be ruled in firmly, so as to show out well from the construction lines, *which must not be rubbed out*, and should be ruled in either with a very light or dotted line. For children probably a fine continuous line is preferable, as it is more quickly done. Dotted lines do not

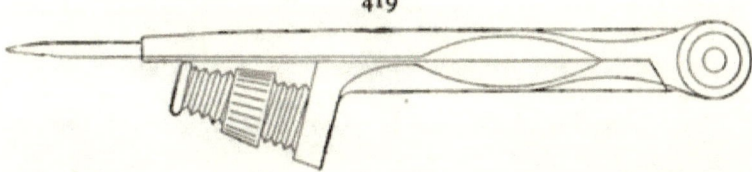

419

look well unless the dots are kept very even, and to do this takes a much longer time. The page should always be divided by ruled lines into spaces, so that each problem is kept distinctly to itself, and the figure should be worked as large as the space will allow. It will be necessary for the teacher to watch carefully the method of holding the compass, and to insist upon it being held nearly upright and between the thumb and forefinger, as the proper method of using the instruments is an important factor towards obtaining successful work.

The course required for Standard V embraces the following points. Elementary constructions relating to :—(1) Lines. (2) The drawing of perpendiculars and parallels. (3) Angles. (4) The construction of triangles of various kinds. (5) The square, the rectangle, and the circle. *Definitions* must be frequently given, in order that the pupil may thoroughly comprehend the questions set. It is not advisable to attempt to learn these definitions by heart; frequent questioning and illustration will soon enable the class to explain the terms used. The theory of construction and the uses of the different instruments must also be carefully and frequently explained.

The following course amply covers the requirements, and most of the figures will explain themselves. Notes are only given where specially needed. Attention is again directed to the necessity of drawing the figures large, in a variety of positions, and of forming numerous exercises from them. A few examination cards are given at the end, which should be arranged upon the paper as directed. Longman's 'Practical

Geometry for Standard V' will furnish the teacher with a variety of exercises.

The following problem is worked out fully as an illustration of the points which should be dealt with in a lesson :—

From a given point A, draw a line which shall meet the line BC at an angle equal to the given angle D.

1 Draw two parallel lines on the board with the set-square. Place the 60° set-square as shown in fig. 421, and draw a line *ab* cutting both the parallel lines. Apply the set-square to the angle at *b*, and direct the attention of the pupils to the fact that it exactly fits, and therefore the alternate angles must be equal.

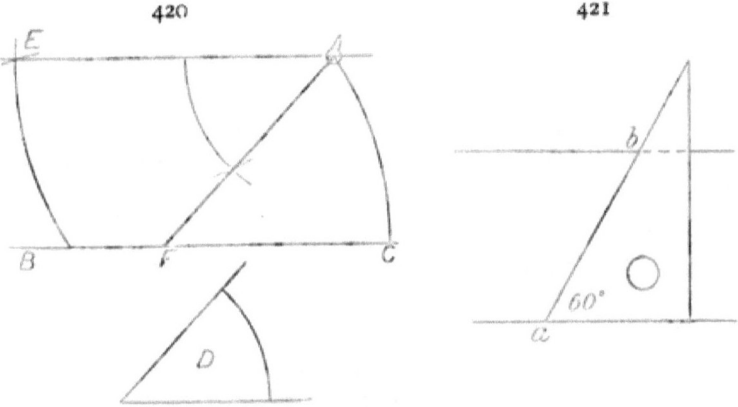

Draw another line with the 45° set-square, and show that there is the same result. Now draw two converging lines, and show that the alternate angles are no longer equal. (Explain 'alternate.')

2. Through *A* draw *AE* parallel to *BC*.

3. At *A* make an angle equal to *D*, and produce the line to meet *BC* in *F*.

4. The angle *AFC* equals the angle *EAF*, as has been previously shown, and *EAF* was constructed equal to *D*, therefore *AFC* must be equal to *D*, and *AF* is the required line.

This is a difficult problem for children, and should be reasoned out as shown above. The parallel line may also be obtained by using the set-square.

Plane Geometry. Standard V

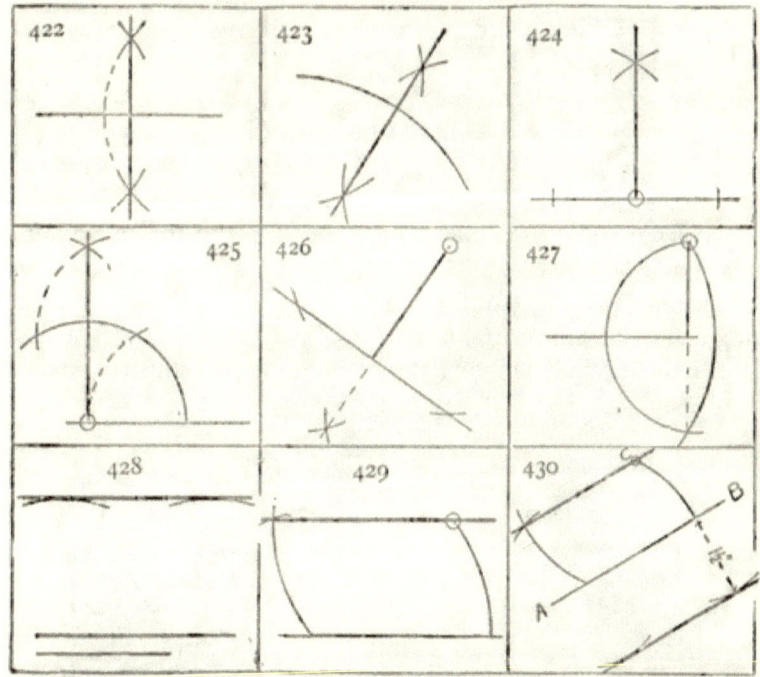

Figs. 422 and 423.—*To bisect lines.*

Be careful to see that the bisecting line goes exactly *through* the intersection of the arcs, and that the arcs are kept equal in length.

Figs. 424 and 425.—*To erect a perpendicular from a point in a given line.*

The method in fig. 422 should be used when the point is near the middle of the line, as it is neater and more quickly performed.

Figs. 426 and 427.—*To drop a perpendicular from a point without a given line.*

The method in fig. 425 is for use when the point is nearly over the end of the line. It can also be used for fig. 426.

Fig. 428.—*To **draw a** line parallel to a given line at **a given** distance from it.*

Fig. 429.—*To draw a line parallel to a given **line** through a given point.*

Fig. 430.—*Draw a line parallel to AB through the point C, and on the opposite side of AB **draw** another line parallel to it and 1½ inches from it.*

Notes.—1. All these perpendiculars and parallels should also be obtained by the use of the set-square.

2. Definitions of the terms 'bisection,' 'intersection,' 'perpendicular,' 'parallel' and 'arc' should be given here.

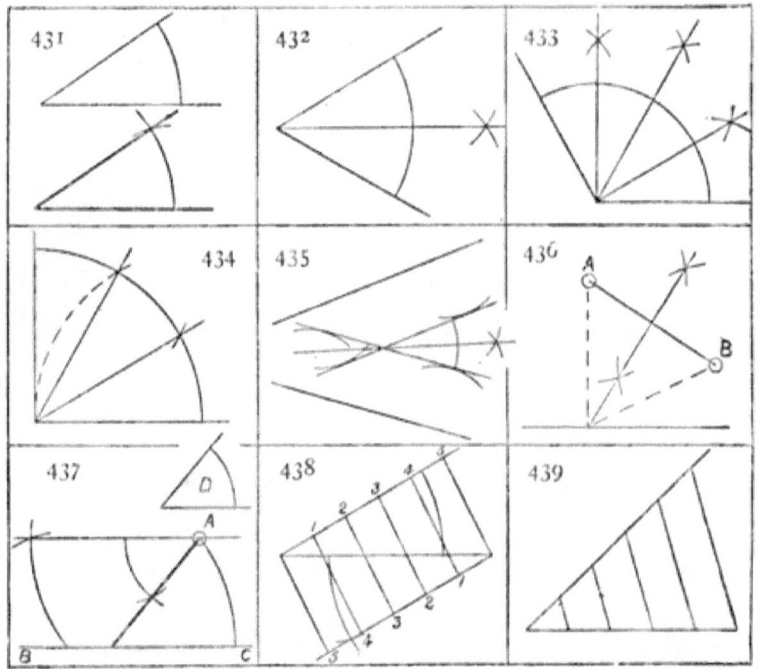

Fig. 431.—*To construct an angle equal to a given angle.*
Fig. 432.—*To bisect a given angle.*
Fig. 433.—*To divide a given angle into four equal parts.*
Fig. 434.—*To trisect a right angle.*
Fig. 435.—*To draw a line that would* bisect the angle between two converging lines without producing *the lines.*

Draw lines parallel to the converging lines and at equal distances from them, as in fig. 428, and bisect the angle thus formed.

Fig. 436.—*Find a point in a* given line equally distant from *the two* given *points A and B.*

Fig. 437.—*To draw a line from the point A to meet BC, and make an angle with it equal to D.*

Figs. 438 and 439.—*To divide a line into any number of equal parts. Say five.*

The pupils should be conversant with both methods, but the method shown in fig. 439 by using the set-square is the most important, as it is the one in practical use.

Plane Geometry. Standard V. 161

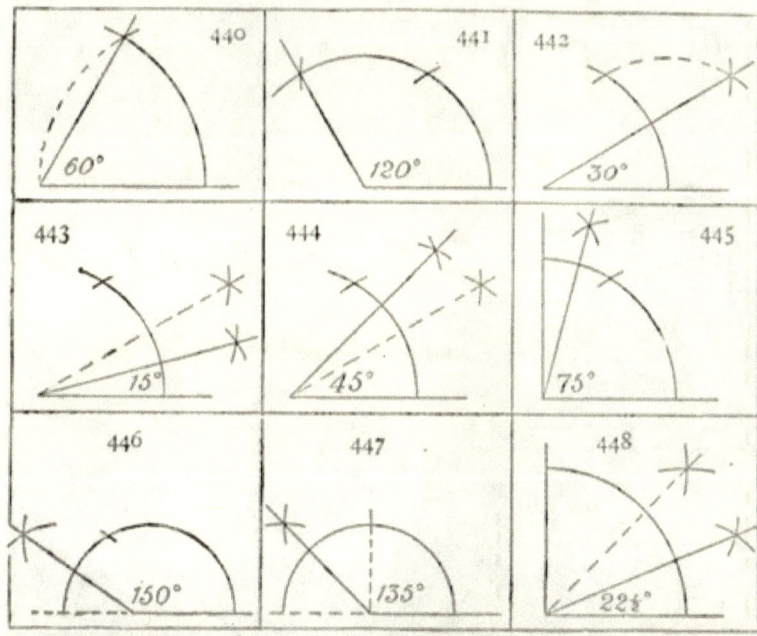

Construction of angles when their size is given in degrees.—Describe a circle, and show that the radius will go exactly six times **round** it. The explanation of a degree is given on page 47, **and** should be recapitulated here. If the circle contains **360°**, then each of the sixths into which it has been divided must equal 60°. Most of the other common angles can be obtained **from** the angle of 60°.

Figs. 440-448.—*To construct angles of* 60°, 120°, 30°, **15°**, 45°, 75°, 150°, 135°, **22½°**.

These may be **easily** followed from the constructions, **and** most of them can **also be** obtained by using the set-squares. The angle of 30° + the angle of 45° will give 75°, &c.

Triangles.—These have previously been **defined and ex**plained in Standard III, and will **now only need** recapitulating.

The number of degrees **in the various** angles will require **constant** practice, and **the pupils must** be well **drilled** in the fact that *the three angles of any triangle contain* **180°**. Plenty of **examples** should be given, **such as,** when two angles are given **to** find the third, and, **in** the case of an isosceles triangle, when the vertical angle **is given to** find the base angles.

M

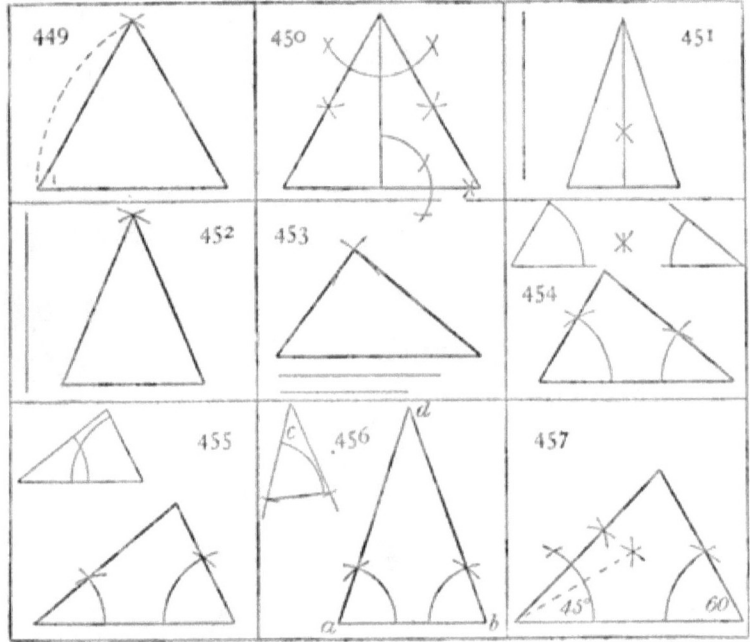

Fig. 449.—*To construct an equilateral triangle on a given base.*

Fig. 450.—*To construct an equilateral triangle, its altitude being given.* Draw the base line first, perpendicular to the altitude.

Fig. 451.—*To construct an isosceles triangle, the base and altitude being given.*

• **Fig. 452.**—*To construct an isosceles triangle, the base and side being given.*

Fig. 453.—*To construct a triangle, its three sides being given.*

Fig. 454.—*To construct a triangle, its base and base angles being given.*

Fig. 455.—*To construct a triangle similar to a given triangle.*

Fig. 456.—*To construct an isosceles triangle having its base and vertical angle given.*

This depends upon the previous problem, and is more easily understood when worked as shown. Convert the given angle c into an isosceles triangle by making its two sides equal and joining them. At a and b construct angles equal to the base angles of c. Then the vertical angle d must be equal to c.

This problem should be practised a number of times until thoroughly understood.

Fig. 457.—*Construct a triangle having a base of 3 feet and two angles of 60° and 45° respectively. What is the size of the remaining angle? Scale = ¾ inch to 1 foot.* [180° − (60° + 45°) = 75°].

Plane Geometry. Standard V. 163

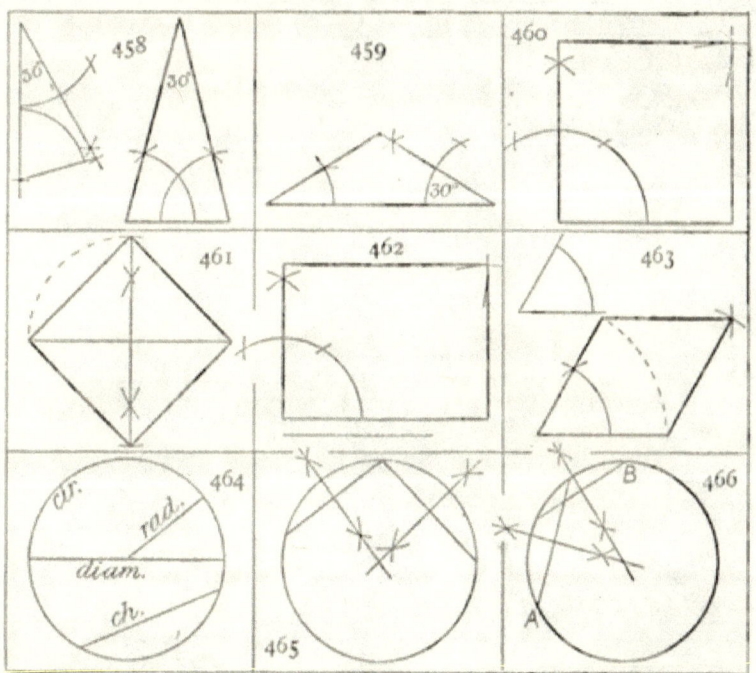

Fig. 458.—*To construct an isosceles triangle with a vertical angle of* **30°** *and a base of* 1 *inch. What is the size of the base angle?*

Construct an angle of 30°, convert it into an isosceles triangle, and then proceed as in fig. 456.

Note.—Practise this problem with a variety of vertical angles, and notice that **to construct an isosceles** triangle having base angles of 75° is only another **way of wording** the above.

Fig. 459.—*To construct an isosceles triangle on a given base and having its base angles 30°.*

It is only necessary to construct one angle, the other is more easily measured from the angle already obtained.

Fig. 460.—*To construct a square on a given base.*

Fig. 461.—*To construct a square on a given diagonal.*

Fig. 462.—*To construct a rectangle, its two sides being given.*

Fig. 463.—*To construct a rhombus, having a side and an angle given.*

The circle.—The various parts should be defined and explained, such as centre, circumference, radius, diameter, **chord**.

Fig. 465.—*To find the centre of a given circle.*

Fig. 466.—*To complete the circle of which AB is a portion.*

164   *The Teaching of Drawing*

In the following card the problems should be arranged as indicated below.

Card I.—1. *Copy the angle ABC, and through D draw a line parallel to AB.*

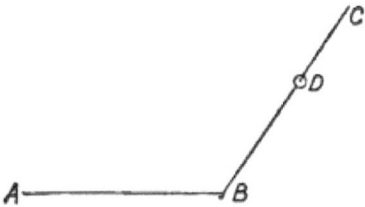

2. *Draw two right lines each 2 feet long to meet at an angle of 90°. Scale = $1\frac{1}{4}''$ to 1' 0".*

3. *Describe two circles touching each other with diameters of 1 inch and $1\frac{1}{2}$ inches respectively.*

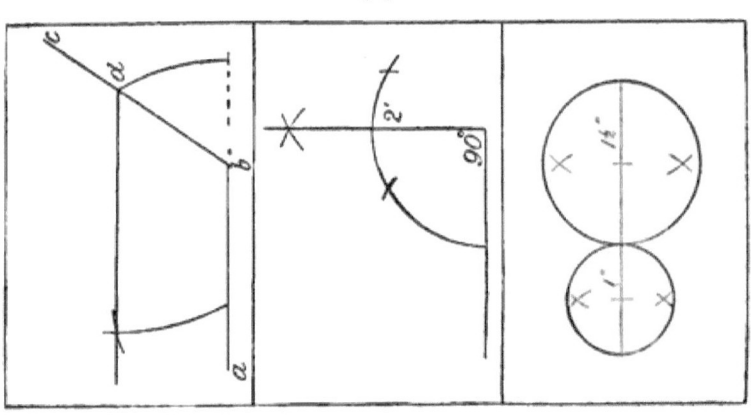

1. To copy the angle, first measure AB. Take BC as radius and describe an arc. Intersect this arc with the distance AC. This method is necessary, as no marks must be made on the cards.

2. As the scale is $1\frac{1}{4}''$ to 1' 0", each line will be $2\frac{1}{2}$ inches long.

3. Draw a line and set off the diameters. Find the centre of each diameter and describe the circles. Be careful to see that the circles touch one another.

Note.—If radii of $\frac{1}{2}$ inch and $\frac{3}{4}$ inch had been set off, the same result would have been obtained.

Card II.—1. *Copy the given triangle,* **and bisect an angle and** *a side.*

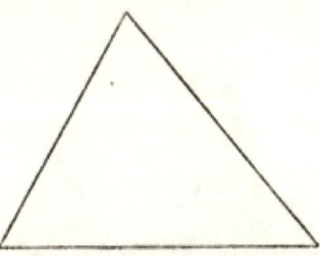

2. *Construct a triangle* **having** *its base* 2½ *inches, and its angles* 45°, 45° *and* 90°.

3. *Construct an equilateral triangle of* 2 *feet sides. Scale* = 1½″ *to* 1′ 0″.

Card III.—1. *Copy the given line AB and the point C,* **and** *through C draw a line parallel to AB.*

2. *Construct a right angle, and* **bisect it.**

3. *Make an isosceles triangle,* **base** 2 *inches and* **angle opposite the base** 45°.

Card IV.—1. *Construct a square on AB.*

2. *Draw two straight lines, each* 2½ *inches long, which shall meet at an angle of* 60°.

3. *Construct a triangle with sides of* 1½ *inches,* 2½ *inches, and* 3 *inches respectively.*

Card V.—1. *Copy the given triangle, and through the point C draw a line parallel* **to the base.**

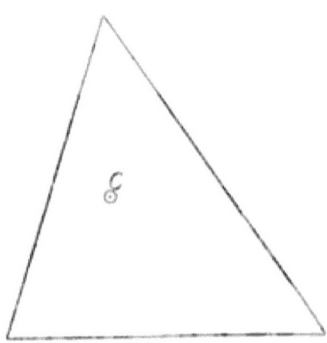

2. *Draw a circle of* 1 *inch* **radius**, *and divide the circumference into four equal parts.*

3. *Draw a line* 2½ *inches long, and divide it into three equal parts.*

Syllabus, Standard VII.—(*b* 1.)   *Geometrical Drawing*, *more* advanced *than in Standard V.*

This section will **include the construction of a** *triangle similar to a* given *triangle and* **standing on a given base.**   *The drawing of two* circles of given radii touching **each other.**   *Construction for* **circles passing** *through three given points, or touching three given* **lines.**   *Tangents to two circles.   Construction of regular polygons* **by any general** *method, together with their inscribed and circumscribed circle.   The* use of plain scales.

This subject may be taken instead of section (*b*.) :—*The drawing of any common objects, and* casts of ornament *in light and* shade.   It is much easier than drawing in light and shade, as it is very difficult to arrange objects and casts with a suitable light in ordinary school-rooms.   There is nothing in the above requirements that cannot be easily covered by the pupils in Standard VII, and it has the advantage of giving a more advanced knowledge of the very useful and interesting study of Plane Geometry which has been already begun in Standard V. The pupils also are now better able to appreciate the value of exactness and finish in the work, and are more skilful in the manipulation of their instruments. To give a complete course is beyond the scope of this book, as there are plenty of text books, such as 'Longman's Plane Geometry, Book 14,' which amply cover all the requirements. A number of examination questions are given which will indicate the character of the work. Solutions are given to the more difficult problems, from which it will be seen that there is no special difficulty to be overcome. These, of course, should be worked to a much larger scale. The scales are all drawn half their proper size, and any necessary notes to the problems are given at the end of the solutions. Three questions are usually given for the examination.

Examination Tests

1. *Draw a line to touch the two given circles* (fig. 468).
2. *Draw a scale of $\frac{3}{4}''$ to $1'\ 0''$ to show $7\ ft.\ 5\ in.$* (fig. 469).
3. *Copy the given triangle at a scale of $\frac{3}{4}''$ to $1'\ 0''$ on a base of $4\ ft.\ 7\ in.$* (fig. 470).
4. *Describe a rectangle of which AB is one side and CD a diagonal* (fig. 471).
5. *Through the point A draw parallels to BC and CD; also from A draw perpendiculars to BC, CD* (fig. 472).
6. *Describe an irregular pentagon of which the sides are $2\frac{1}{2}$ inches, 2 inches, $1\frac{1}{2}$ inches, 1 inch, and $\frac{1}{2}$ inch. The angle which the longest side makes with the shortest side is $100°$, and the angle between the two longest sides is $65°$* (fig. 473).
7. *In a given circle inscribe seven equal touching circles* (fig 474).
8. *Divide a given quadrant into halves, thirds, and sixths* (fig. 475).
9. *From three given points A, B, C, draw three right lines equal to one another, to meet in the same point* (fig. 476).
10. *Construct a trefoil of tangential arcs* (fig. 477).
11. *About a given circle construct an octagon* (fig. 478).
12. *Trisect a given arc* (use the dividers).
13. *Draw a scale to show $3\ ft.\ 7\ in.$ when $1\frac{1}{2}$ inches represent $1\ foot$* (fig. 392).

168 The Teaching of Drawing

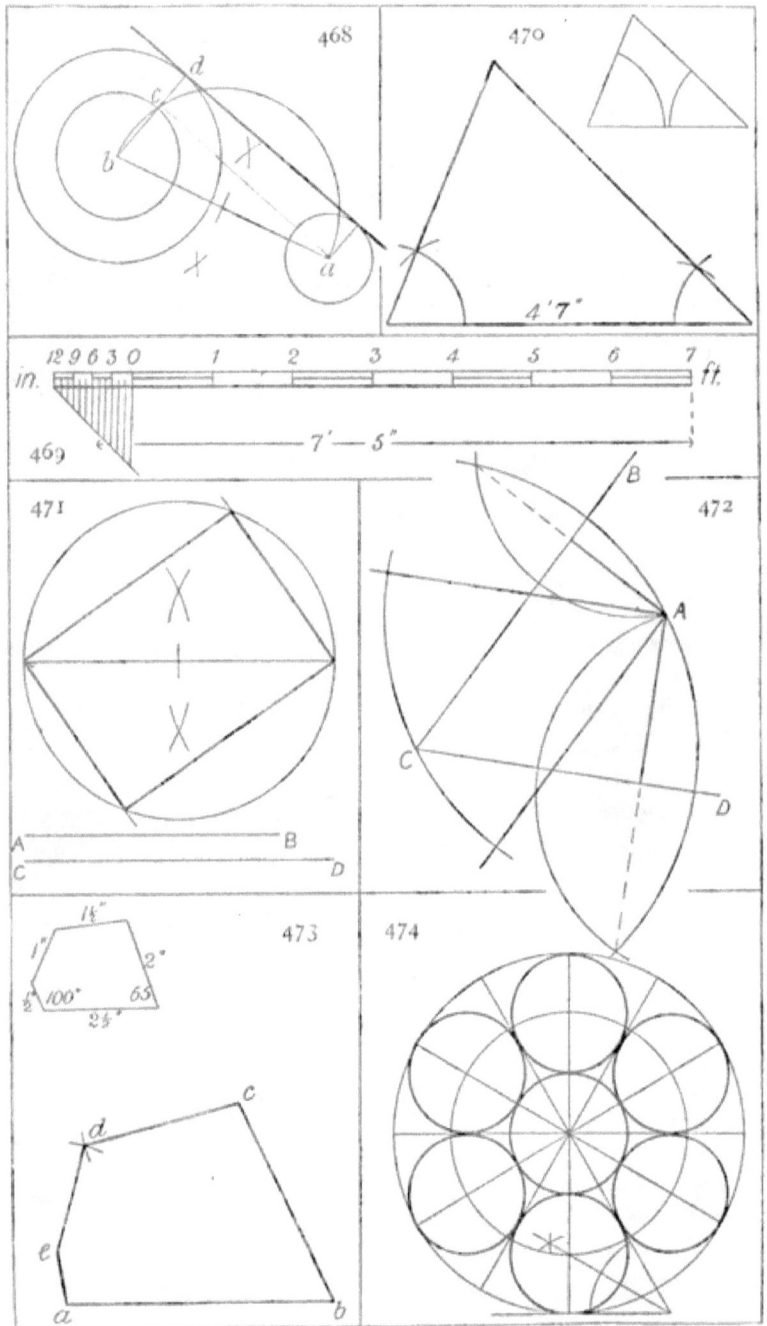

Plane Geometry. Standard VII.

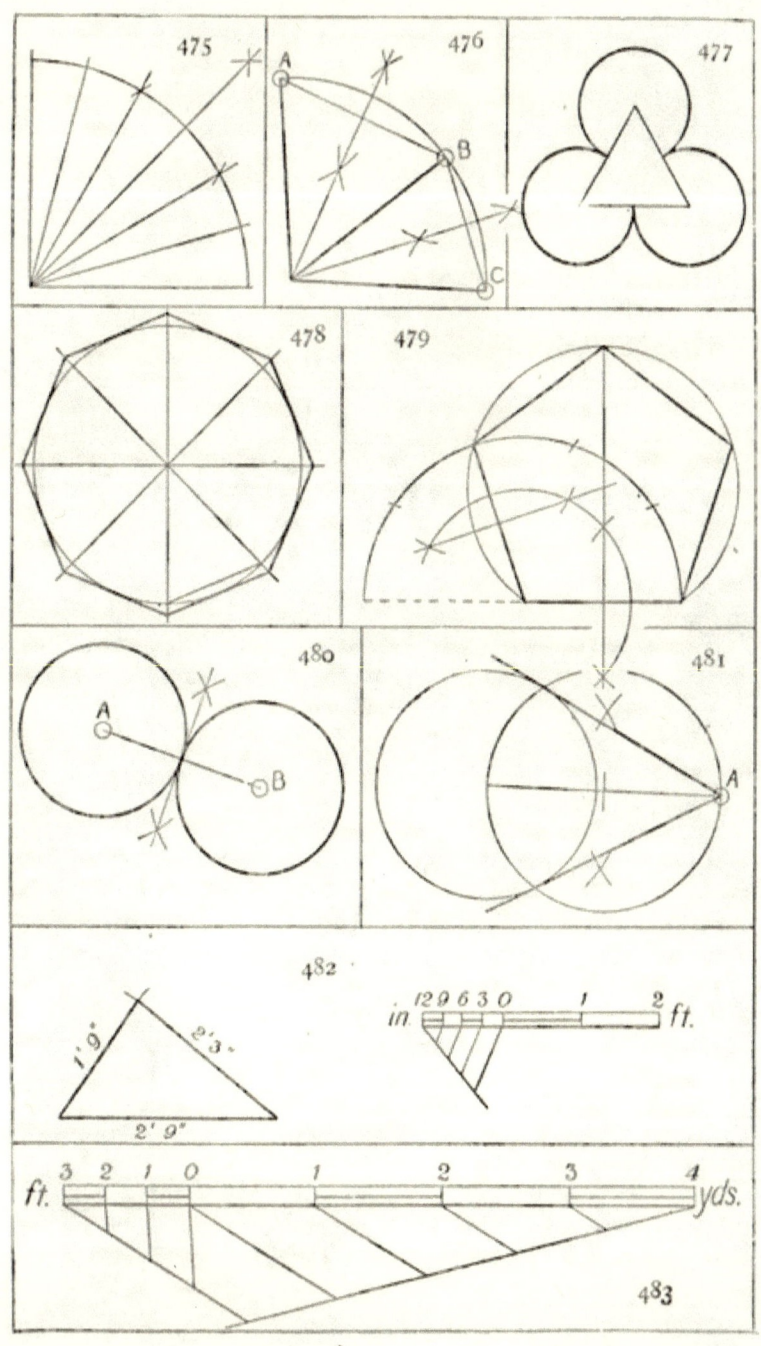

14. *Describe a regular pentagon on a base of* 1½ *inches* (fig. 479).

15. *From two given points, A and B, draw two circles of equal radii touching each other* (fig. 480).

16. *From a given point A draw two tangents to a given circle* (fig. 481).

17. *Construct a triangle with sides* 2 *ft.* 9 *in.*, 2 *ft.* 3 *in., and* 1 *ft.* 9 *in. respectively. Scale* = ¾' *to* 1' 0" (fig. 482).

18. *Draw a scale of* 1/30 *th to show yards and feet, and long enough to measure five yards* (fig. 483).

Notes on the Examination Tests

Fig. 468.—As the two circles are copied, their centres are already found. Join the centres, and describe a circle with the *difference* of their radii. From *a* draw a tangent *ac* to the described circle. Produce *bc* to *d*, and from *a* draw a line parallel to *bd* and rule the tangent.

Fig. 470.—The scale constructed in fig. 469 will give the base.

Fig. 472.—The readiest method for obtaining the perpendiculars is to use that shown in fig. 427, as the same arc which was used for the parallels does also for the perpendiculars.

Fig. 473.—Make a rough sketch first, showing the position of the angles. Draw *ab*. Set out the angles of 65° and 100° with the protractor, and complete the sides *bc* and *ac*.

Fig. 474.—The problem does not state that the circles are to touch the given circle. If six circles be inscribed, the seventh will exactly fit in the centre. If the circles had to touch the given circle, then the circumference would require dividing into fourteen equal parts.

Fig. 476.—As the lines drawn from A, B, C are to be equal, they must be radii of a circle; therefore join AB, BC, and bisect.

Fig. 477.—The arcs are to be tangential—that is, if the circles were completed they would not cut each other. Construct an equilateral triangle with each side double the radius of the arc, and with each angle as a centre describe the arcs. For a quatrefoil, construct a square, &c.

Fig. 482.—First construct the scale, and make it long enough to measure 3 feet. As no smaller measurements than 3 inches are required, it will be sufficient to divide the first unit into four parts.

Fig. 483.—A scale of $\frac{1}{30}$th to show yards means that the unit to be taken is $\frac{1}{30}$th of a yard. The scale has to measure 5 yards, therefore its total length will be $\frac{5}{30}$ of a yard = 6 inches. Draw a line 6 inches long, and divide it as shown into five equal parts, each of which will represent one yard. Subdivide the first part into three for the feet.

CHAPTER IX

SOLID GEOMETRY STANDARDS VI AND VII

Syllabus, Standard VI.—*Plans and elevations of plane figures and rectangular solids in simple positions with sections.* (Girls are not required to take solid geometry in either Standards VI or VII.)

Apparatus.—Same as for plane geometry for the pupils. Drawing-boards and T-squares are very useful, but not essential.

The teacher must also be provided with :—

1. **Plane figures,** such as the triangle, square, rectangle, circle, &c., cut out in cardboard ; black is preferable to white, as chalk marks can be made on it.

2. **Models of the Solids** used, some of which should be cut to show the sections. These can be bought in sets, or the teacher, if fond of tools, may construct them in wood. The easier plan, however, is to make them of cardboard by developing the surfaces. It is a capital exercise for each pupil to make his own set of models in this manner, as it encourages manual dexterity and gives a thorough familiarity with the various models—a most important acquirement in this subject, as it is impossible for pupils to represent a solid unless they can imagine its appearance. The method of constructing some of the easier solids is given, as no successful work can possibly be done unless models are well used and handled by the pupils. For rapid illustration, when a variety of sections, &c., require showing, a piece of soap is a useful substitute.

3. **Model** to show the position **of the** two planes.—Two small black-boards fastened with a hinge is the most useful.

Folded paper or cardboard answers very well when the folding board is not obtainable.

4. Some **wire,** to show the projecting lines.

The principal solid forms and terms connected with them are defined here:—

A cube is a solid figure contained by six equal squares.

A prism has its two ends equal, similar, **and parallel, and** each of its sides is a parallelogram.

Prisms are named from the shape of their ends; thus, a square prism has a square for each end, a pentagonal prism has a pentagon for each end, &c.

A pyramid has a plane figure for its base, and each of its sides are triangles, which meet at a point above the base called the **apex.**

Pyramids are named from the shape of their bases.

A sphere is generated by the revolution of a semicircle about its diameter; every part of its surface is equally distant from the centre.

A cone is generated by the revolution of a right-angled triangle about its perpendicular.

A cylinder is generated by the revolution of a rectangle about one of its sides.

The axis is the line passing through the middle of the solid; when it is perpendicular to the base or ends of the solid, the figure is termed a **right prism** or **pyramid.**

To make Simple Solids from Cardboard

Figs. 484-490 show the shapes to which the cardboard must be cut to form the solids. The figures must first be accurately drawn to the required size, and carefully cut out along the *outer* dark lines. A knife should then be drawn along the *inner* light lines, taking care not to cut quite through the cardboard. Turn up the surfaces on the *opposite* side to that which is cut, as this gives a clean unbroken edge. Finish by gumming thin paper over the joints. Other solids may be made in a similar manner, and the teacher thus secures a good set of models at little cost. They may be made solid by filling with plaster of Paris.

Fig. **484** shows the development of the surfaces of the cube; **figs. 485 and 486** of the square prism and pyramid; **figs. 487 and 488** of the equilateral triangular prism and pyramid; **figs. 489 and 490** of the hexagonal prism and pyramid.

Note.—The equilateral triangular pyramid is usually termed a **tetrahedron.**

Sections.—There is generally a little difficulty in showing sections. These may be easily made in cardboard. Suppose, for example, a section is required through the square pyramid. After cutting out the surfaces, turn up the sides and mark in pencil on the edges where the section is required; turn the sides down, and cut off the parts above the section line. Finish the model by turning up the edges and gumming as before.

The method in this branch of the course is treated rather more fully than in some of the previous portions, as it is felt that solid geometry is the most difficult part for the pupils to understand. All the main difficulties and important principles are dealt with, and test problems given at the end. The ordinary books, such as Longman's Book 10 for Standard VI, and Book 15 for Standard VII, will afford plenty of examples.

This subject is generally taught in a less satisfactory manner than any part of the drawing syllabus, partly on account of the difficulty of the subject in itself, as, although very little is required, the pupil must imagine the position of the object and reason out the solution. In actual practical work it is really the most useful portion of geometrical drawing, as by its aid we represent not only *length and breadth*, but *thickness* also. Carpenters, engineers, and mechanics generally, make more use of this branch of drawing than any other. When taught well it is not only very interesting to the pupils, but it affords excellent mental training. Examples of working drawings can easily be obtained to show to the pupils. This arouses their interest, as the practical use of plans and elevations is at once brought before their minds.

The earlier lessons should be entirely taken up with repre-

Solid Geometry. Standard VI. 175

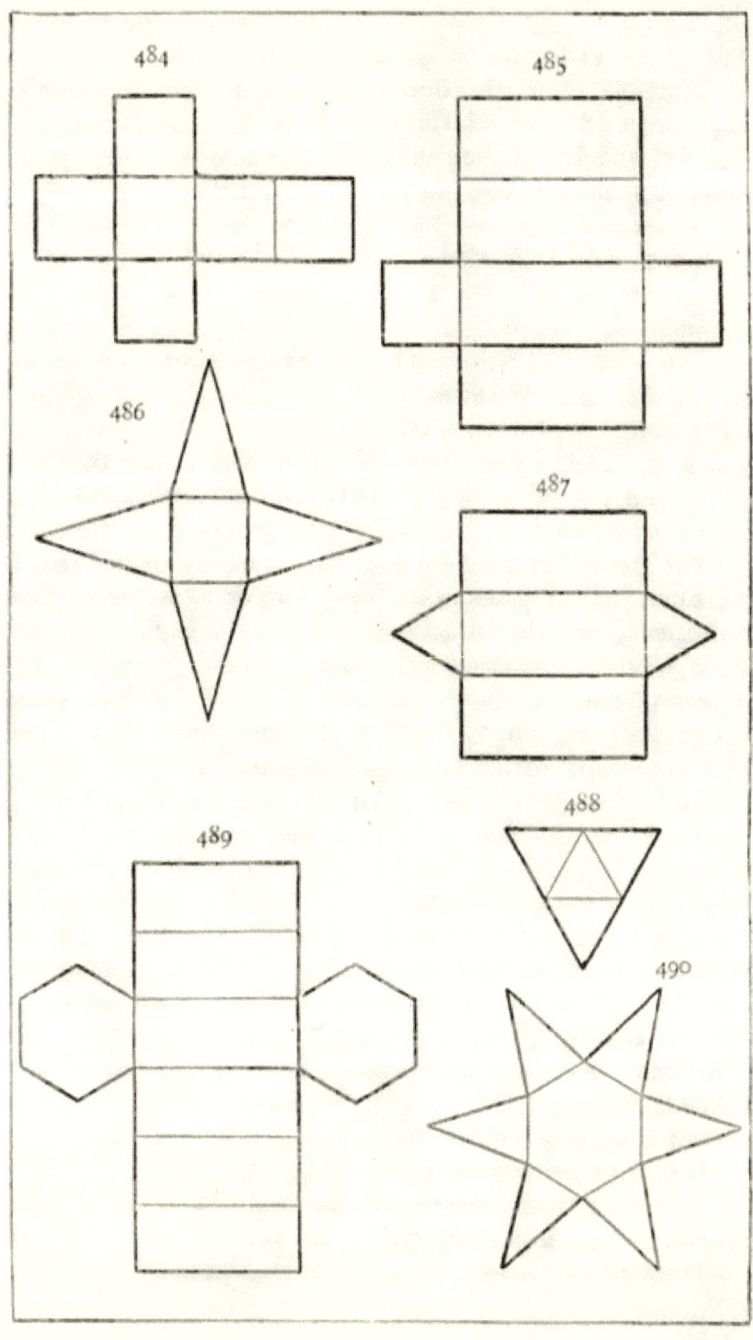

senting plans and elevations **of common** objects in various positions. These should **be drawn roughly on** the blackboard, the **pupils** working with **a slate** and pencil. A line should be **drawn across** to separate **the** plans from **the** elevations. **This method** enables the **teacher to** deal with **a** great number **of objects,** and thoroughly familiarises the **pupils** with the idea **of** representing objects **in a variety** of positions. To begin with definitions and a description of the planes **is** almost sure **to disgust the** pupils, **and to** effectually **kill all** interest **in the** subject.

Three simple rules should **be** laid down : —

1. **The plan** *of an object is seen when* **we look vertically downwards upon it.**
2. **The** elevation *is seen by looking horizontally forwards.*
3. *Every point in* **the plan is exactly** *under the corresponding point in the elevation.*

Let the pupil see the objects, as it is perfectly useless **giving** theoretical demonstrations unless the pupils can see and **carry in** their minds the appearance of the model when viewed **from** different positions. This may be varied by taking some **common object that the** pupils are familiar with, and questioning **as to its** appearance when seen from various positions, without **showing** the model. This **cultivates and trains the** mental powers in the very important **faculty of** remembering what is seen. **Figs. 491-512** show **the** plans and elevations **of** a number of objects suitable **for** the earlier lessons. These should be drawn approximately correct, as previously suggested. The pupils' attention should be directed to the fact that **one** *drawing shows only* **two** *dimensions, as* **length and** *breadth, and* **that** *the two drawings are necessary to show the* **height** *as well.*

When the pupils have thoroughly grasped **the** idea of what **plans** and elevations really represent, then **the** teacher may show how these drawings **may** be accurately constructed from definite statements.

The **vertical** and **horizontal planes** may now be explained, and their relation to one another illustrated. To do this, fold **a piece** of paper at right angles, and place **it** on a board or **table** adjoining a wall, so that one half of the paper rests on

Solid Geometry. Standard VI

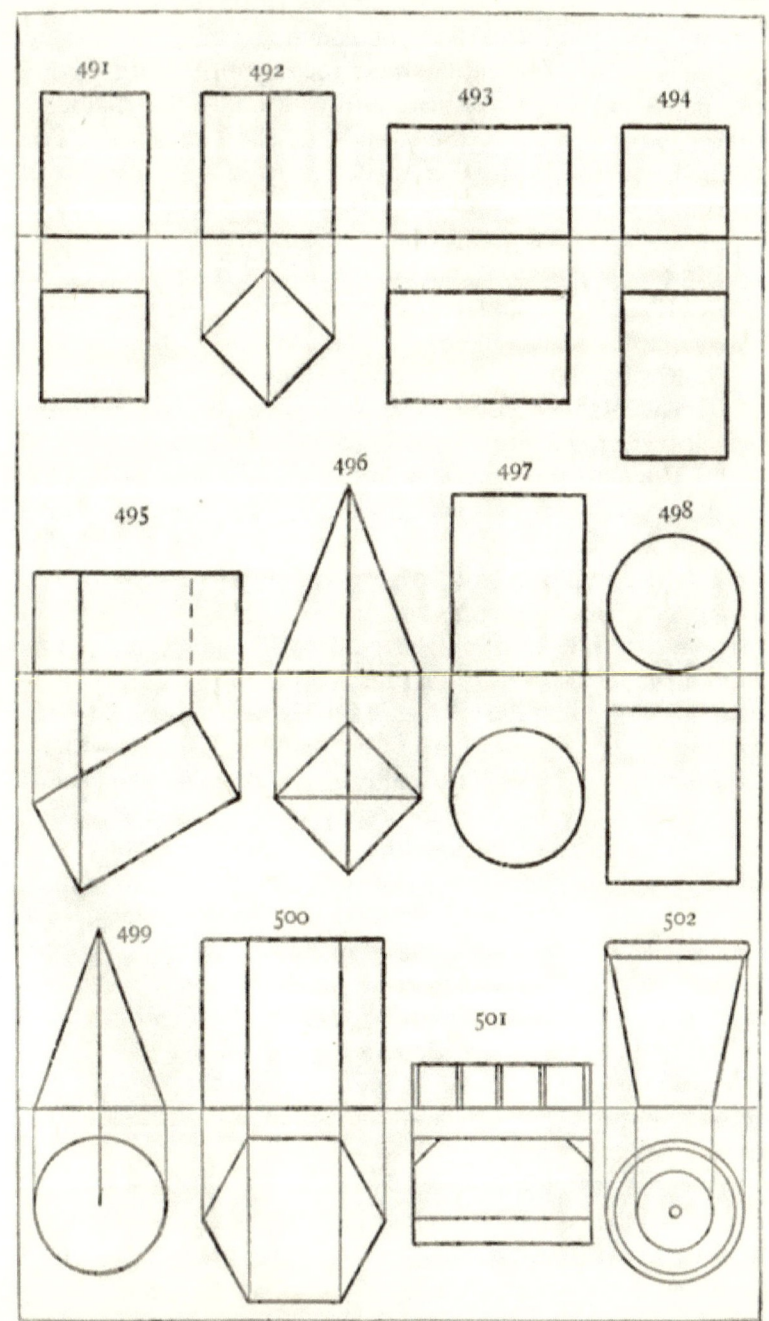

178 The Teaching of Drawing

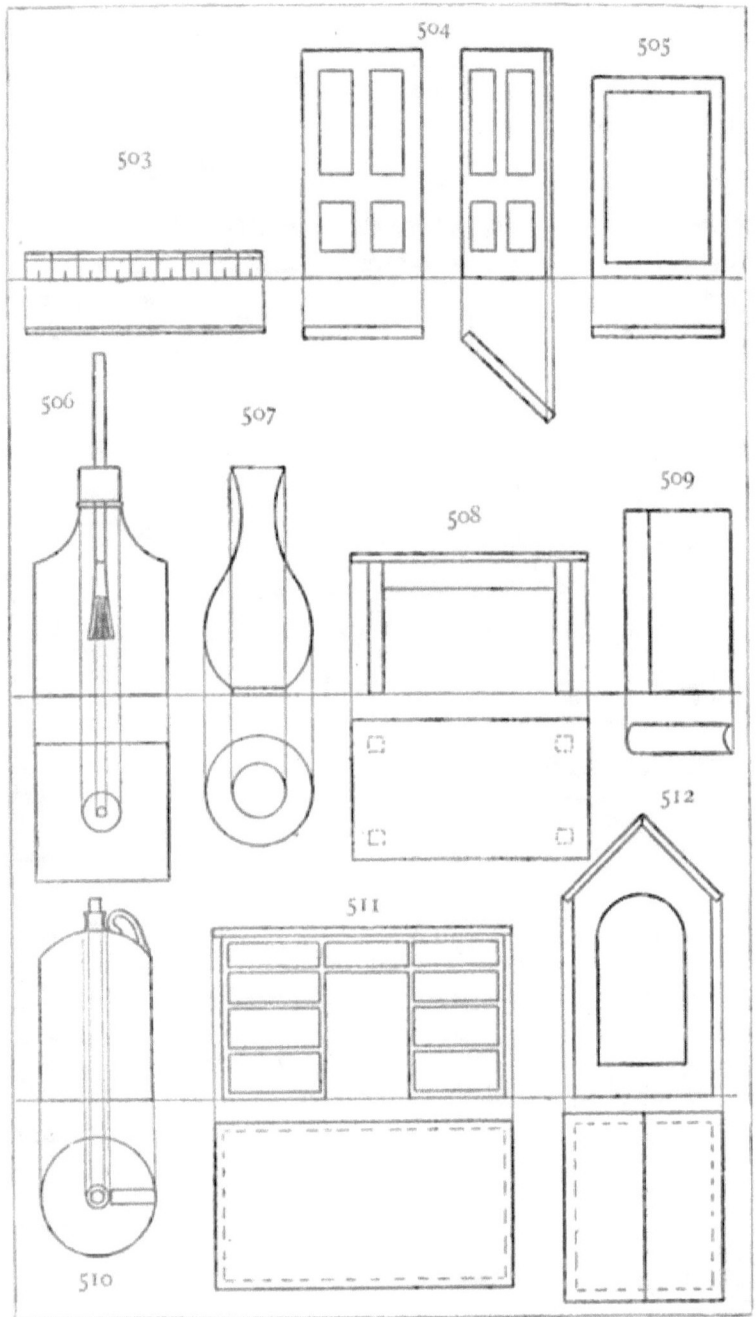

Solid Geometry. Standard VI

the table and the other half against the wall (fig. 513). Explain that any perfectly flat surface is called a plane. Illustrate by reference to the carpenter's plane and its uses. There are two plane surfaces here, one upright and the other level; the upright one is called the **vertical** plane, and the level one the horizontal **plane**. The angle which they make with one another is a right angle, and the line where the two planes intersect is called the **intersecting line**.

Place a small box or any simple object on the horizontal plane, and trace its shape, *abcd*, on the paper. This will evi-

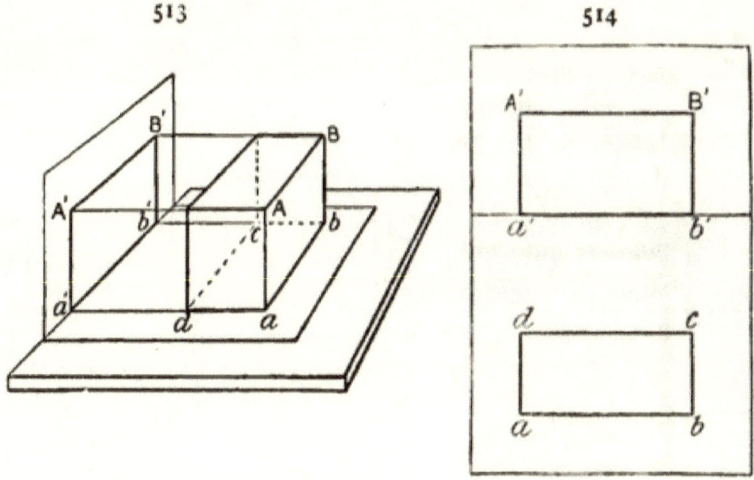

dently show the length and breadth of the box, and, as it shows the space covered by the box on the **horizontal** or **ground plane** and its distance from the vertical plane, it is its **plan**. Next, with a long pencil, trace the outline on the vertical plane, A'B'a'b'. This shows the height, and, as it represents its appearance when looked at horizontally forwards, it is its **elevation**. If the paper be now held up, the plan and elevation will be seen, as in fig. 514, one exactly under the other.

SOLIDS STANDING ON THEIR FACES

Lesson I.—A problem similar to the following may now be worked out on the blackboard.

A cube stands on the H.P. with two of its faces parallel to the V.P. Draw the plan and elevation when the back face is 6 inches in front of the V.P.

Note.—The contractions H.P. and V.P. will be used in future for horizontal and vertical planes respectively.

1. Place the paper showing the planes as in fig. 513. Now elicit the position in which the cube is to be placed and its distance from the V.P. Trace its plan. Remove the cube and show the plan.

2. Draw the intersecting line *XY* on the board; let the pupils show it on the paper, and explain its use. Draw a line 6 inches below the intersecting line, parallel to it, and equal to an edge of the cube. Construct a square *abcd* on this line, and show that this square corresponds with the traced plan.

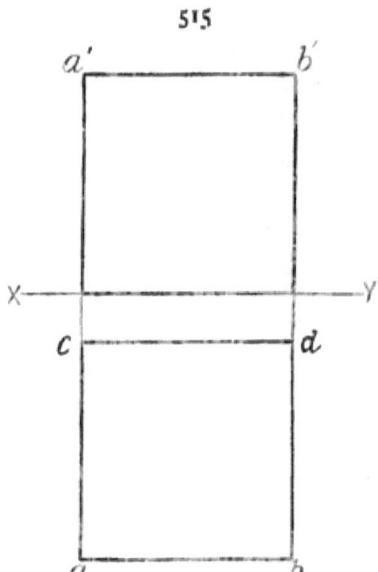

515

3. Replace the paper and cube, and trace the elevation on the vertical plane. Remove the cube, and show the plan and elevation.

4. Draw projectors from the plan on the board. Elicit the height of the cube, and complete the elevation.

5. Show that the constructed drawing corresponds with the traced one, and explain that it would be inconvenient to draw with the planes at right angles to each other, although the pupil must continually bear this in mind while working.

Solid Geometry. Standard VI

6. Letter the figures, and explain that the same point always keeps the same letter. If A be a point on a figure, then a will be its plan and a' its elevation. Find the points at first by referring to the model.

7. Let the class repeat the drawing to a suitable scale.

Lesson II.—Arrange the planes as before, place a cylinder standing with its end on the H.P. and proceed as follows. (Work out each step on the board as it is elicited from the class.)

What position is the cylinder in? '*Standing on its base.*'

In what direction must I look to see the plan? '*Vertically downwards.*'

What shape do I see if I look down on the cylinder? '*A circle.*'

I must now decide where to draw the circle; how shall I find this out? '*By measuring its distance from the V.P.*'

Draw a line at right angles to XY and set off the distance eb. Measure the diameter ab of the cylinder, and describe the circle.

What does the circle represent? '*The plan of the cylinder.*'

Why? '*Because it is the space the cylinder covers on the ground.*'

Could it represent the plan of anything else? '*Sphere cone, &c.*'

Where must the elevation be drawn? '*Above XY and exactly over the plan.*'

In what direction must I look to see the elevation?

What shape do I see then? '*A rectangle.*'

Project the width from c and d. Measure the height, and set it off on the board.

Letter points c' and d'.

Where is b'?

Lesson III.—Place the cube with its sides making angles with the V.P., and point out that its exact position with reference to both planes must always be stated. Now write a problem on the board as follows:—*Draw the plan and elevation of a cube with one of its faces in the H.P., its nearest corner 1 inch from the V.P., and with one side making an angle of 30° with it.*

1. Question out every step with regard to its *position*.

Is it on its face or edge?

Place the model on the plane.

Is it in the required position?

'*No.*'

Why not? '*Because its sides do not make 30° with X Y.*'

Place it in position with the aid of the 30° set-square.

2. What shape will the plan be? '*A square.*'

Draw a line at 30° with XY, and on it construct a square.

How many sides are seen in the elevation? '*Two.*'

Do they appear to be squares? Why not?

3. Project lines from each angle of the plan.

Elicit the height, and complete the elevation.

4. Where will b be in the elevation? Mark it.

Why not at the bottom? '*Because the bottom is not visible in the plan.*'

Elicit the position of the other angles in the same way. Frequent reference to the model will be found necessary, as it is rather difficult for the pupils to find these points at first.

5. Thicken in the visible lines, and explain that the line from c, not being visible, should be dotted.

Notes.—1. The teacher will find it easier to take simple positions of the rectangular solids first, and afterwards proceed to the more difficult ones. The square prism, box, &c. should now be treated in a similar manner.

2. The projectors should be shown with **very** fine lines, **and** care must be taken to see that they are drawn **at** right angles to XY. To do this when the **ruler** and set-square only are used, place the ruler above XY, and with the set-square draw one projector, **say** from a; now place **the** ruler below **the** figure, and with the set-square rule parallels to the projector already drawn.

SOLIDS STANDING ON AN EDGE

Three positions require illustration :— I. When the **edge** is **perpendicular** to the V.P. II. When the edge is **parallel** to the V.P. III. When the **edge** is neither perpendicular nor parallel to the V.P.

I. Edge perpendicular to the V.P.

This is perfectly simple. The three figures given below illustrate what is necessary in this case.

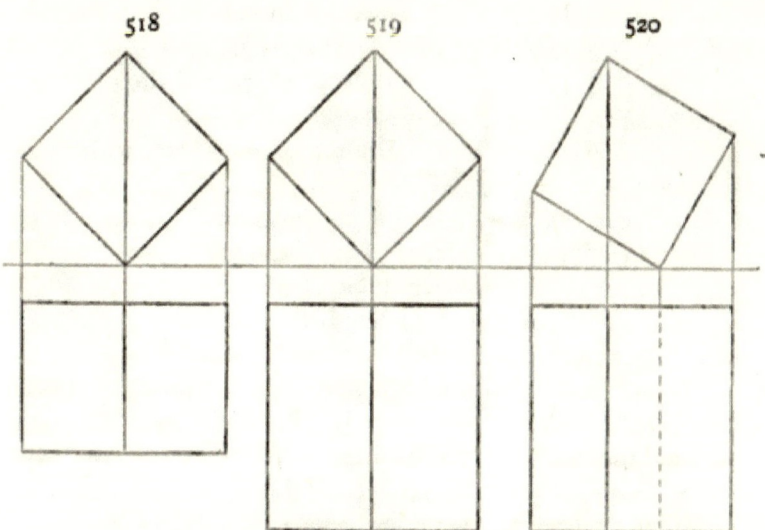

II. **Edge parallel to** the **V.P.**

The pupils will soon discover that when the model is in this position its elevation cannot be determined directly, as the edges of the ends are in an oblique position, and consequently do not show their true size. The true size of the edges can only be determined when the end is parallel to the V.P. Hence we get this general principle, *that when the axis of the solid is not at right angles to the V.P., a third view showing the true shape of the end must be obtained first.*

The following example illustrates the mode of working :—

Draw the plan and elevation of a cube standing on one edge with its axis parallel to the V.P., and with two of its adjacent faces making equal angles with the H.P.

1. Elicit its position, and place the cube on the planes as required. Now show that if we turn it round at right angles all its dimensions can be ascertained.

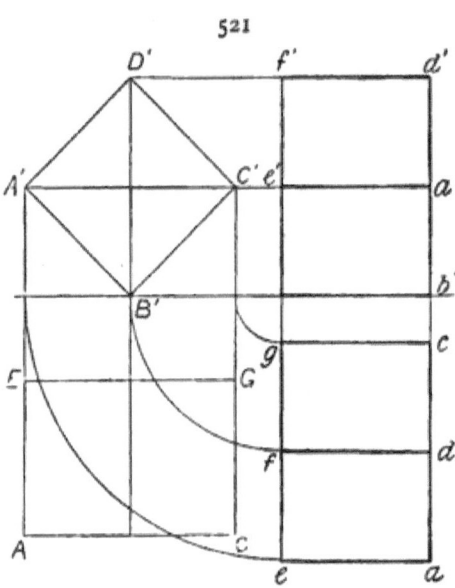

521

2. As two of the adjacent faces of the cube make equal angles with the H.P., they will be at angles of 45°. With the 45° set-square draw $B'A'$ and $B'C'$, make them the required length, and complete the square. Then $A'B'C'D'$ will represent the true shape of the end. Obtain the plan $ACGE$ as in fig. 518.

3. If the plan and elevation thus found be each turned at right angles, the required plan and elevation will be obtained. In actual practice it is not necessary to draw the light-lined plan $ACGE$. It is put in here, as experience shows, that the pupils can readily grasp the idea that the required plan *eacg* is simply the plan $EACG$ turned at right angles.

Project horizontally from A' and D'. Set off the width fd', and complete the elevation.

Solid Geometry. Standard VI

4. Let the pupils look at the model and notice the shape of the plan. It will be found to correspond exactly with the elevation. This is always the case when either the cube or square prism have their axes parallel to the V.P. Project vertically for the plan, and obtain the width as shown.

Note.—The pupils should first draw the elevation and plan as shown in light line, and then turn them at right angles; and afterwards obtain the plan and elevation without using the first plan, transferring the widths directly from the intersecting line as shown by the arcs.

Figs. 522 and 523 *show similar positions of the square and triangular prisms.*

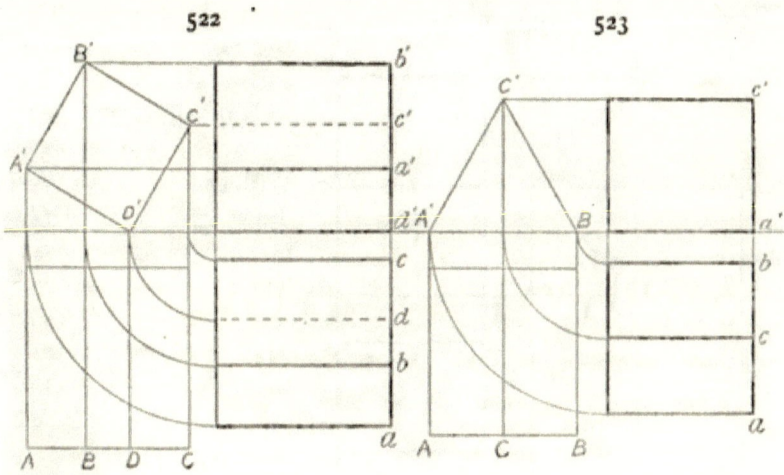

All four views are shown for the sake of clearness. Remember that the required plan is the light-lined plan turned at right angles, and that after the principle is understood the first plan may be dispensed with and the widths transferred directly from the intersecting line.

III. **Edge neither perpendicular nor parallel to the V.P.**

Draw the plan and elevation of a cube standing with its edge in the H.P., and with its axis making an angle of **30° with the V.P.**

This is a rather more difficult position than is usually given to Standard VI. The principle is exactly the same as that used in the previous problems, so that it is included here for the sake of completeness. It is more usual to give the plan, and require the elevation to be drawn from it.

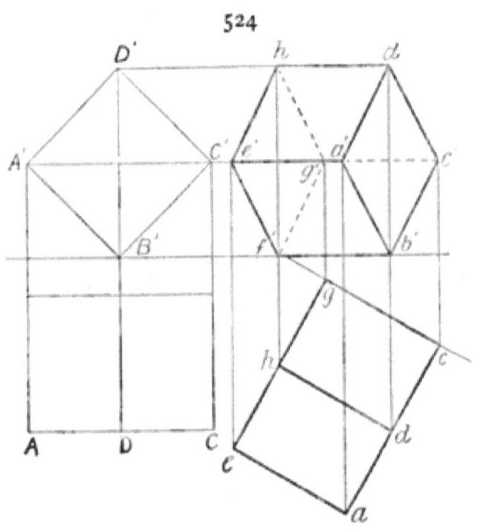

524

1. Draw the elevation and plan when the end is parallel to the *VP* as before.

2. Place the plan so that its axis makes 30° with the *V.P.*; *ADC* then becomes *adc*.

3. Project horizontally from *A'* and *D'* for the heights.

4. Use the model well, and project from *d* and *h*, giving the top and bottom edges. Thicken these lines in when obtained, as it helps to keep the figure clear. Complete the front vertical face by projecting from *a* and *c* to the line from *A'*. Finish the back face, showing the unseen edges with a dotted line.

The square prism should be similarly dealt with.

This problem may be worked more quickly by the device which is constantly used in more advanced solid geometry, viz., *changing the position of the intersecting line* and assuming a fresh vertical plane. The problem may then be solved by using three figures instead of four. The method is as follows:—

1. Obtain the elevation and plan as before (fig. 525).

2. Instead of moving the plan, move the intersecting line *XY*, so that it makes the required angle with the edge of the plan, *X Y*. If we now imagine the figure to be turned so that *X' Y'* is horizontal, the plan *acge* will be in the required position.

3. Project as before from *d* and *h* at right angles to *X' Y'*.

Set off *b'd'* and *f'h'* equal to *B'D'*, and thicken in *d'h'* and *b'f'* for the **top** and bottom edges. Complete the front face, making

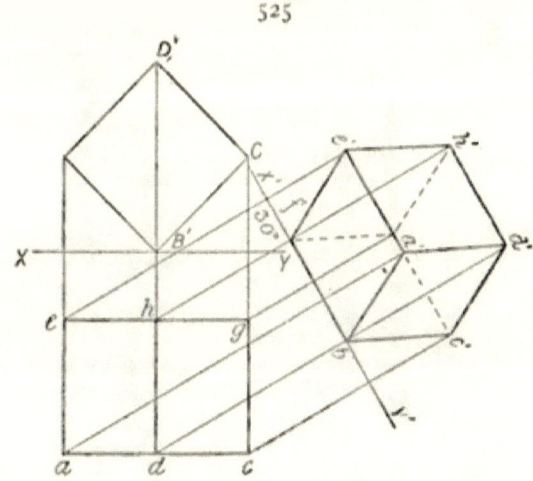

525

a' and *c'* the same distance above *X'Y* that *A'* and *C'* are above *XY*.

4. Complete the back face, and thicken in as before.

PLANE FIGURES

These will present no special difficulty after **solids have** been dealt **with.** Use cardboard figures to illustrate the various positions. A door opened at **various angles shows** the varying width.

Two positions require special attention :—**I.** When the figure is **vertical and makes an angle with the vertical plane** like an open door. II. When the figure **makes an angle with the horizontal plane** like a trap door when **opened.**

I. *A square standing vertically upon one edge makes an angle of* 45° *with the V.P. Draw its plan and elevation (fig.* 526).

The same principle must be **used as** in the preceding problem, viz., to draw the plan and elevation when the figure is parallel to the V.P.

1. Draw the elevation *a'B'C'd'*, and the plan *aB*, when the square is parallel to the **V.P.**

2. Turn the plan through an angle of 45° to position *ab*. This will be the required plan.

3. Project from *b*, and obtain the required elevation *a'b'c'd'*.

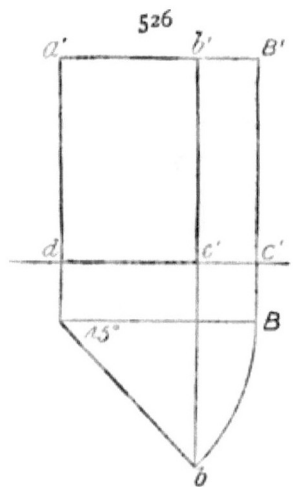

526

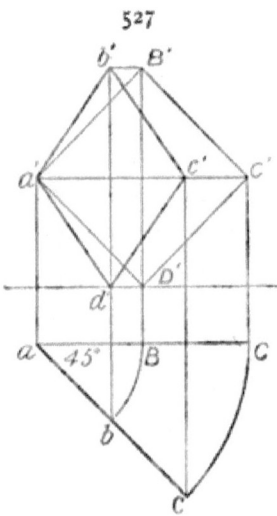

527

The same square has its diagonal vertical. Draw its plan and elevation (fig. 527).

1. **Draw** the elevation *a'B'C'D'* and the **plan** *a BC* when the diagonal *B D'* is vertical and the figure is **parallel** to the V.P.

2. Turn the plan *aBC* into position *abc*.

3. Project from *b* and *c* to the required heights, giving the elevation *a'b'c'd'*.

II. *A square rests with one edge on the H.P. at right angles to the V.P. Its surface makes an angle of 45° with the H.P. Draw its plan and elevation* (fig. 528).

1. Draw the plan *aBCd*, and the elevation *a'B'*, when the surface is horizontal.

2. Turn the elevation *a'B'* through the required angle to position *a'b'*. This will be the elevation of the door.

3. Project from *b'* to the plan, giving *abcd* the required plan.

The same square has one of its diagonals at right angles to the V.P. Draw its plan and elevation (fig. 529).

1. Draw the plan *aBCD* with the diagonal *BD* at right angles to the V.P., and the elevation *a'B'C'*.

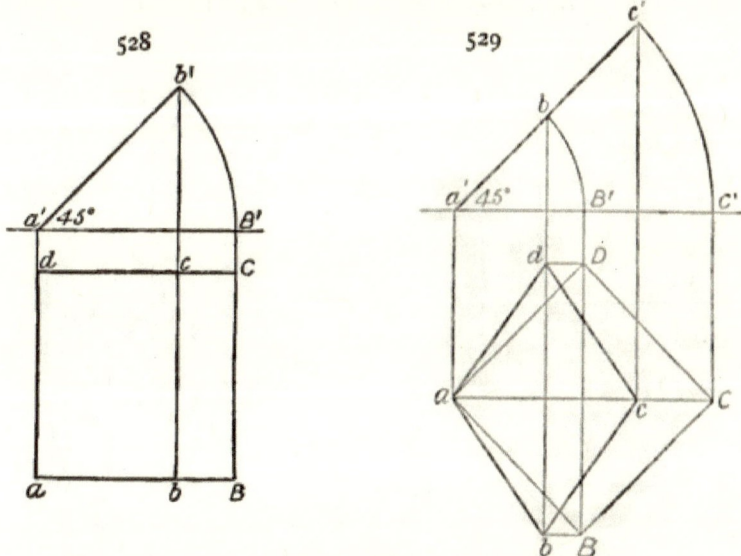

2. Turn the elevation to position *a'b'c'*.
3. Project from the elevation as before for the plan.

SECTIONS

The plan and elevation of an object do not always convey all the information necessary to construct it. The plan and the elevation of a house will not show the position and thickness of the floors, nor would the plan and elevation of a flywheel show the shape and thickness of the arms.

To supply information of this character, drawings showing the shape of the object when supposed to be cut through at various places are given. These drawings are called **sections**.

Sectional plans and elevations are all that are usually required from this Standard. The **true shape** of the section, which is really the most important, is not usually asked for. The difference should be explained to the pupils, and they should be encouraged to draw the true shape for practice. The **sectional plan** is the appearance of the object when viewed vertically downwards from above; the **sectional elevation** is its appearance when looked at horizontally forwards; the **true** shape is seen when the section is viewed at right angles to the plane of the section.

To illustrate these it is necessary to have either models cut in various sections or else made in cardboard, as suggested at the commencement of the chapter. As no fixed section will illustrate every variety of cut, a piece of soap is very useful for this purpose.

The line of section should be indicated by figures to avoid confusion, and the section should be ruled with lines put in with the 45° set-square about one-eighth of an inch apart. This will be quite close enough, and permits of the lines being ruled evenly and carefully. Close section lines are confusing, and cannot be done neatly by the pupils. If the set-square be slipped an eighth on the ruler for every line, perfect uniformity of space between the lines will be secured. The appearance of a neatly ruled section will amply repay the pupil for the trouble bestowed on it.

Figs. 530 and 531.—*The plans are given of two cubes cut by a plane passing through* 1, 2. *Draw the elevation.*

The construction lines show what has to be done. The portions below the section line should not be projected, as they are supposed to be cut away. The **true** shape in fig. 530 would be a rectangle having 12 for its base and its height equal to the height of the cube. It may be shown at right angles to 12 as in 12 *ab*, or by the side of the elevation as in $1''2''$ $a''b'$.

Figs. 532 and 533.—*Elevations of cubes are given. Draw the sectional plans made by a plane passing through* $1'2'$.

The portions above the section lines are not projected, as they are supposed to be removed. In fig. 533 the true shape is shown as well.

Fig. 535.—*The plan of a cube cut by a vertical plane passing through* 1, 2 *is given. Draw the sectional elevation.*

This is rather more difficult. First obtain the elevation of the cube as in fig. 524. The section should then be found in the following manner. Point 1 is on line *ae*, therefore its elevation will be on $a'e'$. Point 2 cuts the edges *ab* and *ad*, therefore its elevation will be the points marked 2′, on lines $a'b'$ and $a'd'$. If each point of the section be traced out and marked in this way very little difficulty will be found.

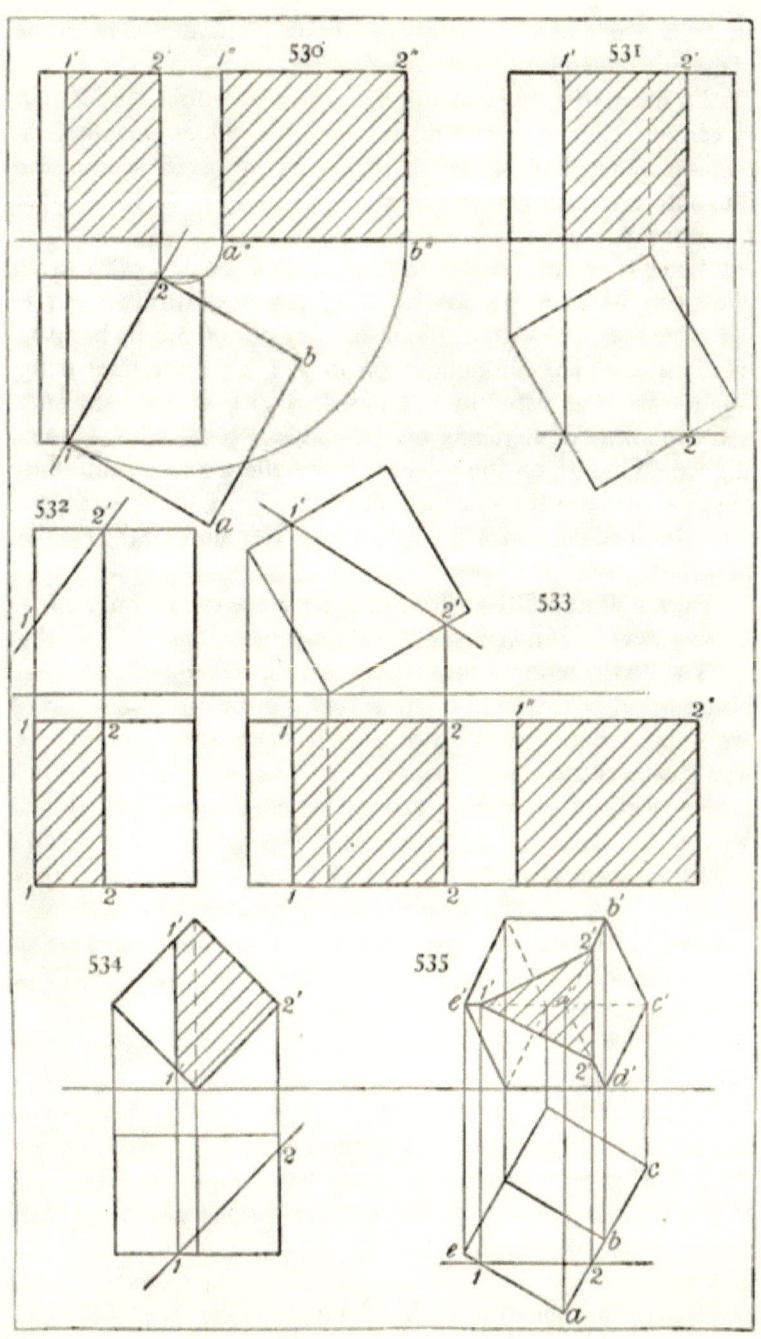

Fig. 536.—*The elevation of a cube is given. Draw the sectional plan when cut by a plane passing through* 1′3′.

As the plan of the cube when in this position is of the same shape as its elevation, it can at once be projected. For the section proceed as follows :—Point 1′ is on line $a'e'$, therefore its plan will be on line ae. Point 2′ is on line $b'f'$ and the line behind it $d'h'$, therefore its plan will be on bf and dh. Join the points already found. It is evident that 3′ cannot be projected, because the ends of both plan and elevation are in the same straight line. The true shape of the end must be drawn, and 3′ projected to it, giving 3″3″ as the width of the cut on the end. Set off 3 3 equal to 3″3′. The corners b and d are not shown thickened in, as they would be cut away.

Fig. 537.—*The plan of a square prism cut by a section plane 13 is given. Draw its elevation.*

The elevation of the prism will be the same shape as the plan. Project points 1 and 2 for the section as before. Point 3 must be dealt with in the same manner as in fig. 536.

Fig. 538.—*The elevation of a square prism is given. Draw its plan when cut by a section plane passing through* 1′3′. Carefully project the plan of the prism. Trace out each point, marking it when found by a small dot. Thicken in the figure, and shade the section.

Fig. 539.—*The plan of two steps is given, each of which is as high as it is wide. Draw the elevation when cut by a plane passing through* 1, 3.

This is rather confusing to young pupils. First project the two steps and rule in. Remember that in the section, 1 and 2 are on the top step. Point 3 is on the bottom step, and must only be projected to it.

Solid Geometry. Standard VI

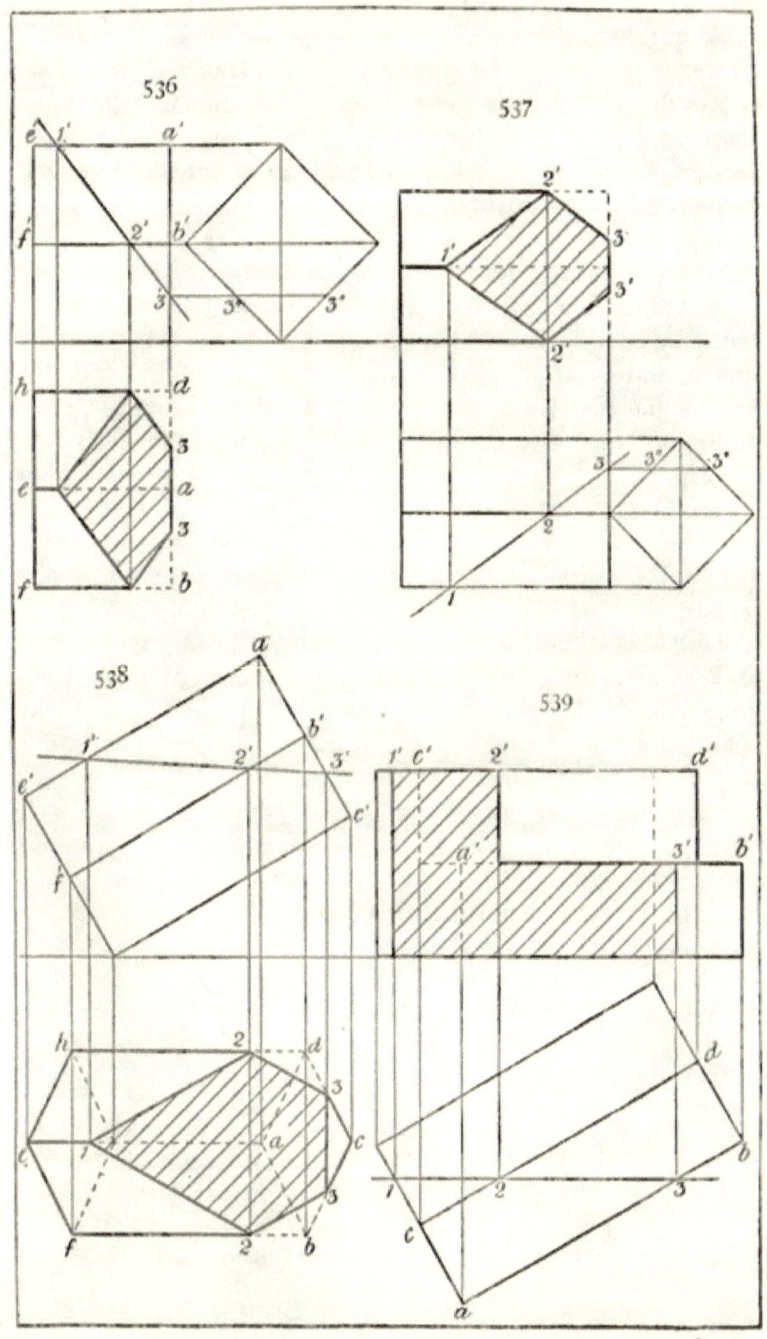

The Teaching of Drawing

Examination Tests.—Two problems are usually given on each card, which should be arranged on the paper as shown in fig. 540. The figures given in the tests should be drawn about three times the given size.

1. *AB, BC are the elevations of two straight lines parallel to the V.P. Draw their plans.*

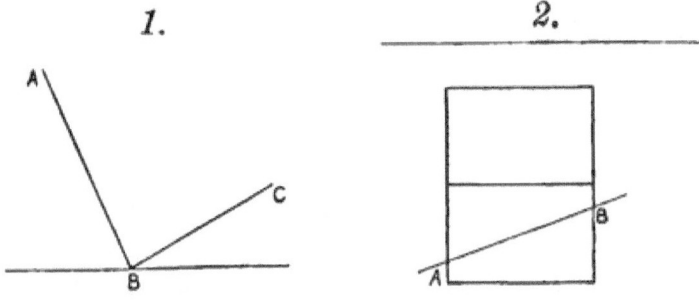

2. *The given figure is the plan of a **cube**. Draw its elevation, and the elevation of the section made **by a plane** passing through AB.*

Problem 1 presents no special difficulty. Remember that the true length of a line is shown when the elevation is parallel to the *V.P.*, or when the plan is parallel to the *H.P.* *AB* and *BC* in the question represent the true lengths of the lines.

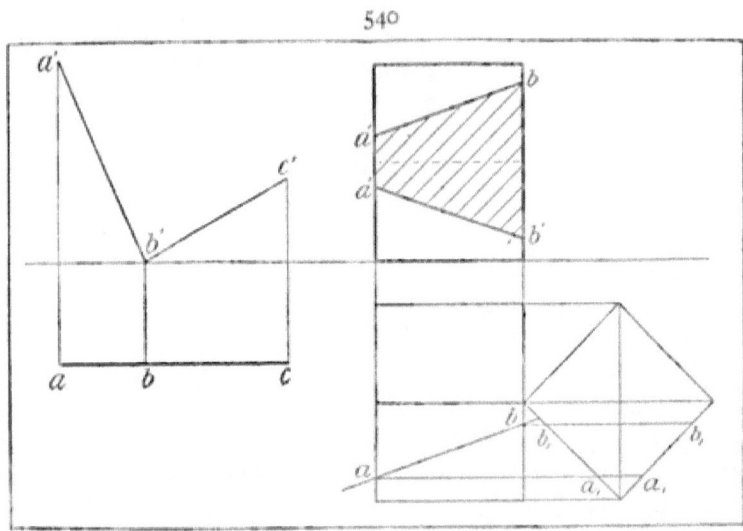

540

In **problem 2** the elevation will be of the same shape as the plan. The points 1 and 2 cannot be projected to the elevation, and the true shape of the end must be drawn. If the points be projected to this end the widths of the section will be shown by the lines $a_1 a_1$ and $b_1 b_1$. Make $a' a'$ and $b' b'$ equal to these widths.

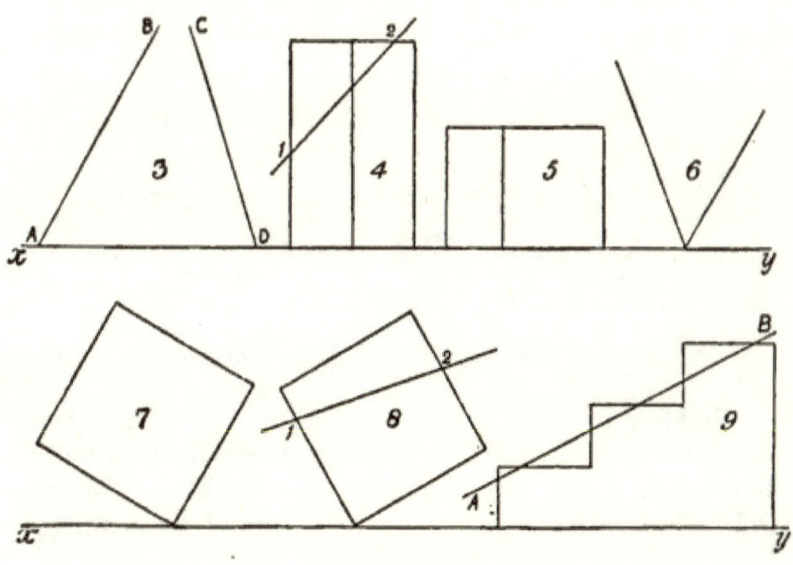

3. *AB* and *CD* are the elevations of two squares having two sides parallel to the V.P. Draw their plans.

4. The given figure is the elevation of a square prism. Draw the section when cut by a plane passing through 1, 2.

5. Draw the plan of the cube of which the given figure is the elevation.

6. The given lines represent the elevations of two squares each of which has a diagonal parallel to the V.P. Draw the plans.

7. The elevation of a square prism $2\frac{1}{2}$ inches long is given. Draw the plan.

8. The given figure represents the elevation of a cube. Draw its plan when cut by a plane passing through 1, 2.

9. Three steps are given in elevation. Draw the plan, and the plan of the section made by the line *AB*. The steps are $3\frac{1}{2}$ feet wide. Scale $= \frac{1}{2}''$ to 1' 0".

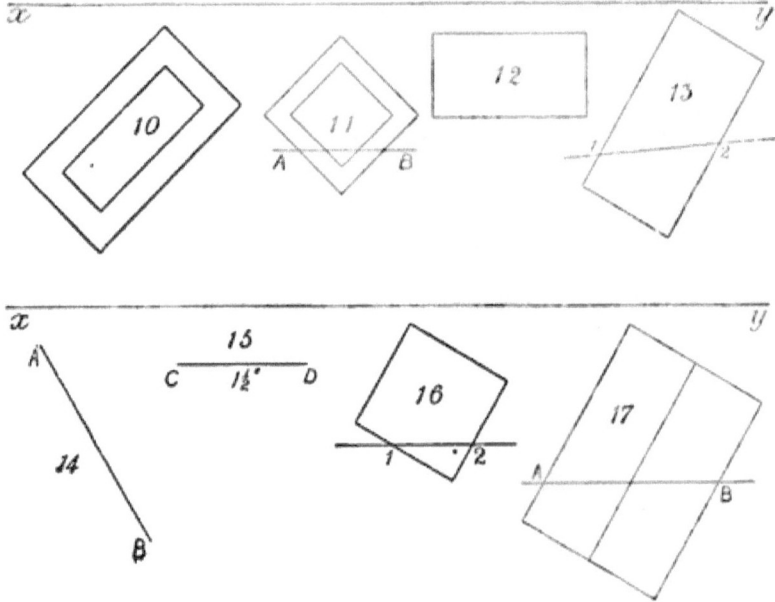

10. The plan of two slabs each 1 inch thick is given. **Draw** their elevation.

11. The plan of a square slab 1 inch thick surmounted by a cube is given. Draw the **sectional** elevation when cut by a vertical plane AB.

12. The given figure represents the plan of a square prism. **Draw** its elevation.

13. **Draw the elevation of** the **square prism, and the** elevation of the **section made by the vertical plane 1 2.**

14. AB is the plan of a line parallel to the H.P. and 1 inch above it. Draw its elevation.

15. CD is the plan of a line 3 inches long. Draw its elevation.

16. The given figure is the plan of a cube. Draw its sectional elevation when cut by a plane passing through 1, 2.

17. The given figure shows the plan of two steps in each of which the width equals the height. **Draw the** elevation when cut by a vertical section through AB.

Solid Geometry. Standard VII

Syllabus. Standard VII.—*Plans and elevations of rectangular and circular solids, with sections.*

The work of Standard VI must be continued in an increased degree of difficulty. Rectangular solids, both singly and combined, must be drawn in more difficult positions. In dealing with the circular solids great care must be taken to keep the construction lines, which are rather numerous, neat and distinct. In setting off the widths for the elliptical ends, the greatest exactness must be insisted upon, or it will be found impossible to secure good curves. When the points for the curve are obtained, it must be very lightly sketched in first, and thickened in after an accurate shape has been obtained.

Any number of points may be taken in the curve. It is convenient to take either 8 or 12, as the circle can be readily divided into either of these parts by means of the set-squares.

A few typical positions of the circular solids are shown, with some examination tests to show the character of the work required.

Figs. 541-548 show easy positions of the circle, cylinder, and cone.

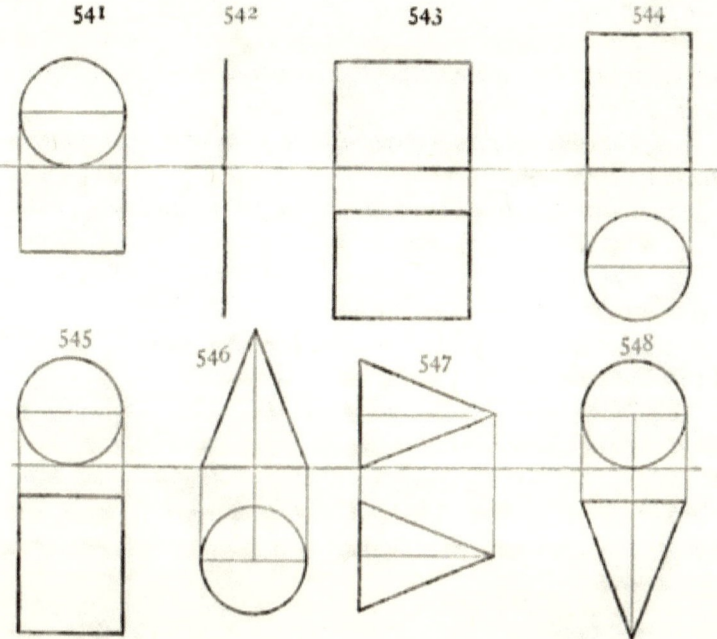

Figs. 549-556 show easy sections of the cylinder, cone, and sphere. In fig. 549 the true shape, as well as the plan of the section is shown.

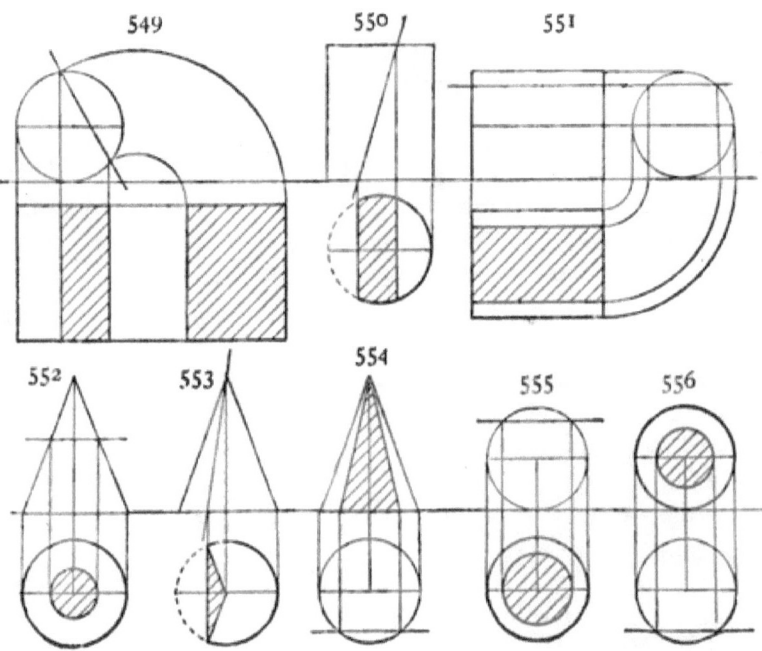

Figs. 557 and 558.—*Draw the plan and elevation of a circle:*—1. With its plane vertical and making an angle of 45° with the V.P. 2. With its plane perpendicular to the V.P. and inclined at 60° to the H.P.

1. The plan will evidently be the line *ab* inclined at 45° to the V.P. Its elevation will be an ellipse having its longer diameter $c'c'$ equal to *ab* and its shorter diameter $a'b'$. As, however, an ellipse cannot be accurately drawn when only four points of its curve are given, four additional points in the circle will be taken. The same method as that used in fig. 521 and the following figures is used here, viz. drawing the true shape of the figure. In the case of the circle it is neither necessary nor advisable to put in the whole of the figure on account of the multiplicity of lines, the semicircle giving all the necessary measurements.

On *ab* describe a semicircle and divide it into 4 or 6 parts, as at *E, C* and *F*. From *E, C* and *F* draw perpendiculars to *ab* giving widths across the circle at those points. (The complete circle is inserted here, the unnecessary part being in dotted line.)

From *a, e, c, f, b* project to the V.P. Set off *c'c'* equal to *ab*, and draw *a'b'* midway between *c'* and *c'*. On each side of *a'b'* set off the distance *e*E, giving the points *e'e'* and *f'f'*. Through the eight points thus obtained draw the elliptical elevation.

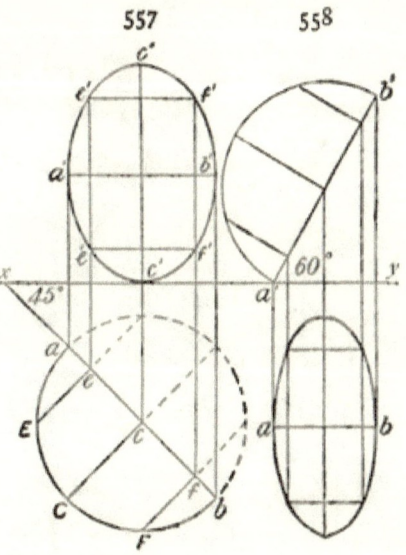

2. The elevation will be a line at 60° to the H.P. For the plan proceed in a similar manner to that shown in the preceding figure. After projecting from the points, draw *ab* at any convenient distance from *xy*, and set off the widths from the semicircle on each side of it.

Fig. 559 shows the plan and elevation of a cylinder when its axis is inclined to the V.P. The method is only a repetition of that explained in fig. 557. Two circles are projected and joined.

Fig. 560 shows the plan and elevation of the cylinder when its axis is inclined to the H.P., and also a second elevation when the cylinder is viewed from the left at right angles to its former position.

Note.—The second elevation will be readily followed if the figure be turned so that *V' P'* is horizontal. The first elevation then becomes the plan for the second, and the lines are merely repetitions of those in fig. 559.

Fig. 561 shows the plan and elevation of a cone, with its axis inclined at 30° to the H.P. and parallel to the V.P. Also a side view similar to that shown in fig. 560.

200 The Teaching of Drawing

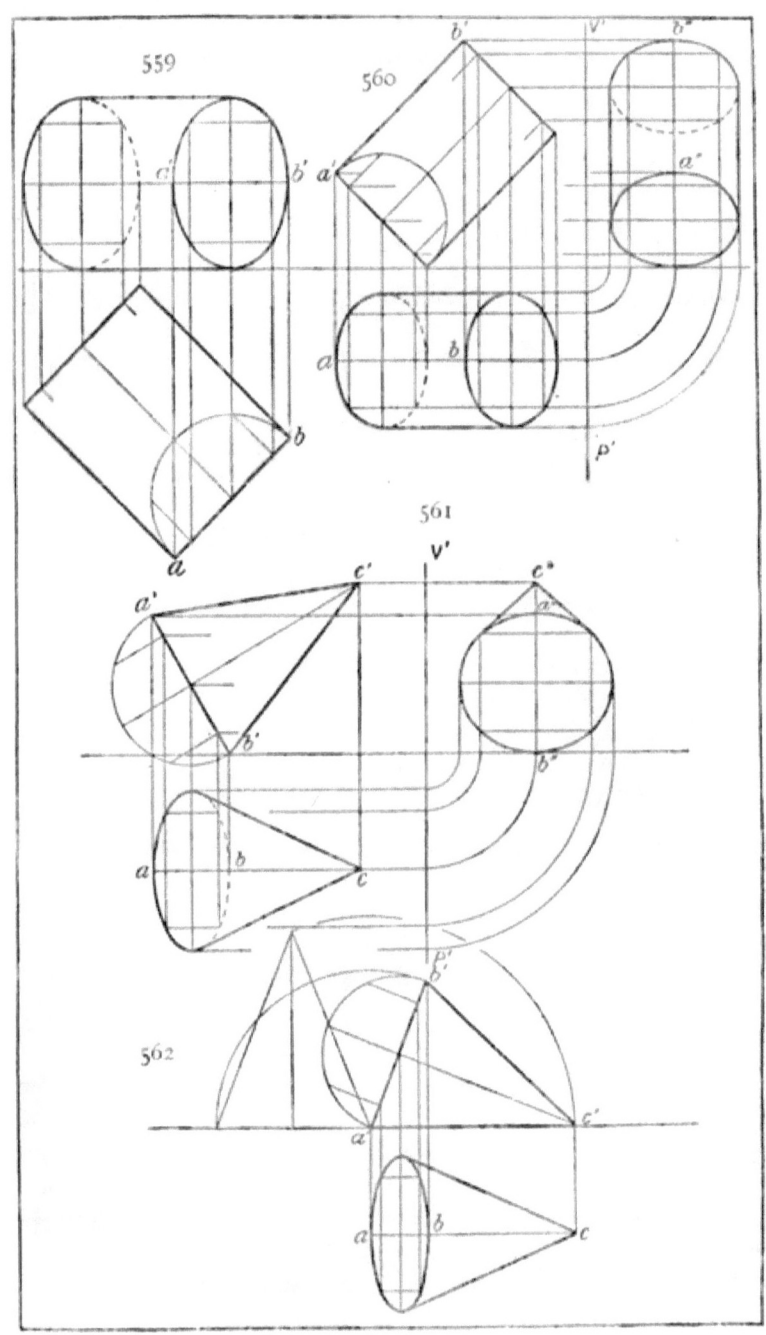

Solid Geometry. **Standard VII** 201

Fig. 562 shows the plan and elevation of the cone when lying on its side with its axis parallel to the V.P. Notice that the cone must first be drawn in an upright position, and then turned so as to bring the side into the H.P. for the required elevation.

Fig. 563 shows the plan of the sphere cut by the section plane 1′2′.

Fig. 564 shows the elevation of the sphere when cut by a vertical plane 1 2.

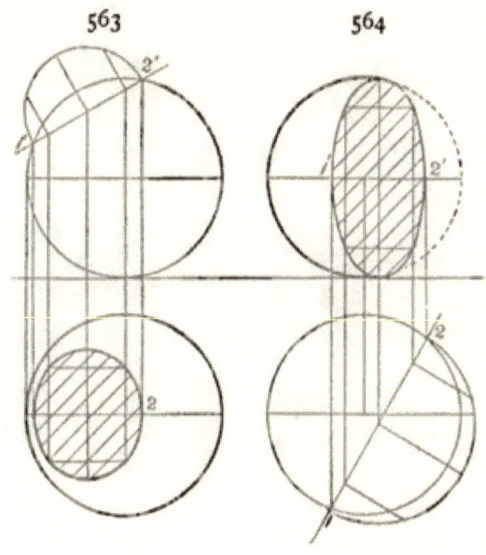

Fig. 565 shows the sectional plan **and true** shape of a cylinder when cut by the plane 1′2′. All oblique sections of the cylinder are ellipses or portions of ellipses. After drawing the plan of the cylinder, draw the centre line 1*p*. Point 1 will be the extremity of the longer diameter of the ellipse. Describe a semicircle on the elevation, showing half the shape of the end, and draw 2′2′. On each side of *p* set off the distance 2′2′, giving 2 2, the width of the section on the end of the cylinder. Through the centre *a* of the semicircle draw *ab*, and produce it to meet the section line at 3′. Project from 3′ to the plan, giving the points 3, 3, where the section will be widest. The

curve might now be drawn, but its accuracy will be better secured by fixing at least two more points. Mark point 4', and project horizontally and vertically. Set off the distance *cd* on each side of the centre line, giving the points 4, 4. Through the points obtained draw the curve. The true shape is easily followed from the construction lines. Project at right angles to the section, and draw the centre line. The widths will be exactly the same as in the plan.

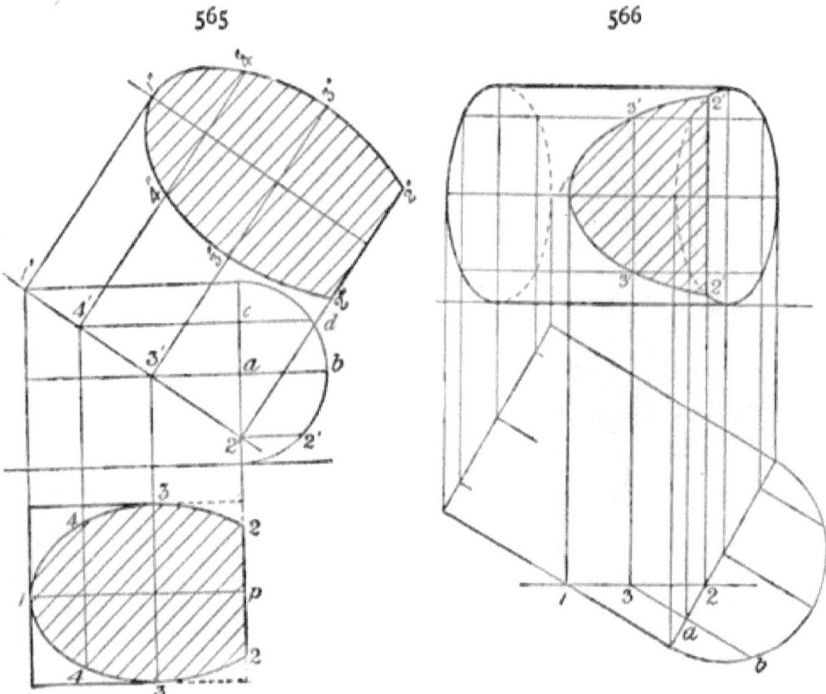

Fig. 566 shows the elevation of a cylinder cut by a vertical plane 1 2. After obtaining the elevation of the cylinder, project from 1 to the middle line of the elevation, giving 1', and from 2 to the end, giving 2'2'. Produce *ab* to meet the section line at 3. From 3 project to the elevation, setting off the distance *ab* on each side of the centre line for the points 3' 3'. Through the points thus obtained draw the curve.

Fig. 567 shows the plan of a cone when cut by the section plane 1′2′. When the cone is cut by a plane which passes through both sides, the section is an **ellipse**. Project from 1′ and 2′, giving points 1 and 2, the length of one diameter of the ellipse. Take point 3′ on the section line, and suppose a *horizontal* section to pass through this point. The plan of this section would be a circle, and if 3′ be projected to this plan two more points 3, 3 in the section will be obtained. Take other sections, and proceed in a similar manner. Draw the curve through the points obtained.

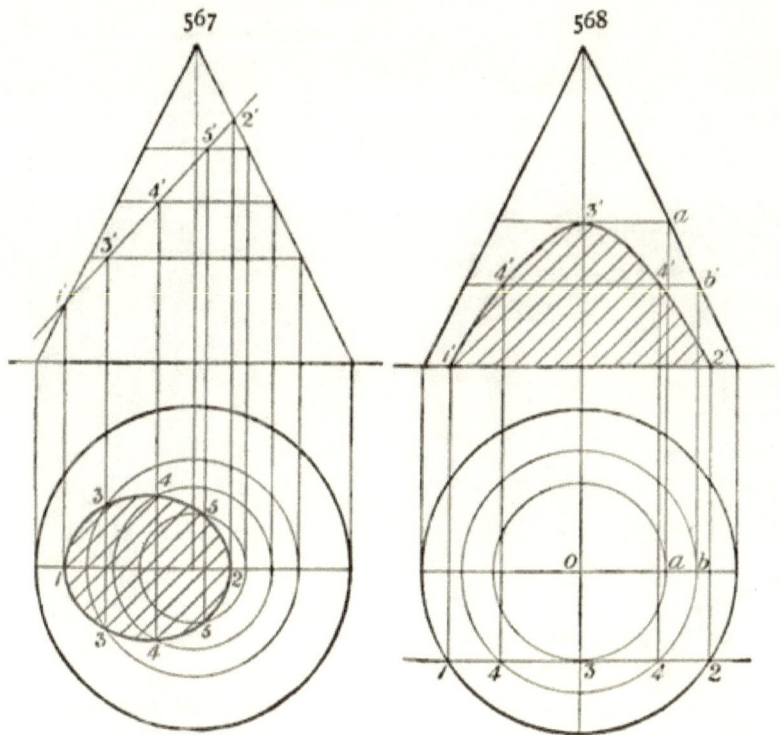

Fig. 568 shows the elevation of a cone cut by a vertical section through 1, 2. After obtaining the elevation of the cone, project points 1 and 2, giving 1′2′ the width of the section. Next obtain the height. From the centre *o* draw a line at right angles to the section, and with *o* as centre describe a circle

touching the section. From *a* project to *a'*, and from *a'* draw a line representing the elevation of the circle described. A projector from 3 will give 3', the top of the section. To obtain other points in the curve, mark 4, describe a circle passing through it, project the elevation of this circle at *b'*, and from the points 4, 4 project for 4'4'. Other points may be obtained in the same way. This section is called the **hyperbola**.

Fig. 569 shows the plan of a section made by the plane 1'2' parallel to the side of the cone, also the true shape of that section. Project the points 1' and 2', giving 1 1, the width, and 2, highest point of the curve. To find other points in the curve, take any number of points, as 3' and 4', and draw horizontal section lines through these points. Obtain the plans of the

569

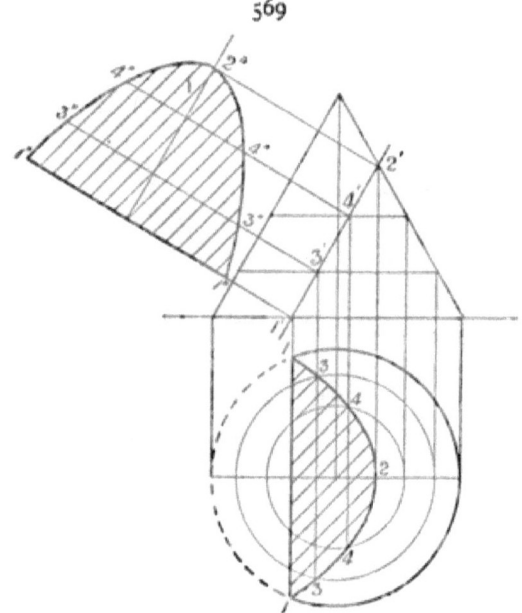

circles of which these lines are the elevations. Project from points 3' and 4' to the plans of these circles, giving the points 3, 3 and 4, 4, and draw the curve. For the true shape project at right angles from each point of the section, draw a centre line, and set off 1″1″ equal to 1 1, 3″3″ equal to 3 3, &c. The curve drawn through these points will be that known as the **parabola**.

Solid Geometry. Standard VII

Examination Tests.—Solutions or references are given where needed. All the figures must be copied to a much larger scale.

1. *The given figure represents the plan of a right cylinder, with an axis of* $1\frac{1}{2}''$. *Copy the plan, and draw the sectional elevation.*

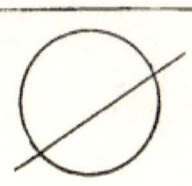

2. *The elevation of a cube surmounted by a sphere is given. Copy the elevation, and draw the plan, showing the section made by AB.* (*Fig.* 563.)

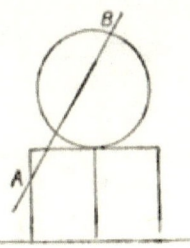

3. *AB and BC are the elevations of two circles. Draw the plans.*

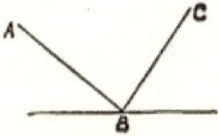

4. *The given figure shows the elevation of a cone. Draw the plan and plan of section made by AB.* (*Fig.* 567.)

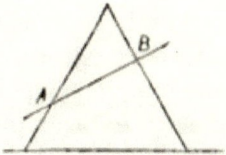

5. *The given figure is the plan of a cone with a section passing through its centre. Draw the elevation.* (*Fig.* 570.)

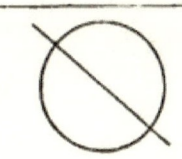

6. *The given figure is the elevation of a cylinder. Draw its plan, and the plan of a section made by AB.* (*Fig.* 571.)

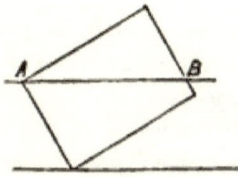

7. The elevation of a cone is given. Draw its plan. (Fig. 562.)

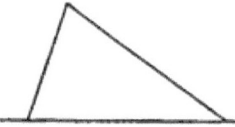

8. The given figure is the elevation of a cube with a hemisphere placed upon it. Draw the plan, and show the section on AB. (Fig. 572.)

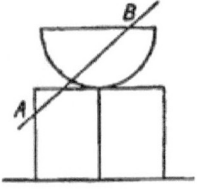

9. The figure is the plan of a circular slab 2 inches thick, with a cube of 2-inch edges placed centrally on it. Draw the elevation, and show the section made by AB. (Fig. 573.)

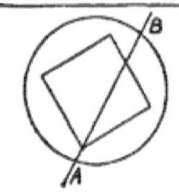

10. The figure is the plan of a cube pierced by a cylindrical tube. Draw the elevation, and show the section on AB. (Fig. 574.)

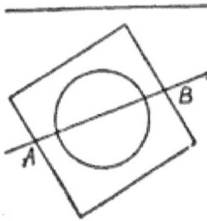

Solid Geometry. Standard VII.

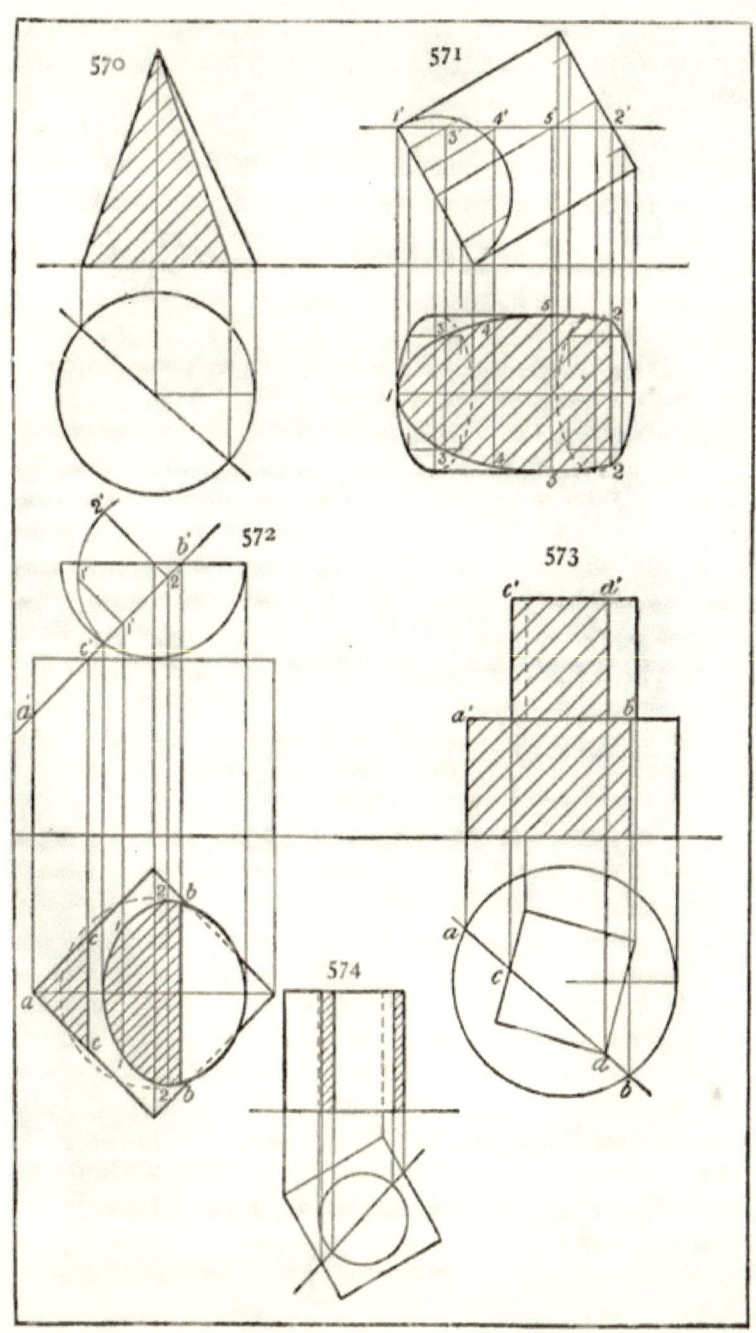

CHAPTER X

MODEL DRAWING. STANDARDS V AND VI

Syllabus. Standard V.—*Drawing from* **simple rectangular** *and circular models, and easy common objects.*

Model drawing requires both greater skill **in teaching and** increased dexterity **in** drawing from **the** teacher. **In** freehand drawing **all draw the same view, hence** class teaching has been **easy ;** but in model drawing class teaching can only be used to **demonstrate the principles, and to** show how the model would **appear under certain conditions.** The fact that every pupil **sees a different view of the** object necessarily prevents them **from** clearly comprehending **the** illustrations **drawn** upon the board, simply because **they do not** appear **so to them.** So that although the board may **be used to a great** extent, it is absolutely necessary, **if** really **good work is to be secured,** that there should be a large amount **of** individual supervision. The **teacher** will find it necessary to go to each pupil, take the same **position, and then show how to obtain a** correct **representation of the object.** Attention to good methods **and plenty of practice are the two great secrets of** success. **As the pupils understand the methods** adopted, only the slower ones need so much **individual supervision,** and if plenty of practice be given, this **branch of drawing** becomes very attractive, especially when common **objects are taken.** When the pupils can successfully represent some **object with which** they are familiar, their interest is **aroused and stimulated, as they see some** tangible result of this **drawing of cubes, cylinders, &c., which** must certainly appear somewhat unattractive and monotonous to them if not sufficiently varied.

The pupils having already acquired the knowledge of how

to draw straight lines, how to ascertain the various proportions of a copy, and how to apply this knowledge so as to secure an accurate drawing, it is now only necessary to show how this knowledge may be applied to the drawing of objects.

Introductory Lessons.—These should be taken on slates, as their object is to cultivate the observing and reasoning faculties, and to bring clearly home to the minds of the pupils important principles upon which success in model drawing largely depends. The lessons should be short, with plenty of illustrations, and the sketches should be rapidly made.

First Lesson.—The door will form a suitable example.

1. Let the pupils commence by drawing a vertical line *ab* to represent one side (fig. 575). Now ascertain the width as compared with the height, and complete the rectangle.

2. Open the door at an angle, and let the pupils now measure the width as compared with the height. They will discover that the width has decreased and that

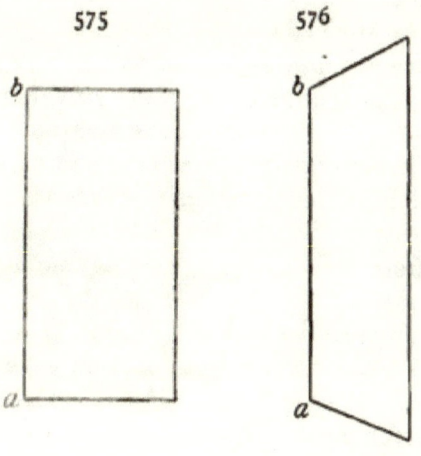

the upright lines must now be drawn closer together (fig. 576). This shows the variation in the width of a plane surface when seen at various angles.

Second Lesson.—Take a piece of cardboard about 2 feet square. Place it so that all can see as nearly as possible the same view.

1. Let the pupils rapidly sketch it on their slates, noticing that the sides will be vertical and the top and bottom horizontal (fig. 577).

2. Turn the cardboard at an angle, and let the pupils draw it under fig. 577, step by step from the teacher's direction, and working with him.

P

Draw the nearest vertical edge *ab*.

Is the width the same as in the first drawing?

Measure the width, and compare with the height. Draw the other vertical side *cd*.

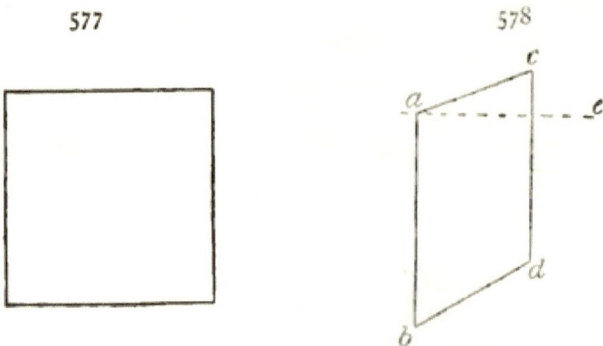

577   578

Is the top edge now horizontal? They will not all be able to decide this.

Let all hold their pencils in a horizontal position level with point *a*.

Is the back corner above the pencil? ' *Yes.*'

Then the line must run up. Draw *ae* to represent the level of the pencil. Notice the angle made by the edge of the cardboard with the horizontal pencil, and draw it as nearly as possible. This will give the top edge *ac*.

3. Measure the back vertical edge of the cardboard, and compare it with the front. They will discover that it measures a shorter distance. Make *cd* less than *ab*, and draw the bottom edge *bd*.

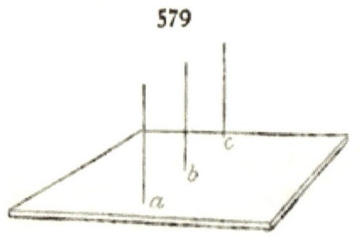

579

4. Change the position of the card again, and note that the width appears still less and that *ac* makes a greater angle with *ae* than before.

Another illustration that is very convincing to children is to arrange a board in a horizontal position and on it to place three objects of equal height, one at *a*, another at *b*, and a third at *c*. Let the pupils measure

c with the pencil, and apply this distance to b. It will be found that it only covers part of b, and on applying the distance to a a larger portion still is not covered by it.

The pupils will now have been familiarised with two most important principles in model drawing :—

1. *The varying width of a plane surface when viewed at different angles.*

2. *The smaller space occupied by an object when it is removed farther back.*

Now hold the card above the eye, and direct attention to the fact that the top and bottom lines appear to run down. Place it level with the eye, and show that the back corner is level with the front. This will enable the pupils to grasp the idea of lines vanishing to the level of the eye. The fact that the top line of the door runs down will be demonstrated directly the pencil is held horizontally level with the front top corner, when the back corner will be found to be below it; and in the same manner if the pencil be held level with the front bottom corner, the back corner will be seen above the pencil, and the bottom line of the door will consequently run up.

Several short lessons of this character, well illustrated and rapidly drawn, will do more to fix these important truths than the drawing of many models before these ideas are understood.

After the teacher has drawn the various views on the board, the pupils should always be allowed to make their own representation of the object. Care should be taken to keep as nearly as possible the same view before all the class. It is very necessary that the teacher should be able to sketch these views correctly on the board, as otherwise much mischief will be done. A little previous practice and forethought will enable almost any teacher who can draw a straight line to illustrate all that is necessary.

The various models will now be treated separately in typical positions, such as lend themselves to demonstration on the blackboard. After the pupils have gone through these carefully, they will experience but little difficulty in dealing with other views. It is very desirable that the ordinary models should be followed up by a judicious selection of common objects. Instead of going through all the models first, it will be found far more interesting to combine the drawing of the models with common objects. When the cube and square prism have been dealt with, a box or any similar simple object should be drawn. Children do not associate the drawing of the cube with anything useful, but when able to draw a box or a book they feel that considerable strides have been made.

Arrangement of the models.—In the earlier lessons it is very desirable that, as far as possible, only one view should be drawn, as the teacher's difficulties will be very much increased if more than one view has to be dealt with in the same lesson. To secure this, if the class be large several models should be used. This is only necessary when dealing with the model for the first time, as after the pupils have drawn two or three views they will be able to apply the principles to other views without much difficulty. Fig. 580 shows the arrangement for a lesson. *a*, *b*, *c* show the position of the models, which should be large and placed as far from the class as possible, as by that means it is more easy to secure a similar view for all the class.

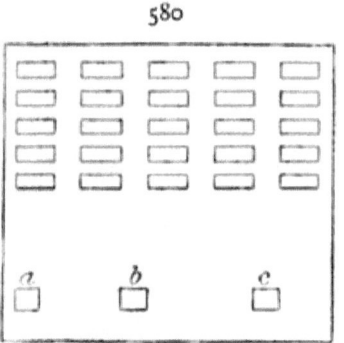

THE CUBE

First Lesson.—1. The easiest position in which to draw the cube is evidently when one vertical face only is visible. Place the models as shown in fig. 580. If only one cube be obtainable, square boxes, or cubes made of mill board, will make very good substitutes.

Question rapidly as follows:—
What is the object called? '*A cube.*'
How many faces has it? '*Six.*'
How many edges?

Model Drawing. Standard V

What is the shape of each **face**?
What is a square?
How many faces can you see? '*Two.*'
What positions are they in? '*One vertical and one horizontal.*'
Which face can you see most of? '*The vertical face.*'
What shape is it? '*A square.*'
Draw a square *abcd* of about 4-inch sides.

2. Beginners generally make the error of drawing the top face too wide. To prevent this careful measurement is necessary. To assist the pupils, place a ruler on the edge *cd* of the model, and gradually raise it until it is in a line with the back edge *ef.* Now hold the ruler still, and let the pupils take the vertical distance from *cd* to the edge of the ruler and compare it with the height of the model.

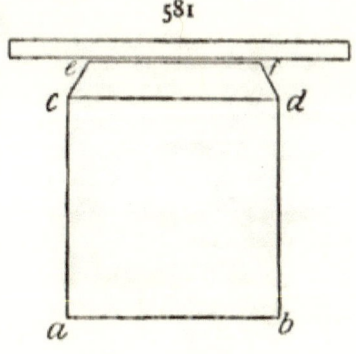

Before doing this, let the pupils estimate the distance with their eye. Most of them will be astonished at the difference.

Now mark the distance and draw the line *ef.*

3. The next point is to decide upon the length of *ef.* Let the teacher place a pencil vertically upon the corner *c* of the model.

Which side of the pencil is the back corner? '*Right.*'
Mark it on the line *ef.* Now place the pencil on *d.*
Which side of the pencil is the other back corner? '*Left.*'
Mark it, and join *e* and *f* with *c* and *d.*
Ought *ef* to be less than *cd*? '*Yes.*'
Why? '*Because it is further away.*'

4. Now show a *large* drawing previously made in which the back lines are equal to the front, fig. 582. On being questioned the pupils will probably say that 1 is longer than 2. Measure the lines, and show that they are equal. Now explain that we always draw objects not as they really are, but as we see them.

All this can be shown from the board, but it will also be necessary to visit each pupil to see that the drawing is generally correct.

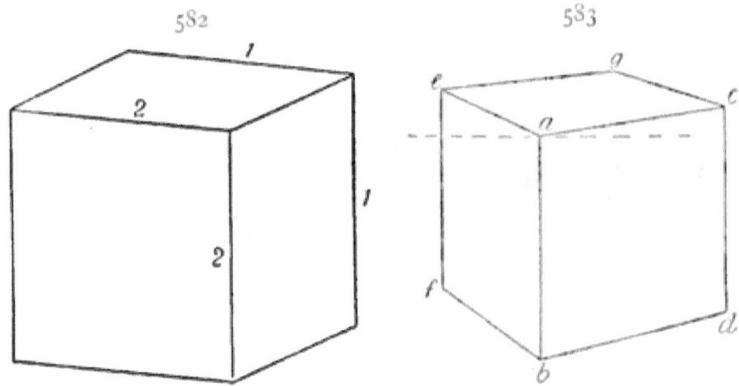

Second Lesson.—Place the cubes so that three faces are visible (fig. 583).

1. Begin with *ab*, the nearest vertical line, and fix its length.

2. Measure the width of the widest face, and compare with *ab*. Mark this width, and draw *cd*.

3. Compare the narrower vertical face with the wider one and draw *ef*. Before anything else is attempted the horizontal distance between *ef* and *cd* should be compared with *ab*. It will be found to be greater.

4. Draw a very light horizontal line through *a*. Hold the pencil in a horizontal position level with point *a* on the model, and notice carefully the angle made with the pencil by the wider edge *ac*, and from *a* draw *ac* making a similar angle. Direct attention to the fact that the wider the side the less this line will slope.

Find the inclination of *ae* in the same manner.

These lines *ac* and *ae* should be carefully verified before proceeding, as the rest of the model depends upon them.

5. Look at *ac*, and draw *eg* slightly converging towards it.

From *c* draw *cg* converging slightly towards *ae*.

6. Recall the exercise in measuring in fig. 579.
Is *cd* shorter than *ab*? Why?
Is it much shorter? '*No.*'
Why not? '*Because it is not much farther off.*'
Then make *cd* slightly less than *ab*, and draw *bd*.

Elicit that *ef* is shorter than *cd* because it is farther back, and draw *bf*.

Third Lesson.—The cube may now be drawn when its vertical faces appear equal as in fig. 584. This will present no special difficulty.

The lines should be drawn according to the order in which they are numbered.

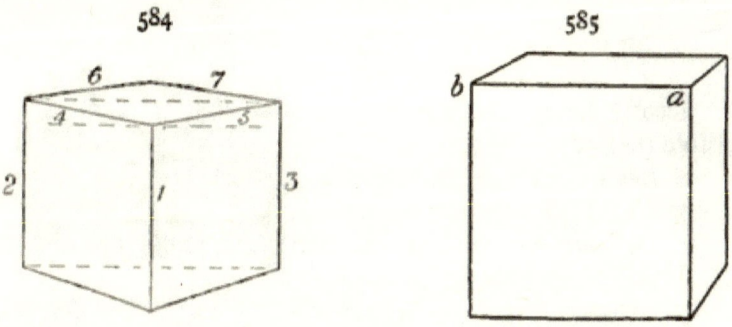

Common errors.—Fig. 585 shows a very common error, arising from the fact that the teacher has drawn such views in perspective. In this the pupil is supposed to be drawing the cube when looking at something else, an impossible task. The error may be easily demonstrated by holding the edge of the drawing-book horizontally level with *a*, when the sides of the cube will be seen making an angle with the edge of the book. The pupils are liable to make the error, because the face of the cube is parallel to the front of the desks. The simplest way to avoid the error is to lay down the rule that *ab can only be horizontal when the pupil is quite in front* and sees only that vertical face. From this deduce the rule that *when nearly in front ab will be nearly horizontal, &c.*

Fig. 586 shows another common mistake. Here the lines vanish too much, producing a distorted representation of the object.

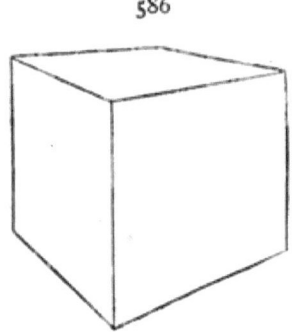

586

The **height of** the eye and the position of **vanishing lines** may now be explained. Draw a horizontal line *ab* on the board to represent the edge of the horizontal plane upon which the model stands (fig. 587). Let the pupils point out on the wall the level of their eye Draw a line *cd* to represent this. Draw a cube as shown, and explain that the edges, if carried far enough, would appear to meet at the level of the eye as shown.

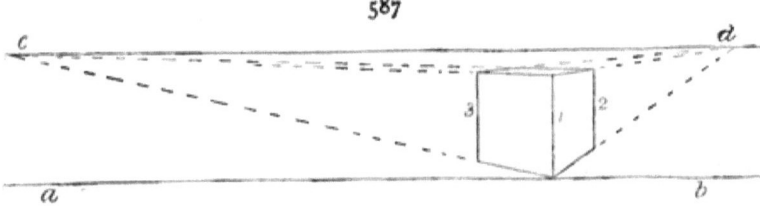

587

The square prism.—The only fresh point is that one of the sides is longer than the other. The prism may be easily converted into a box, as in fig. 588.

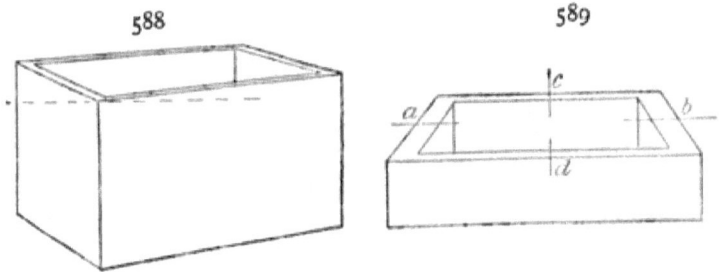

588 589

The square frame is very useful for showing how to obtain the width of the sides. The sides *a* and *b* will be seen wider than *c* and *d*. To decide what this width should be, point out that if from *c* to *d* equals ⅓ of the distance from *a* to *b*, then the thickness of the wood at *c* and *d* should be ⅓ of the thickness at *a* and *b*.

A box, such as that shown in fig. 590, is a suitable model to take next. After drawing the box, and marking the position of the lid, obtain the keyhole by drawing the diagonals for the centre of the side. Through this centre draw a vertical line, and on it place the keyhole. Notice that the half *ab* will be slightly larger than *bc*, because it is nearer to the spectator.

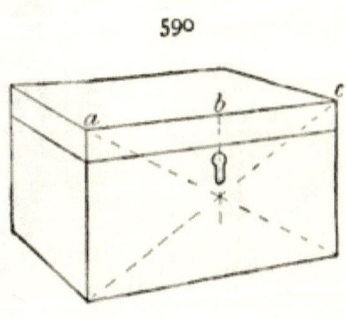

590

A slate may now be attempted. This is a rather difficult object, and at this stage should only be drawn in an easy position. A number of slates can easily be arranged so that all the class may see a similar view.

1. Draw *ab*. Obtain the side *cd* and the points *c* and *d* in the same manner as shown in fig. 581.

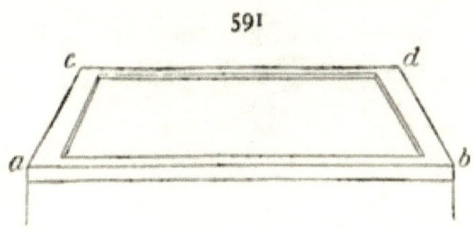

591

2. Draw the width of the frame as in fig. 589.

3. For the thickness of the frame draw vertical lines from *a* and *b*, and on them mark off the thickness. A common error is to make these lines slope outwards.

4. It may be left at this stage if thought fit. If where the slate fits the frame be indicated, then direct attention to the fact that this distance is ⅓ of the thickness of the frame.

The book.—Let the pupils draw a rectangular prism similar to fig. 592 from a copy on the board. Turn it into a book as shown in fig. 593. They **will thus see the** principles upon which the book is drawn.

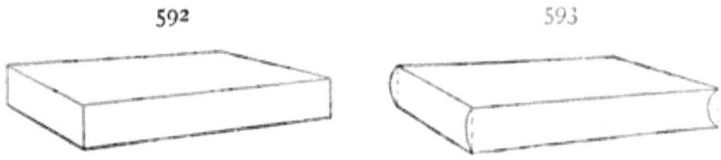

592   593

Now put up a sufficient number of books **so** that all have a similar view, and draw as shown in fig. 594. Notice that the edge **of the** leaves falls within the cover. If the drawing be a

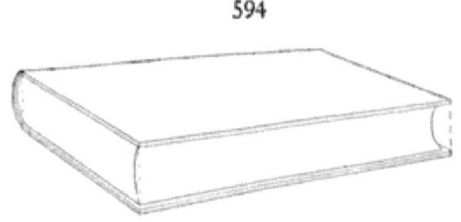

594

large one the thickness of the cover may be indicated. On a small drawing the thickness is better left out for the present.

Other rectangular objects, **such** as bricks, &c., may **now be** taken. Probably a sufficient number are given here **for the** present. It is not advisable at this stage to draw **difficult** positions ; a few familiar objects in easy positions **interest the** pupils more and secure better results. If difficult positions are given at this early stage the pupils cannot make creditable drawings and are more likely to be disgusted at their attempts to represent the object.

THE CYLINDER

This is a very important model, as it enters into the formation of such a large number of objects.

Axis vertical. First Lesson

1. Draw *ab* and fix its length. Compare the width of the cylinder with its height, and **draw** *cd*. Join *a* with *c*, and *b* with

d. Examine the drawings at this stage to see that the proportions are correct.

2. Take a circle cut out of cardboard, and show the variations in its shape as the circle is changed from a horizontal to a vertical position.

3. Draw ellipses on the board, showing the most common errors.

Question on these, elicit the defects, and correct. Fig. 596 is too flat. Fig. 597 is made up of two curves meeting and forming angles at *a* and *b*. This error is best remedied by drawing the curved portions at *a* and *b* first. Fig. 598 is not symmetrical. This may be easily tested by holding the drawing so that *ab* is vertical. The defect is then easily detected.

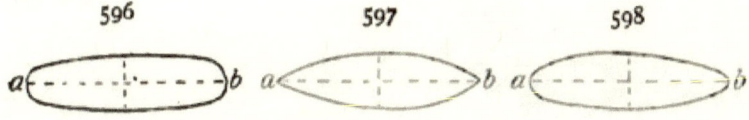

4. Find the centre of *ac* and *bd*, and draw the shorter diameters. Compare the width *ef* with *ac*. Draw the rounded portions at *a* and *c* as shown in fig. 599. Complete the ellipse. Test it as explained in fig. 598.

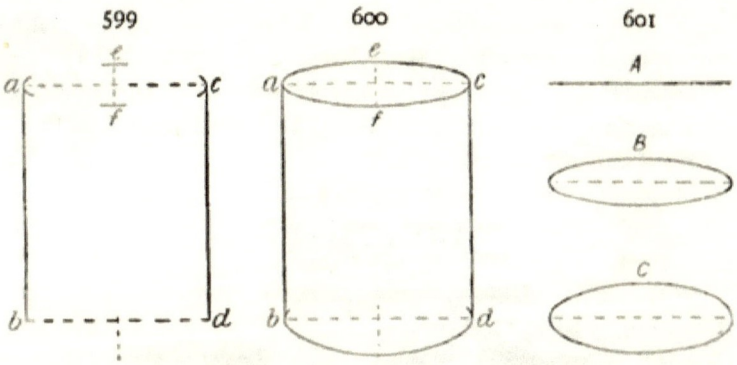

5. Take the circular card again and hold it in a horizontal position, level with the eye. Its shape will be a line (fig. 601 A).

Place it lower down, level with the top of the cylinder. Its shape will now be represented by B. Now place it level with the bottom of cylinder, and compare its width with the width when at B. Its shape will now be represented by the wider ellipse C. Hence the bottom of the cylinder must be drawn slightly wider than the top. Why? '*Because it is more below the level of the eye.*' It is advisable to draw the rounded ends at *b* and *d* (fig. 600). If not, the tendency is to make a corner at these points, as in fig. 597.

A number of easy common objects should follow this lesson. Let the teacher draw several cylinders on the board, and illustrate how they may be converted into representations of objects, as in figs. 602–605.

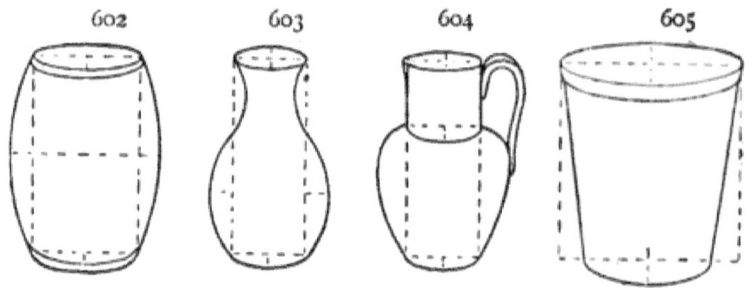

These may be drawn from the blackboard copies by the pupils, as they form good exercises in freehand as well as model drawing. This is generally a fascinating lesson for children, and may be used as an exercise in memory drawing. They also make good examples for dictated drawing, given as follows :—*Draw a cylinder half as wide as it is high. Turn this drawing into a jug, showing a handle and a spout.* An exercise of this kind helps to develop the inventive faculties, as a great variety of curves will be produced. It is, however, of no use doing this until after exercises similar to figs. 602 to 605 have been shown.

Axis horizontal.—This is a much more difficult position, and much care must be bestowed upon it. It is easier to adopt two fixed methods. I. *When the end of the cylinder is facing or*

Model Drawing. Standard V

nearly facing the pupil. II. *When the axis is inclined to the picture plane.*

I. First Lesson.—1. Arrange several cylinders before the class so that all see a similar view—viz., end nearly facing the pupil. This is easier to draw than when the end is exactly opposite. Rolls of paper or jars will make suitable substitutes if a number of cylinders are not available.

2. Draw *ab* and *cd* (fig. 606). Let the pupils test whether *cd* be less than *ab*, and draw the front face. This will be nearly a circle.

3. Measure the distance from the front edge to the back edge. Compare with *cd*, set this distance off from *ab*, and draw *ef*. Why is *ef* shorter than *ab*? '*Because it is farther back.*'

Through the centre of *ef* draw *gh*, and make it a little less than *cd*. Draw the back curve. These two curves should be similar in shape, but the back one a little smaller than the front one.

4. Join the two curves.

Note.—When the drawing is lined in, all the portions shown in dotted line should be omitted.

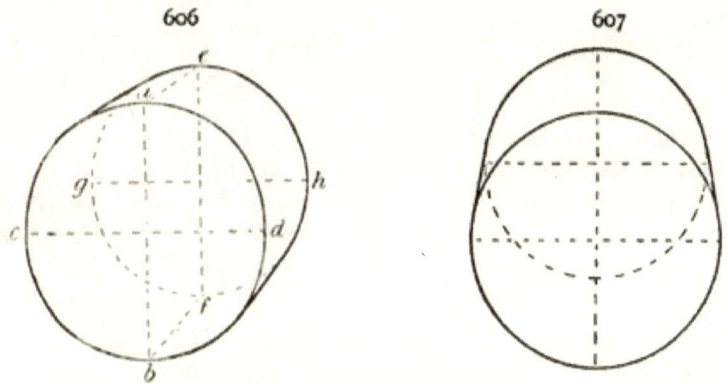

606   607

Fig. 607 shows the cylinder when the end is exactly opposite to the pupil. Draw two circles and join them. This is not so easy to demonstrate as fig. 606, as the construction lines of the back circle clash with those of the front one. The back circle is, of course, smaller than that in front.

II. Axis inclined to the picture plane.—This position of the cylinder is the real difficulty, not on account of the actual drawing, but from the fact that it is difficult for the pupil to correctly estimate the angle of inclination. When in this position **it is easier to draw the** inclination of the axis first, instead **of the** longer diameter of the elliptical end.

1. Arrange the model **so that** a somewhat similar view is **seen by** all. It is not now so essential that all should see exactly the same view. Explain the term 'axis,' and mark point *a* for one end. Through *a* **draw a** horizontal line. To get **the** inclination of the axis, hold the pencil in a horizontal position level with point *c*, and notice the angle made between it and the top edge *ce* of the cylinder. Through *a* draw *af* at this inclination.

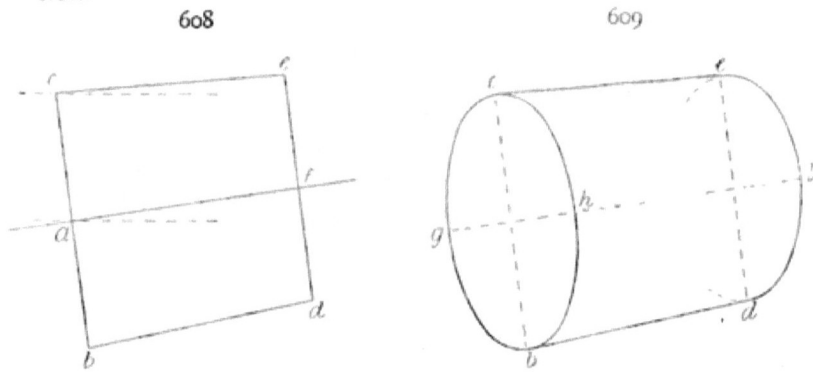

608   609

Note.—This is quite accurate enough for all practical purposes; strictly speaking, the angle of inclination at *a* is slightly larger than that at *c*. It is, however, impossible for the pupil to measure the inclination at the axis, as it is not visible. This angle should be tested repeatedly until the pupil has obtained it fairly accurately. It is a good plan to call several pupils out to the board, and let them draw the inclination which they see. This prevents the lazy ones shirking this most essential step, as if the inclination be incorrect the rest of the model will be wrong.

2. Through *a* draw *bc* at *right angles* to the axis, and fix its length. If the axis and this line be obtained correctly, the rest of the model presents no special difficulty.

3. Compare the length of the cylinder with *bc*, and set it off

from *a*. Through *f* draw *ed* parallel to *bc* and slightly shorter. Draw *ce* and *bd* (fig. 608).

Notes.—1. In estimating the length of the cylinder, measure from *h* to *l* (fig. 609). This is easier than from *c* to *e*. Common errors are to make the length too great and the back end too small.

2. The figure, when in the stage represented by fig. 608, should be carefully examined to see that the proportions are accurate.

4. Compare the width *gh* with *bc*, and draw the ellipse. Complete the back in the same manner Remember that the back ellipse is slightly rounder than the front ; *hl* should be a little longer than *ce*.

THE CONE

1. **Axis vertical.**—Commence with the ellipse. Produce *ab* for the height, and draw the sides (fig. 610).

II. **Lying on its side.**—This is a very awkward position, as it requires considerable judgment to estimate the slope of the axis.

1. Mark a point *a* for the centre of the base, and through it draw a horizontal line. Hold the pencil so as to be in line with the axis, and with the other hand hold a pencil or ruler horizontally level with *a*. The angle between the two pencils

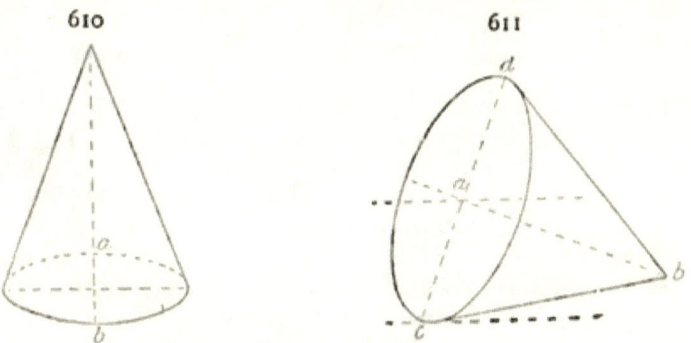

610 611

will be the inclination of the axis. The line *ab* represents the position of the right-hand pencil, the dotted line that of the other. Test this until sure of the inclination, and draw *ab*.

2. Through *a* draw *cd* at *right angles* to *ab*. Determine the length of *cd*.

3. Compare the width with *cd*, and draw the ellipse.

4. Compare *ab* with *cd*, and draw the sides. Notice that these lines do not touch the ellipse at *d* and *c*.

Notes.—1. The drawing may be additionally verified by testing the slope of *cb*.

2. As the ellipse widens, the distance *ab* will decrease.

The principles of construction involved in the preceding figures are applicable to all rectangular and circular models. An increased number of common objects can now be drawn. A few typical examples bringing in fresh points are now given.

Fig. 612 shows a box with the lid partly open. The fresh point here is the obtaining of the point *a*. Hold the pencil vertically and notice the position of point *b*, which is directly under *a*. Draw an upright line *ab*. Compare the height *ab* with the height of the box, and draw *ac*. To obtain *d*, draw a line *be* vanishing with the length of the box, and from *e* draw a vertical line *ed* a little less than *ab*. Join *a* with *d*.

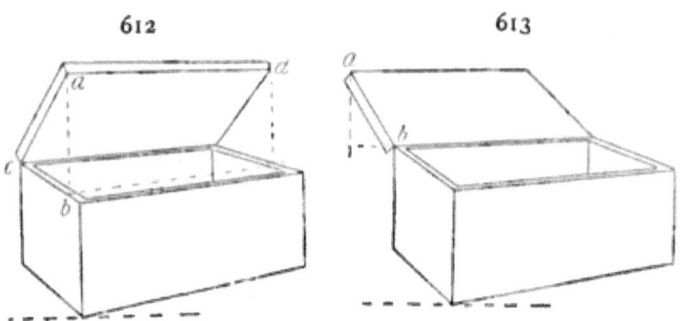

612   613

Fig. 613 shows the lid open at a different angle. To obtain *a*, find its horizontal distance *from*, and its vertical distance *above*, *b*.

Fig. 614.—To obtain the open cover of the book, produce *ab*, make *ac* slightly less, and draw *cd*.

Fig. 615.—Draw *abcd*. Find the centre by drawing the diagonals, and draw *ef* vanishing with *ab* and *cd*. Obtain the line above *ef*, showing the opening of the leaves. Notice that the leaves open like the box lid, in a circle of which *eb* is the radius. Of course this circle will be represented as an ellipse in the drawing. Draw the top leaves first, and observe that all

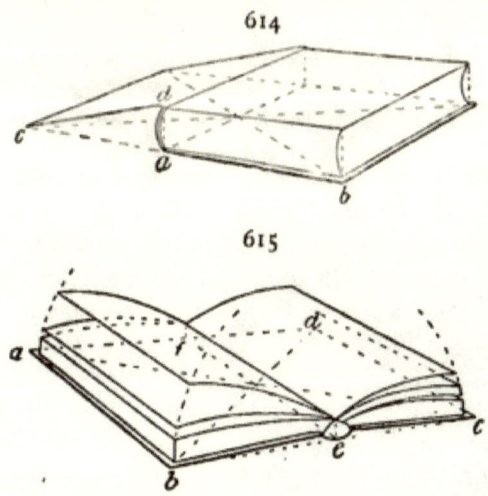

the openings radiate from the back, and that the long edges of the leaves vanish in the same direction.

Fig. 616 shows the cylinder standing on a board. (*Always draw the board last.*) Having drawn the cylinder after estimating the space necessary for the board, notice the distance between *ab* and the edge of the cylinder. Fix point *a* with reference to the side of the cylinder, and after noting the inclination draw *ab*. Find how far *b* is from the side of the cylinder. Draw *ac*. Very carefully notice where the back line of the board cuts the cylinder. Mark this point, and draw through it to meet *ac*.

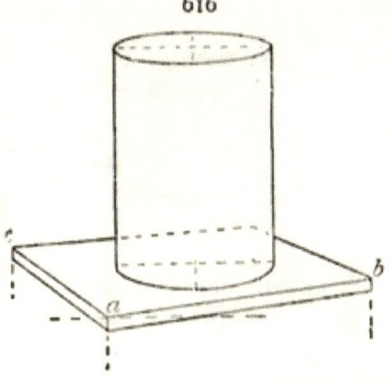

Note.—A board presents considerable difficulty to young pupils at first. The tendency to make it too wide seems inevitable. This can only be remedied by careful measurement.

Draw vertical lines from *a*, *b* and *c*, and set off the thickness. If these lines are drawn longer than the required thickness as shown, the common error of making these short lines sloping will be avoided.

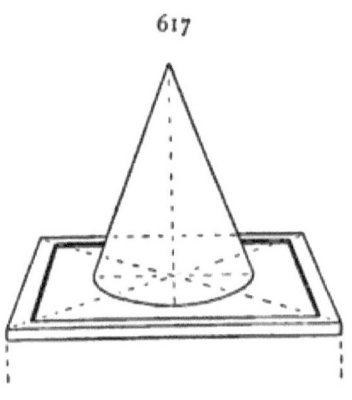

617

Fig. 617 shows the cone with a slate. Proceed as in the previous figure. The width of the slate frame may be obtained by drawing diagonal lines as shown, or as in fig. 591.

Fig. 618 shows an ordinary jam pot. Draw the rectangle *abcd*. Next obtain the bottom ellipse. Find the position of the shoulder *ef*, and draw the ellipse. Divide the space from *e* to *c* for the rim and neck. Find the size of the mouth and draw the ellipse. Two similar ellipses on *lm* and *gh* will give the neck. In showing the thickness be careful to represent the greatest width at the parts nearest to *c* and *d*.

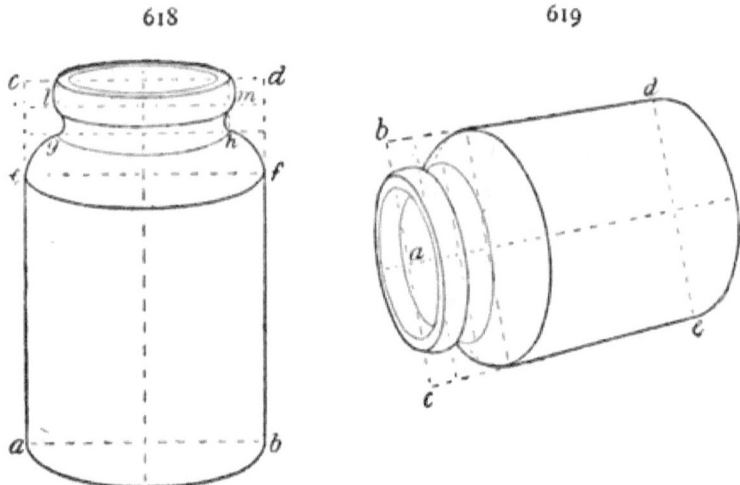

618   619

Fig. 619 shows the same object when lying on its side. After obtaining the inclination of the axis as in fig. 608, draw *cbde*. Obtain the mouth and foot of the jar. The ellipse for the shoulder will fall on the ellipse forming the neck, as shown. The neck will be represented by the inner ellipse.

Figs. 620-622 show a common jug in three positions. Handles are always difficult to represent well, so that three views are given here. Notice in all that a line through the centre gives the position of both handle and spout. In fig. 620 the handle is not so difficult; the thickness is represented by

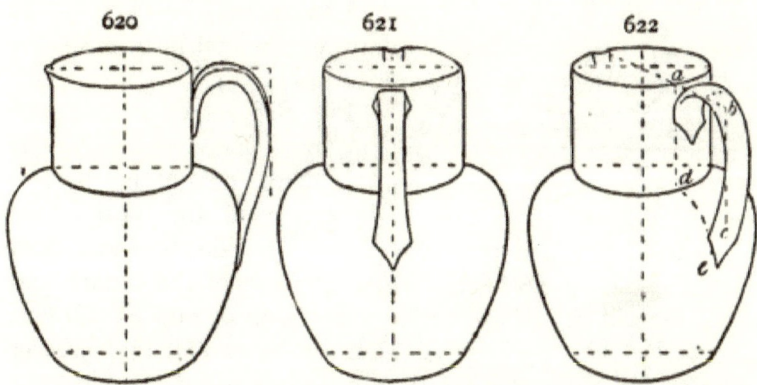

two parallel lines, and the width by a line which gradually runs into the thickness. Lines drawn as shown are of considerable assistance in obtaining the curve. In fig. 621 the handle is a band slightly broadening out where it is attached to the jug. It is in fig. 622 that the real difficulty presents itself. Fix the position of the spout and draw a line from this point through the centre, produce this line to *b*, and draw a vertical line *bc*. The handle will fall within these lines. To obtain its position on the neck, draw a vertical line *ad* from *a*. From *d* draw the curve *de*, giving the position of the handle on the body. Now, using these lines as a guide, draw the curve The right-hand curve is drawn in a similar manner to that on the left, as in the handle shown in fig. 623. Join the two curves at the top and complete. All handles of this kind should be obtained in this way.

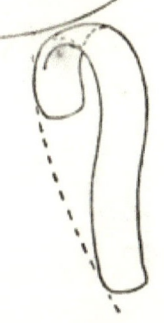

228   *The Teaching of Drawing*

The drawing of a **bucket** is shown in fig. 354. Notice the method of obtaining the handle. A bell is shown in fig. 327. The glue pot shown in fig. 356 forms an excellent model, giving double practice in the drawing of handles.

Fig. 624 shows an ordinary gallon bottle. After obtaining its proportions, draw the rectangle *abcd*, **and the ellipses for the bottom,** shoulder, and commencement **of the neck.** Now

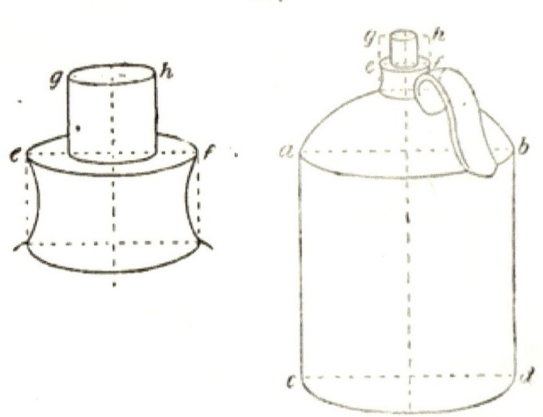

624

set off the lines *ef* and *gh* **for** the neck and cork. An enlarged drawing of this part is shown with the necessary construction lines. **The** handle is **obtained in** a similar manner to that of the jug.

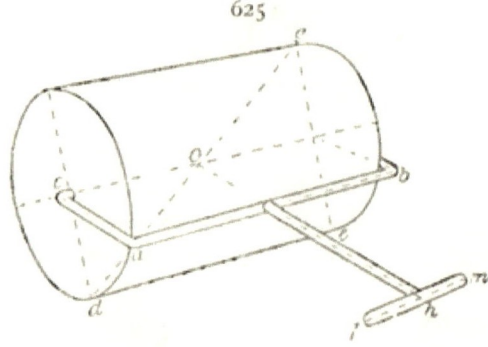

625

Fig. 625 shows an ordinary roller. The fresh point to notice is the method of drawing the handle. After obtaining the roller, draw *ab* vanishing with the length, and join *a* and *b* with the ends of the axis. Draw the diagonal *dg*, and from the centre draw *oh* vanishing with *ac*. Fix the length and draw *lm* vanishing with *de*.

Fig. 626 shows how to obtain the handle of a common tin saucepan when it is turned either towards or from the pupil. Mark the position of the handle, and draw a line *ab* through the centre of the top ellipse. Draw *bd* about the height that the handle stands above the mouth. Draw *dc* vanishing with *ab*, and produce it towards *e*. The top of the handle must lie in this line. Mark its position *e*, and draw the centre line of the handle. The rest of the drawing is easily completed.

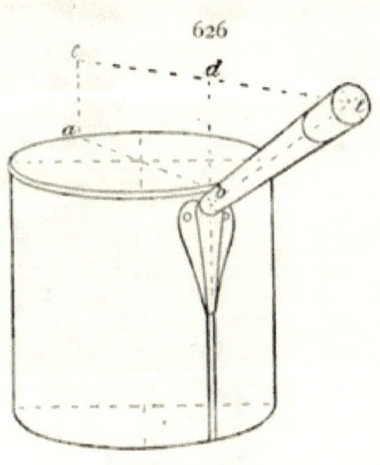

Note.—This is a very important principle, and is applicable to many objects. The handle of a hot-water can or of a kettle would need the same lines of construction.

THE HEXAGONAL PRISM

This important model is not often set for Standard V, as it is not strictly speaking a purely rectangular model. It is, however, very commonly set for the other standards. If the proper principles of construction are not understood it is by no means easy. The following methods, if followed out carefully, will secure an accurate drawing without much difficulty.

Axis Vertical. First Lesson.—1. Arrange the prism so that the pupils are opposite one of the rectangular faces. Draw *ab*, and decide upon its length. Compare the width of the front face with the height and draw *cd*. Complete the rectangle *abcd* (fig. 627).

2. Estimate the distance that *ef* appears to be from *ac*, as in fig. 581. Make *ef* a little less than *ac* and draw *ae* and *cf*.

3. Draw the diagonals *ec* and *af*. Through *o* draw a line parallel to *ac*. Make *gh=go* and *lm=lo*. (*These four distances are always equal in the hexagon.*)

4. Complete the top by drawing *ah*, *he*, *fm*, and *mc* (fig. 628).

5. Draw *hn* and *mp* each a little less than *ab*, and complete the figure.

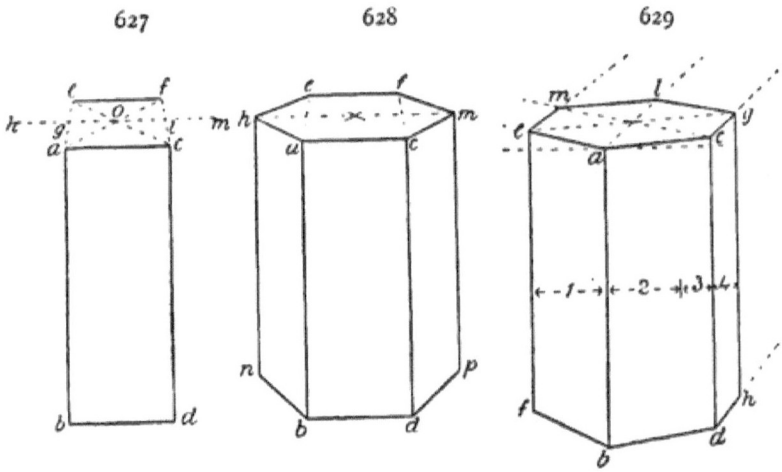

627   628   629

Second Lesson.—1. Arrange the prism so that its rectangular faces appear of unequal widths. Draw the vertical edge *ab*, which is nearest to the pupil. Compare the width of the widest face with *ab*, and draw *cd*. (*This measurement should be carefully tested before proceeding further, as the proportions of the other faces depend largely upon this.*) Compare the next widest face with *ac*, and draw *ef*.

2. Set off the width of the narrower face on the wider so that 1=2. On the right of *cd* set off a little less than the distance marked 3, and draw *gh*. Then 2+3 will be a little greater than 1+4.

3. Test the inclination and draw *ac*. (*This will be almost horizontal.*) Draw *ae* sloping a little more than *ac*. From *e* draw *eg* vanishing very slightly with *ac*. Join *c* and *g*.

Model Drawing. Standard V

4. Find the centre of *eg*, and draw *al*. From *e* draw *em* vanishing with *al*.

5. From *c* draw a line through the centre to meet *em*. Draw *gl* vanishing with *cm*. Join *m* and *l*.

6. Complete the prism by drawing *bd*, *bf* and *dh*, vanishing with the corresponding lines on the top.

Notes.—1. The pupil must bear in mind that the lines of the top vanish very slightly, as they are not very far from each other.

2. Particular attention should be given to the inclination of *ac* and *ae*, as if these lines slope too much the top of the prism will appear distorted.

3. The pupils' attention should be directed to the fact that there are three sets of parallel lines in the top of the figure.

4. In fig. 628 the two narrower sides could be made each a little less than half the middle face, and the hexagon finished in a similar manner to fig. 629.

Axis Horizontal. I. End parallel with picture plane

1. Draw a vertical line *ab* to represent the height of the end. As the pupil is directly in front, draw a horizontal line *ac* for the top side of the end. Compare *ac* with *ab*, and draw *cd* and *bd*. The width *ac* should be very carefully verified in all cases before proceeding any farther, as if that be incorrect the whole of the end will be wrong.

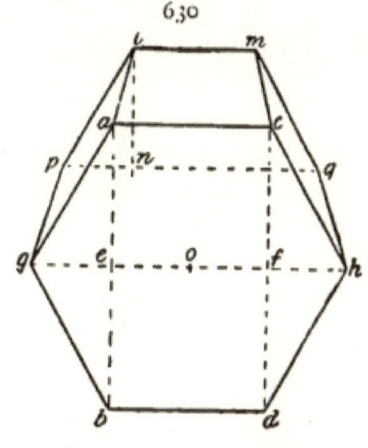

2. Bisect *ab* and *cd*, and draw *ef*. This is preferable to drawing the diagonals of the rectangle *abcd*, as the pupil has two points through which to draw *ef* instead of one.

3. Bisect *ef* in *o*. Set off *eg* equal to *eo* and *fh* equal to *fo*. Complete the end by drawing *ag*, *gb*, *dh* and *hc*.

Note.—These construction lines should be drawn with chalk on the end of the model.

4. Measure the distance to the back line *lm*, find the position of the back corners in exactly the same manner as shown in fig. 581, and draw *al* and *cm*.

Note.— *lm* will, of course, be less than *ac*.

5. Draw one vertical line *ln* less than *ae*. Complete the top half of the back hexagon, and draw *gp* and *hq*.

Note.— The advantage of drawing *pq* is, that the corners *p* and *q* are then accurately shown. There is a tendency to let the lines *gp* and *pl* run into each other instead of showing an angle.

II. End nearly parallel with the picture plane.

1. This is similar to the last figure. Draw *ab*. Find the width between the vertical lines, and draw *cd*. Test the inclination of *ac*. (Nearly level, because the end is nearly opposite.) Draw *bd*, making *cd* very slightly less than *ab*.

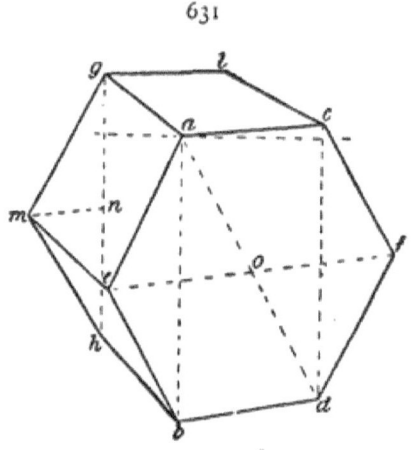

631

2. Bisect *ab* and *cd*, and draw *ef*. Be careful to see that all three lines vanish in the same direction. Find the centre *o* as before, or by drawing the diagonal *ad*, and set off the distances as in the previous figure. Draw *ae*, *eb*, *df*, and *fc*.

3. Test the inclination of *ag*, bearing in mind that if *ac* is nearly horizontal then *ag* will have a considerable slope. The easiest way to find the position of *g* is to hold a pencil vertically in line with *g*, and notice its distance right or left of *e*.

4. From *g* draw a vertical line *gh*, and make it shorter than *ab*. Draw *bh*.

5. From *e* draw *em* vanishing with *ag*, and draw *hm* and *gm*. The point *m* may also be obtained by drawing the line

nm from the centre of *gh* and making it slightly less than the corresponding distance on the front end.

6. Draw *gl* vanishing with *ac*, and *cl* vanishing with *ag*.

Note.—*em* will be slightly longer than *ag*, as it is nearer.

III. End at an angle to the picture plane.

1. Draw the vertical lines *ab* and *cd* as before. Great care is necessary in deciding upon the width between these lines when the model is in this position. Test the inclination, and draw *ac*. Make *cd* a little less than *ab*, and join *b* with *d*.

2. Bisect *ab* and *cd*, and draw *ef*. This must be carefully scanned to see that *ef* vanishes with both lines. Find the centre, set off the distances, and complete the end.

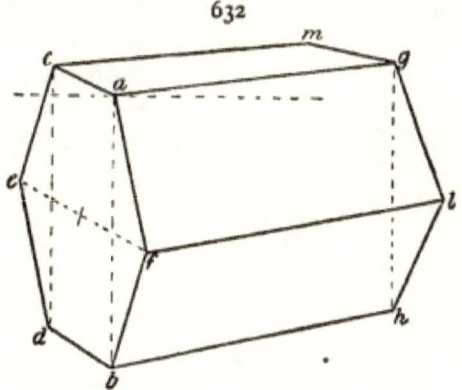

632

Note.—These four distances are, of course, only exactly equal when the hexagon is quite opposite. Strictly speaking, they gradually diminish from *f* to *e*. In a very large drawing it would be more accurate to draw the diagonals *ad* and *bc*. This would give the first distance slightly larger than the second.

3. Find the inclination of *ag*, remembering that if *ac* be much inclined then *ag* will be nearly level. Determine the length of *ag*, and draw a vertical line *gh*. Make *gh* less than *ab*. The difference between them may be tested by measuring. Draw *bh*.

4. Look at *ag* and *bh* and draw *fl*. Make *fl* slightly longer than *ag*, and draw *lg* and *lh*.

5. Notice *ag* and draw *cm*. Make *cm* less than *ag*, and draw *gm*.

THE TRIANGULAR PRISM

The only point that calls for mention here is the method of obtaining the height of the prism. Draw the rectangular face *abcd* in the usual manner. Find the centre, and draw *ef* vanish-

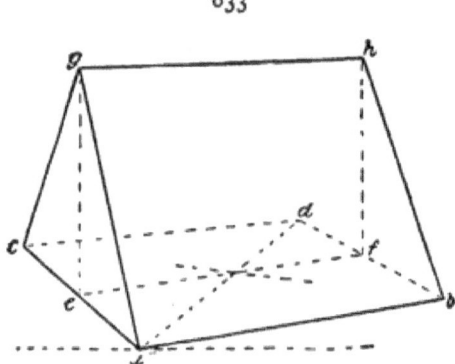
633

ing with both *ab* and *cd*. At *e* draw *eg* and set off the height. Join *g* with *a* and *c*. For the farther end draw *fh*, and make it a little less than *eg*. Draw *gh* and *bh*.

PYRAMIDS

I. **Axis vertical.**—For all pyramids when the axis is vertical the method is the same, viz. :—

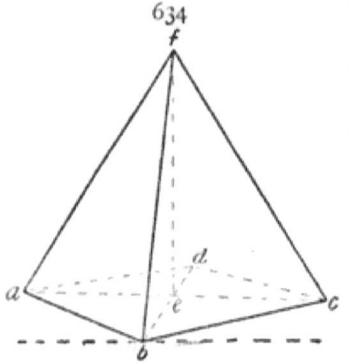

1. Draw the base. 2. Find the centre. 3. Set up the height from the centre. 4. Join the apex with the angles of the base.

Fig. 634 shows a square pyramid standing upon its base. Draw the base *abcd* in the usual manner. Obtain the diagonals. From *e* draw the axis *ef*, and mark off the height. Join *f* with *a*, *b* and *c*.

Fig. 635 shows the same pyramid when one side of the base is opposite the pupil. Three of the triangular faces are then visible.

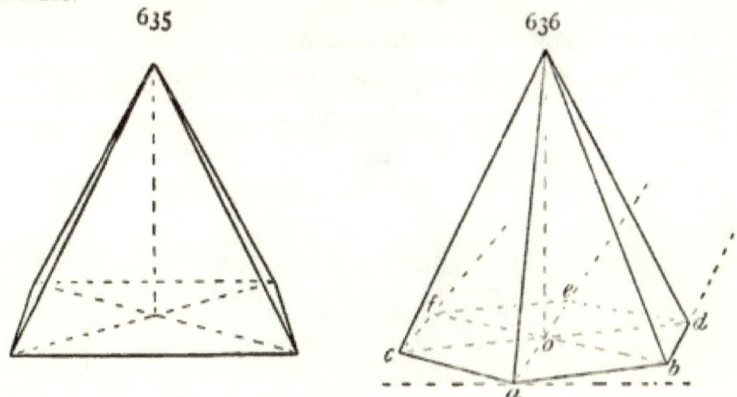

Fig. 636 shows the hexagonal pyramid. Fix point *a*, the angle nearest the pupil. Draw *ab*, the widest side and therefore the least inclined. Draw *ac*, the next widest side. From *c* draw *cd* vanishing with *ab*, and from *b* draw *bd*, the narrowest side of the base, to meet *cd*. Find the centre *o* of *cd*, and through it draw *ae*. Look at *ae* and draw *cf*. Through *o* draw *bf*, and from *d* draw *de* vanishing with it. Join *e* with *f*. Draw the vertical axis from *o*. Set off the height, and join the apex with the angles of the base.

II. **Lying on one of the triangular faces.**—Fig. **637** shows a square pyramid. This is a very difficult position. The simplest plan is to mark point *a*, and draw the line *ab*. To get the slope of *ab*, hold the pencil vertical with *b* and notice the distance that *b* is to the right of *a*. Determine the inclination, draw *ad*, and complete the base.

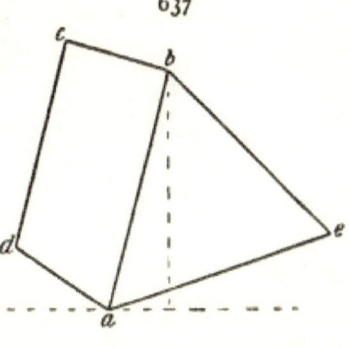

It will not be of much assistance to draw the axis; the easier plan is to determine the inclination and length of *ae*, and join *b* with *e*.

CYLINDRICAL RING

I. **Axis** vertical.— 1. Draw *ab*. Compare *cd* with *ab* and draw the ellipse.

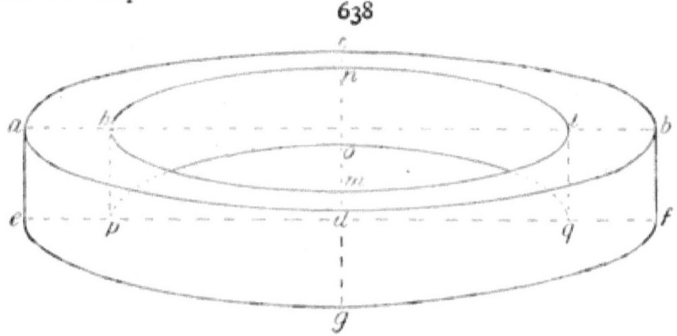

2. Set off the depth, *ae* and *bf*. Draw *ef*. Make *dg* a little longer than *ae* (because it is nearer), and draw the bottom curve.

3. Set off the width of the ring, *ah* and *bl* equal to *ae*.

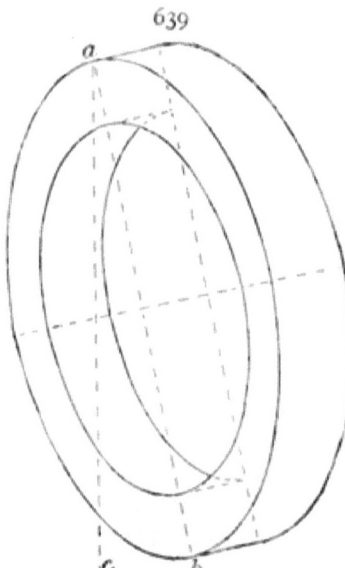

The width at *dm* will be the same part of *ah* that *cd* is of *ab*. Notice that *cn* will be a little less than *dm*. Draw the inner ellipse.

4. For the inner bottom curve draw a semi-ellipse on *pq*. Notice that *no* will be slightly less than *hp*.

II. **Axis horizontal.**— If the ring were level with the eye then the drawing would be similar to fig. 638 turned at right angles; but if below the eye the axis will be inclined and *ab* will not be vertical. In the cylinder the inclination of the axis was first obtained, but in this case the axis is too short to test its inclination. It is, therefore, easier to draw the longer diameter of the ellipse first. The only difficulty here is in determining the inclination, *ab*, of this diameter. Hold the pencil in a line with the longer diameter so as to cut the ellipse into two symmetrical portions, and with the other hand hold a pencil vertically with *a*, as indicated by the dotted line *ac*. This will assist the eye to estimate the slope. The rest of the drawing is done in exactly the same manner as in the previous figure, and may be easily followed from the construction lines.

Note.—Figs. 627-639 are not included in the Standard V syllabus. They are, however, shown here for the sake of completeness.

VASES

Three sets are recommended by the Department.
1. Set of Three Regular Objects of Form in white pottery.
2. Set of Three Earthenware Vases in terra-cotta.
3. Set of Five Vases in Majolica ware.

The first set is the most suitable for schools, as it gives greater variety of shape and simpler lines.

The general contour should be noted, and the fact pointed out that vases with oval or egg-shaped bodies are generally more effective and beautiful in form than those with either circular or elliptical ones.

Simple vases in elevation are shown in figs. 214-218, 324, and 332; while figs. 381 and 382 show more difficult ones. The method of procedure has already been given on page 99, Standard V, Freehand. Figs. 334, 336, and 338 illustrate the method of drawing the three vases of the first set. Figs. 335 and 337 are from the third set. Fig. 330 shows an enlarged drawing of the mouth of fig. 334, and fig. 331 shows the foot of fig. 338. The only additional point needing illustration is the ornamental handle of fig. 336. This is difficult and should be shown on the board, and drawn separately in three positions before drawing it on the vase. If the leaf form to which the ring is attached be examined, it will be found to be of a pentagonal shape and divided into five parts. The shape varies a little on different vases, but the same method of obtaining it should be adhered to.

Fig. 640 shows the handle when seen on the side of the vase.

Fig. 641 shows the front view blocked in. Begin with line *ab*, and ascertain the proportion which *ab* bears to the height of the vase. Find the position of *c*, and draw the base of the pentagon. Mark the width at *d* and *e*, and complete the pentagon. Now draw the ring. Divide the pentagon into five parts as shown.

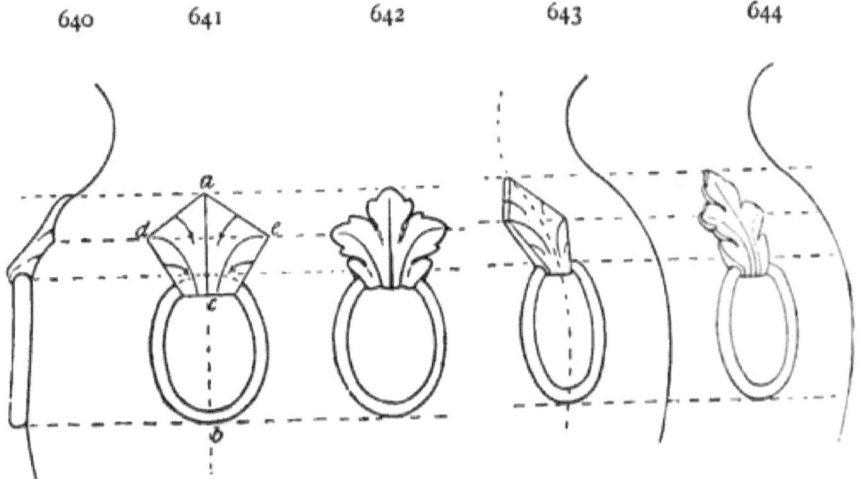

640   641   642   643   644

Fig. 642 shows the completed sketch. Notice that the points of the leaf are not sharp, but blunt and rounded as pottery would naturally be.

Figs. 643 and 644 show the most common and also the most difficult view. In fig. 643 the blocking in is shown. The central line follows the curve of the vase, and the pentagon is foreshortened. In fig. 644 notice that the thickness of the leaf is now visible, and that the right-hand side will not be so clearly defined as the left or nearer side.

Figs. 645-647 show the largest vase from the second set in terra-cotta. It is not recommended for Standard V, as, although of a beautiful shape, it presents too many difficulties

Model Drawing. Standard VI

for the present stage. It is one of the two vases prescribed by the Department for the examination in what is now known as the Elementary stage of Model Drawing, corresponding to what was formerly second grade Model. The other vase is that shown in figs. 338, 648, and 649.

The elevation of the vase in **fig. 645** is shown in order that the lines to be represented may be clearly seen, as about eight ellipses have to be indicated in the drawing.

Fig. 646 shows the construction lines. After obtaining the centre line, draw the lines *ab*, *cd*, and *ef*, representing the widths of the mouth, the widest part of body, and the foot, respectively. Now obtain *gh*, the width of the bottom of the neck, and *lm*, the width of the top of the foot. Draw the mouth and the curve of the body. The general proportions of these parts should now be carefully examined and the rest of the figure completed, as in fig. 647. Notice how the lines 1 and 2 gradually die away before reaching the diameter of the ellipse.

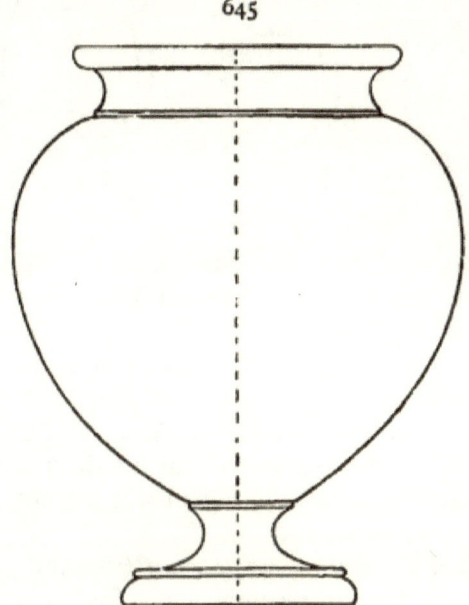

645

240   *The Teaching of Drawing*

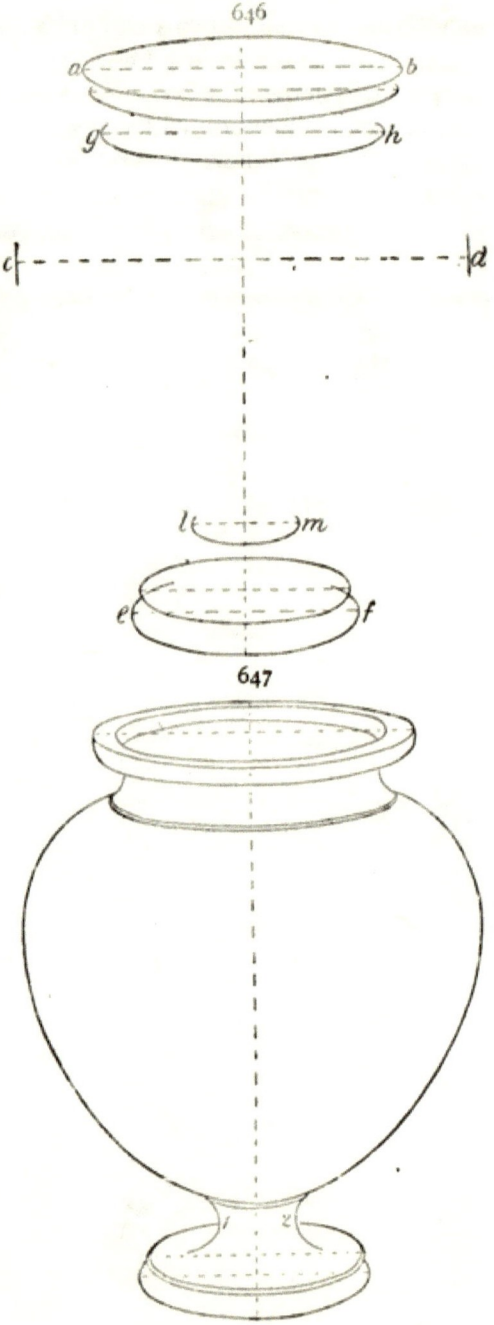

Model Drawing. Standard VI 241

Figs. 648 and 649 show two views of the bottle when lying down. These are not intended for Standard V. In fig. 648 the axis is nearly parallel to the pupil. First draw the axis *ab*. To determine the inclination, hold the pencil in a line with *ab*, and with the other hand hold a pencil in a horizontal position level with *a* ; the angle between the pencils will give the slope of the axis. Draw *cd, ef,* and *gh* at right angles to *ab,* and sketch the outline as in fig. 338.

In fig. 649 the contour is lost in the ellipses to a great extent. After obtaining the axis, draw the three ellipses on *cd, ef,* and *gh.* The curve of the neck loses itself as shown. The lower part of the body is smaller than the upper part, and the curve of the ellipse (shown by the dotted line) will require a little addition at *l*.

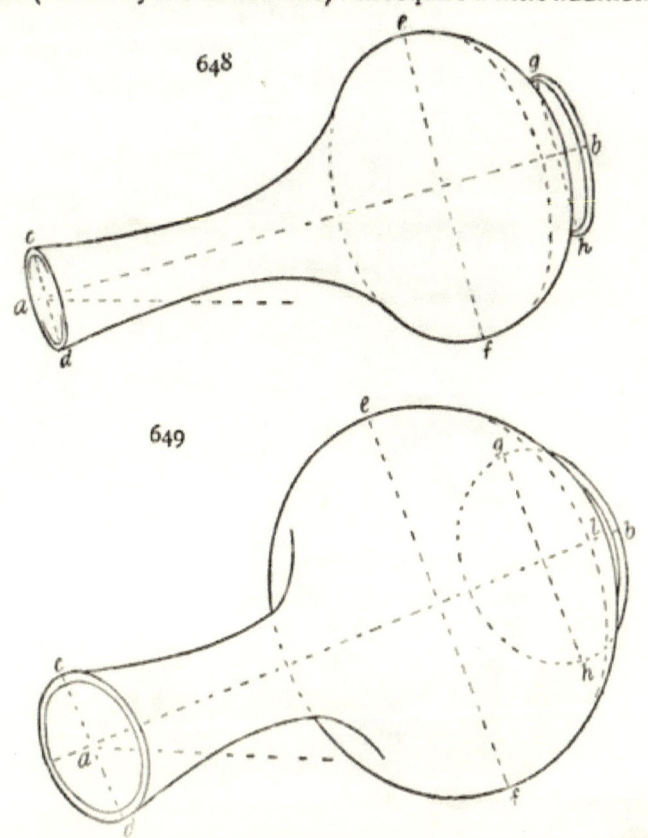

R

Syllabus, Standard VI.—*Drawing from models of regular forms and from easy common objects.*

All the models previously shown are suitable for Standard VI. when grouped. The only fresh point is the arrangement of the models. Usually two models are set, but this is not an absolute rule. Very large models should not be used in combination with the vases or any small objects, as the vases will be so small when drawn as to make it impossible to show their lines with any degree of accuracy.

Fig. 650 shows the examples given in the 'Illustrated Syllabus.'

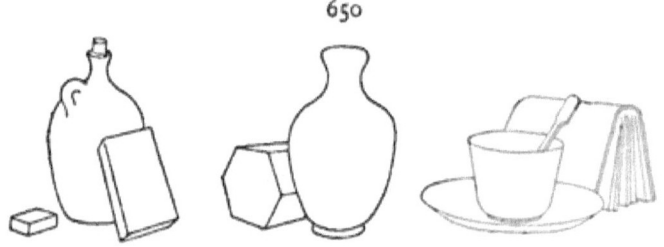

650

Figs. 627-639 and 645-649 all belong, strictly speaking, to Standard VI. course. A few groups will now be given, illustrating difficulties that frequently occur.

Fig. 651 shows a group of average difficulty, to be drawn with the board.

1. Begin by comparing the greatest height *ab* with the greatest width *bc*, so as to obtain an idea of the proportions of the whole group.

2. Next draw the hexagonal prism after comparing its height with *ab*.

3. Hold the pencil vertically in a line with the axis of the vase, notice where it cuts the prism, and draw *de*. Hold the pencil level with the foot of the vase, and notice its position, whether above or below the corner *f* of the prism. Compare the height of the vase with the height of the prism, and complete as previously shown.

4. To draw the board, fix the position of *g*, its distance *below*, and its distance *left*, of *e*. Find the inclination of *gh*. Notice how far *h* is to the right of the prism. Find the inclina-

tion of *gl*, and determine the position of *l*. Notice where the back lines of the board cut the other models. Draw vertical lines from *l*, *g*, and *h*, and complete the figure.

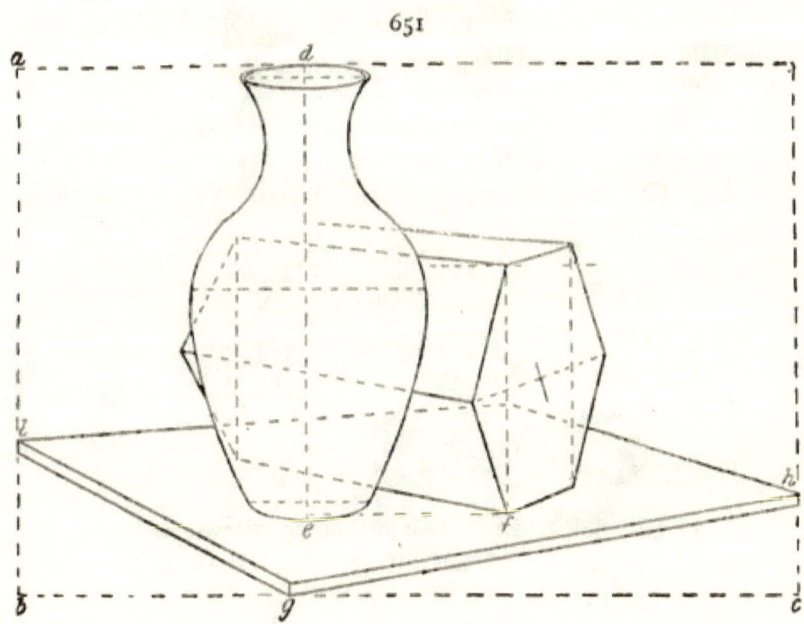

651

Notes.—1. These earlier groups should be composed of a circular and a right-lined **model**, and should be placed in easy positions.

2. They will probably take some time to **draw correctly, but it** will be found **most** profitable to endeavour to **get** the earlier groups well drawn **rather than to attempt a larger number of drawings.**

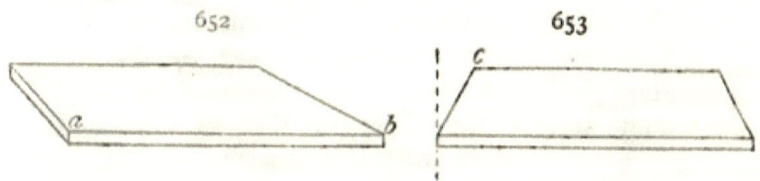

652 653

3. **The board is** generally **difficult to draw** (see fig. 616). Observe that fig. 652 is an incorrect drawing, as if *ab* were level then the sides should be drawn as **in fig. 653.** This may be easily tested

by the pupil holding the pencil vertically in line with *a*, as shown by the dotted line, and noticing on which side of the pencil *c* appears to be.

Fig. 654.—First draw the cylinder. Now determine the position of *a* with regard to *b*, of *c* with regard to the edge and length of the cylinder, and draw *ac*. Test the inclination before

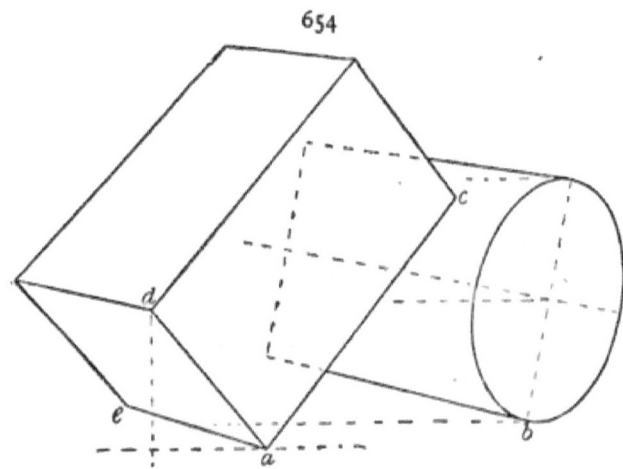

proceeding further. Obtain the position of *d* (*above* and *left* of *a*) and draw *ad*. Find the inclination of *ae*, and complete the figure.

Fig. 655.—This is a very difficult group to draw, and is shown in two stages. The figures should be blocked in as shown in the top drawing, obtaining all the main lines and proper proportions first. Begin with the centre line of the cup, and draw the ellipse on *ab*. Now obtain the diameter *ef* of the saucer; the position for this diameter will be obtained by holding the pencil in a horizontal position level with *e* and *f* and noticing where it cuts the sides of the cup. Draw *gh* for the points of attachment of the handle, and if a line be drawn from the centre through *g* the direction of the handle will be indicated.

For the spoon draw the centre line and block in as shown.
In drawing the book, fix the position of *l* and draw *lm*.

Model Drawing. Standard VI

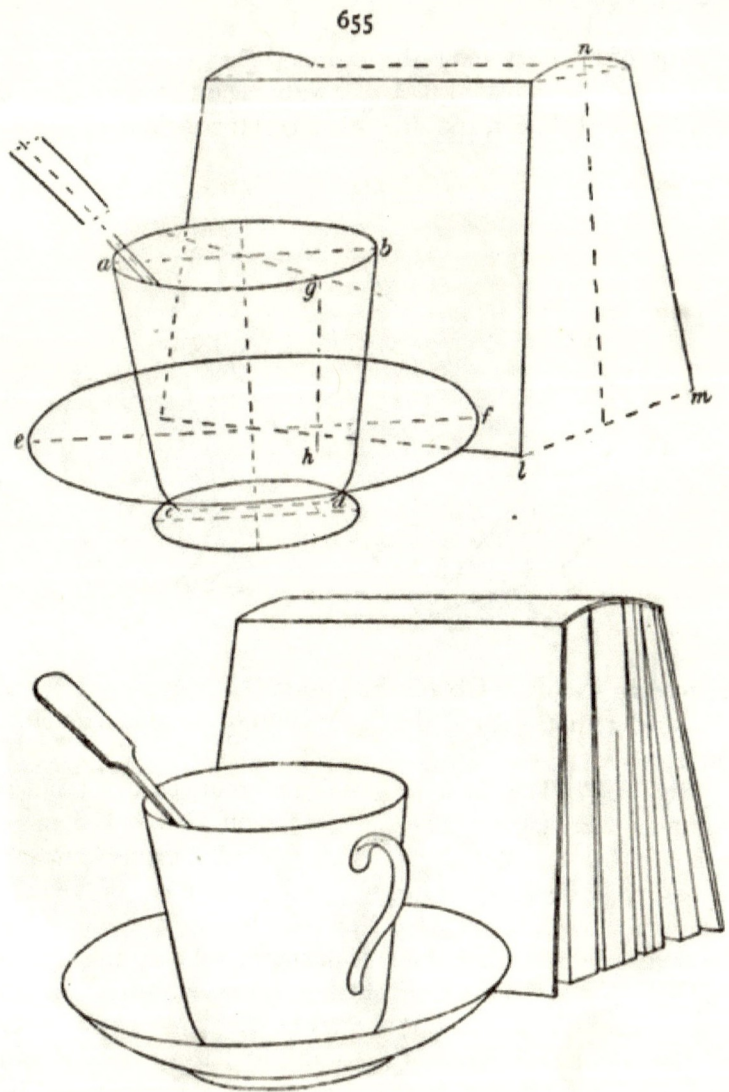

655

Determine the height of *n*, and complete the end. In drawing the leaves, notice that the horizontal edges will vanish with the length of the book.

Objects wholly or partly above the eye should also be practised—such as a door, window, board and easel, swing slate, &c.

Fig. 656 shows the construction for the board and easel. Commence with *abcd*, and set up the height as shown. As the top of the easel is narrower than the bottom, the side rails will not come from the points *e* and *f*. Hold the pencil level with *f*, and notice how much *e* is below *f*. Draw a line H for the

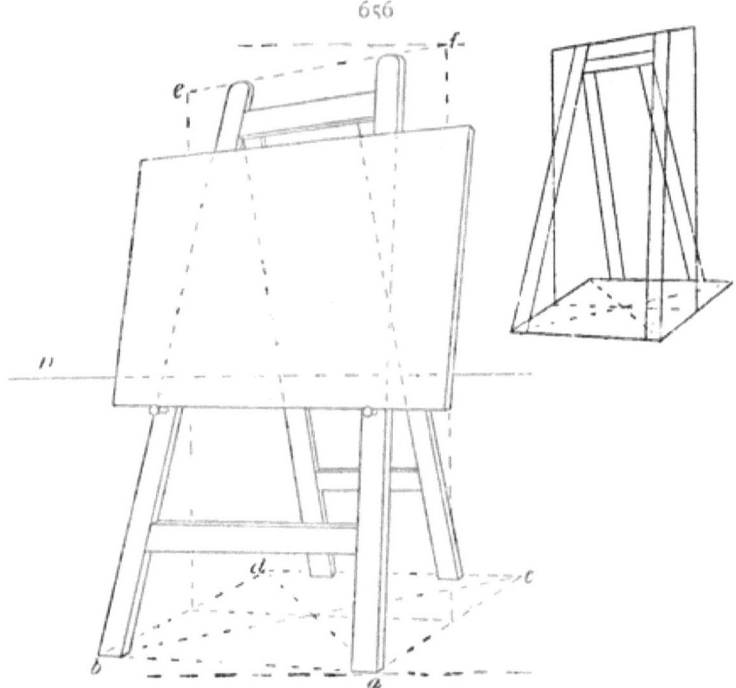

656

level of the eye, and remember that all lines below H run up, and those above it run down towards H. Lines like the bottom of the board which are near the level of the eye will be nearly horizontal. The back legs are not so wide apart as the front ones, and are parallel to each other. They will therefore not be drawn to *c* and *d*.

Fig. 657 shows an ordinary swing slate. The dotted lines show the parts to be drawn first. H marks the level of the eye.

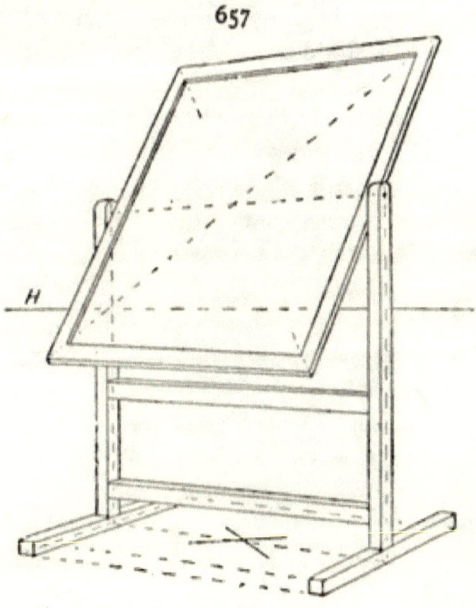
657

CHAPTER XI

LIGHT AND SHADE. STANDARD VII

Syllabus.—*Drawing any common objects and casts of ornament in light and shade.*

This is the most difficult part of the syllabus to carry out in ordinary schools, as the difficulties in the way of securing a proper light are very great. The object should be lighted from one window only (with a northern aspect, if possible), as cross lights increase the difficulty to a very great extent by destroying the effect of the shadows. The only way to prevent this is to fence off the other lights by means of screens. A box with two of its sides knocked out will frequently answer fairly well for this purpose.

It is also necessary that the teacher should possess a higher degree of artistic feeling and knowledge than the previous parts of the syllabus necessitate; practical acquaintance with the subject being absolutely necessary before instruction can be imparted to the pupils. Where these difficulties of teaching, lighting, &c., arise, it is much better to take the alternative subject of *Geometrical Drawing* (*b.* 1.), which is easier and quite as useful to the pupils. (See Chapter VIII. Standard VII.)

Materials.—These are inexpensive and readily procured. They will depend somewhat upon whether the pencil, crayon, or stump is used for the shading. Arguments may be adduced in favour of each, but for producing a good general effect in a short time the stump is preferable. The pupils will need a drawing-board, paper with a rough surface, an F or H pencil for sketching the outline, a piece of indiarubber cut to a sharp point for removing the dark spots, small paper stumps, and prepared stumping-chalk.

Paper.—This must have a rough surface, as smooth paper is perfectly useless. For ordinary practice, French white paper is very suitable, as it is cheap, and has a ridgy surface. Cartridge paper will do if it has a good texture. For examination purposes and for finished drawings Whatman's 'Not' is the best that can be used.

Stumps.—These are made either of leather or paper. The small paper stumps sold at about 3*d*. per dozen are the most suitable for ordinary purposes. The stump should be held between the thumb and finger, *under* the hand, and very gently turned round while being used, so that all parts of the chalked end may be brought into use, thus securing an even texture in the shading.

Stumping-chalk is sold in small bottles by all artists' colourmen. When using it, a small quantity should be rubbed into a piece of wash leather pinned at one corner of the board, and the stump charged by rubbing the point on it. A piece of rough paper, with the bottom corner turned up so as to prevent any of the chalk rolling upon the drawing, will answer just as well.

When the shading is obtained by using the pencil or crayon, then a BB pencil, or a No. 1 Conté Crayon in wood is the most suitable for the purpose. The Conté Crayon is also useful for indicating the edges of the figure, which are sometimes apt to get indistinct and irregular.

First Lesson.—The pupil should begin by practising the laying on of flat even tints of various degrees of darkness. When this has been satisfactorily accomplished, the shading of objects should be at once proceeded with. Copying from shaded drawings is of little use; the pupil needs practice in drawing from the object, and the training of the eye to distinguish the varied gradations of shade between the highest light of the object and the darkest part of its shadow.

There are many ways of using the stump, all having the same end in view, namely, the production of an even tint. Some accomplish this by using broad diagonal strokes, others by a zigzag stroke; probably the easiest for covering a large surface is a rounded zigzag something like the letter S. The method selected must largely depend upon that which the teacher has found most successful. In all, the steps are the same; first, the covering of the surface with strokes, giving a general depth of tone, and then securing evenness by filling up the light spaces and removing any dark spots.

1. Rule a two-inch square. Charge the stump by rubbing it on the chalked leather or paper as previously explained, taking care that no loose chalk is left on the stump, or the stroke will be uneven. Try the stump on a piece of white paper to see that the stroke is of the required degree of darkness; then, holding it as directed, and gently rolling it while working, cover the square as in fig. 658 A.

In working begin at the left side, work towards the right, and try to avoid crossing over a stroke a second time, as this

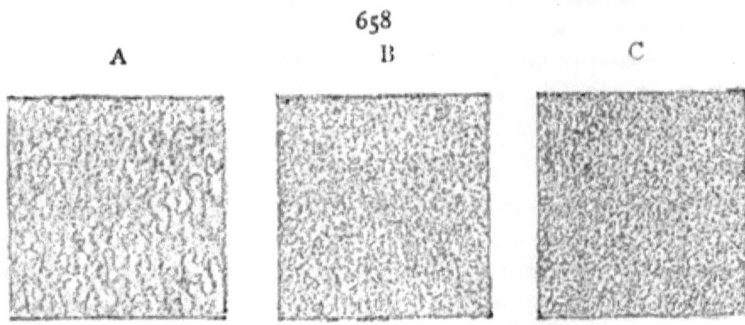

658
A   B   C

will produce a darker spot which will need removing. For the first practice it is desirable to make the strokes rather large and open, as shown in the bottom part of the square. As the pupil acquires more power the strokes may be made smaller and less open, thus securing an even tint at once. The top part of the square where the strokes are smaller shows a fairly even shade with one process. Be especially careful to *use the stump lightly and never scrub the paper.*

2. Fill up the light spaces by gently touching them with the point of the stump as shown in stage B.

3. Remove any dark spots by gently pressing (*not rubbing*) the point of the indiarubber on them. Clean the indiarubber after removing each spot by rubbing it on a piece of paper. The tint should then be even as in C.

Draw another square. Charge the stump more heavily with chalk, and fill up with a darker tint as shown in fig. 659. Finish in exactly the same manner as shown in fig. 658, and the result will be a square of a darker tint than the previous one.

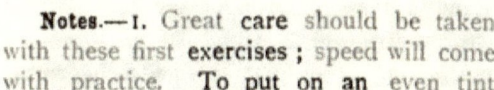

659

A third square might be filled up in the same manner with a still darker tint by charging the stump more fully than in the last.

Notes.—1. Great care should be taken with these first exercises; speed will come with practice. To put on an even tint without much subsequent alteration should be the pupil's aim, as much use of indiarubber or bread is sure to destroy the texture of the shading.

2. Remember that the three steps indicated in the lesson must always be patiently gone through, though practice and care will gradually decrease the time spent on two and three to a small amount. When occupied with these two stages the student should always *sit well away from the work*, as the general evenness of the tint can only be seen when the eye is far enough off to take in the whole of the drawing.

3. A piece of tissue paper should be kept under the hand while working, and the part of the drawing which is not in progress should be covered up.

Second Lesson.—When the power of laying on a flat even tint has been acquired, proceed at once to the shading of a simple rectangular model such as the cube.

1. Place the model on a sheet of white paper so that the shadow may be more distinctly seen (it may also sometimes be desirable to pin a sheet at the back of the model), and draw the cube very lightly in outline, marking the shadow, and avoiding rubbing out as far as possible (fig. 660). Do not make the drawing too large at first: about three inches is quite long enough for the edge of the cube.

Note.—Use an F or H pencil. Charcoal is frequently used for this purpose, as the lines can be readily dusted out. It is not, however, recommended for beginners, as it requires constant sharpening and is easily broken.

2. Direct attention to the fact that some parts of the cube are lighter than others. The top on which most light falls is the lightest; one of the vertical faces is darker than the other, and the shadow thrown on the paper is the darkest of all. If the darker vertical face be looked at carefully with half-closed eyes, it will be noticed that this face is not of the same depth of tone, but that the top part is darker than the bottom part. This is due to the light reflected from the white paper upon which the model stands. Remove the white paper, and place the cube upon a black surface, when this difference will not be seen. To illustrate this further, hold a sheet of white paper opposite to the darkest side of the model; the light reflected from the paper will cause this side to appear much lighter.

The facts observed may now be summarised as follows:

(*a*) The lightest part of the cube is said to be in **high light**.

(*b*) The part of the cube upon which the light does not directly fall is in **shade**.

(*c*) The part of the paper which is deprived of light by the cube is the **cast-shadow**.

(*d*) The parts of the cube made lighter by the paper upon which it stands are in **reflected light**.

(*e*) Place a cylinder on the paper, and in addition to the four preceding points, it will be seen that between the highest light and the shade, there are intermediate tints on the curved surface upon which the light does not fall so directly. This is termed the **half-tone**.

3. Begin to shade the darkest part, that is the cast-shadow. Put on an even tint of the same depth as its lightest part (fig. 661).

4. Shade the darker vertical face with an even tint, as dark as its lightest part.

5. Shade the lighter side in the same manner. The drawing should now show three degrees of shade, all perfectly even as in fig. 661.

6. Put in the gradations on the vertical faces (fig. 662). *The left-hand face is darker towards the top and left*, the paper making the bottom part lighter. *The right-hand face is darkest at the top and at the left*, nearest the light part of the

Light and Shade. Standard VII

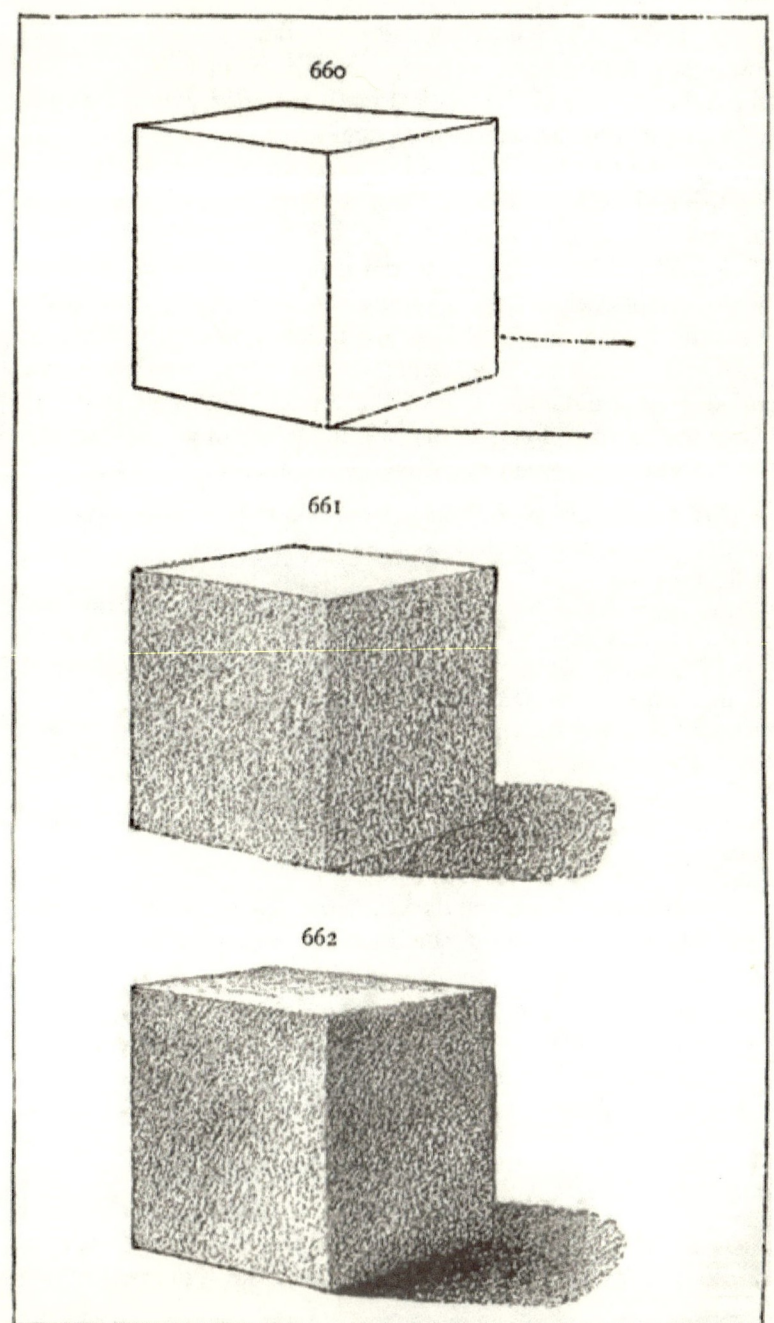

top and the left-hand face. The pupil will notice that the bottom part of the right-hand face is not the lightest part, as the cast shadow prevents so much light being reflected upon it.

7. Darken the cast shadow towards the object.

8. The top of the cube, although the lightest part, is not quite white, and requires a very light tint from an almost clean stump on the part furthest removed. This general principle should be carefully borne in mind : *That a light tone if placed beside a dark one appears lighter where it approaches the darker tone, and the dark tone appears darker where it approaches the lighter one.* This will be seen to be the case on the cube ; the top appears lighter as it approaches the darker vertical faces, the vertical faces appear darker as they approach the lighter top, and the right-hand face appears darker towards the edge nearest the lighter-toned face, &c.

Notes.—1. Be very careful not to make the gradations too dark.

2. As the pupil progresses he will be able to lay on a gradated tint at once, instead of doing it in two stages.

3. The above steps apply to all models, and the rectangular and hexagonal prisms will present no difficulty to those who have mastered the shading of the cube.

The Cylinder.—This is taken as the type for all circular models, as the same rules are applicable more or less to all similarly shaped objects.

1. Sketch the cylinder, mark in the cast shadow, and indicate by a light line the part of the cylinder in *shade*. This line will commence at A, where the shadow is seen to begin (fig. 663).

2. Shade the cast shadow evenly of a depth equal to its lightest part.

3. Lay on an even tint, from the right-hand side to the line marking the extent of the shade, as dark as its lightest part (fig. 664).

4. Notice that the darkest part is not at the edge, and gradate the tint already laid on. The highest light is not quite at the left edge. On each side of the *high light* put in the *half*

tone on the portions of the cylinder upon which the light falls obliquely. Be careful to gradate these tones so that there is a *gradual* darkening from the highest light to the darkest shade.

5. Darken the cast shadow where necessary, and put a very light tint upon the top, decreasing as it approaches the front (fig. 665).

The cylinder lying down should be treated similarly ; its

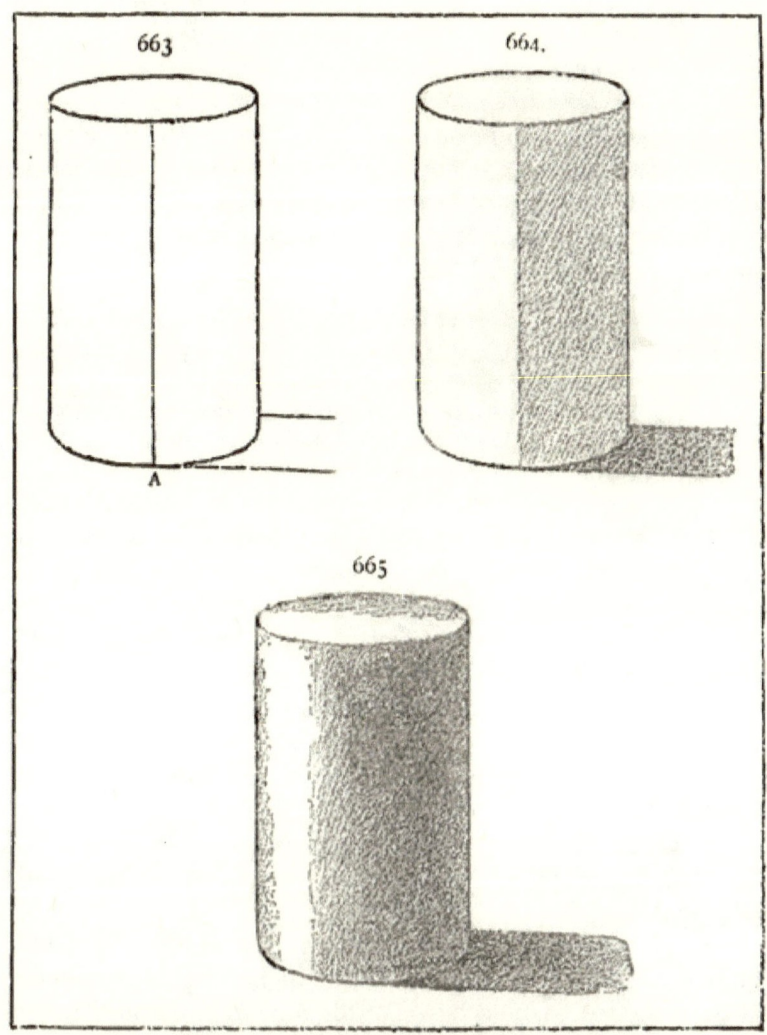

vertical end will get lighter as it approaches the dark part of the shade on its length, as in the left-hand face of the cube.

The **cone** is treated similarly to the cylinder; the only fresh point to notice is that the darkest part of the *shade* is near the apex, as owing to its sloping surface there is less light reflected on this part. The same fact applies to all pyramids when standing on their bases.

The waterbottle from the three objects of form is shown as an example for **vases**, as it is the one prescribed for the elementary stage of model drawing, and is in common use.

1. Very carefully sketch in the outline; mark the cast shadow and the line of shade (fig. 666).

2. Lay on the shade with an even tint as dark as its lightest part.

3. Put in the cast shadow in a similar manner (fig. 667).

4. Gradate the shade on the neck as in the cylinder, bearing in mind that the darkest part is not quite at the edge. The darkest part will be at *a*, as here the shadow from the neck falls upon the shoulder of the vase. The darkest shade on the body is some distance from the edge, owing to the reflected light from the ground. Add the half tones. The lightest part of the body will be at *b*, as the light falls most directly upon the vase at this part.

5. Complete the cast shadow. Notice that it falls on the foot with a rather sharp edge; on the ground its edges should be kept soft. The middle part of this shadow is lighter than the outside, owing to the light reflected from the body of the vase.

6. Blend the tones carefully, and complete as in fig. 668.

When the pupils have shaded several of the models singly, they may at once proceed to the shading of a group. The 'Illustrated Syllabus' shows, as an example, a group of three objects lightly shaded. The pupils should notice the cast-shadow thrown upon the book by the other two objects. Any group of models of about the same degree of difficulty as is usually set for Standard VI will make a suitable group for shading.

Shading from Casts.—The syllabus specifies shading from

Light and Shade. Standard VII 257

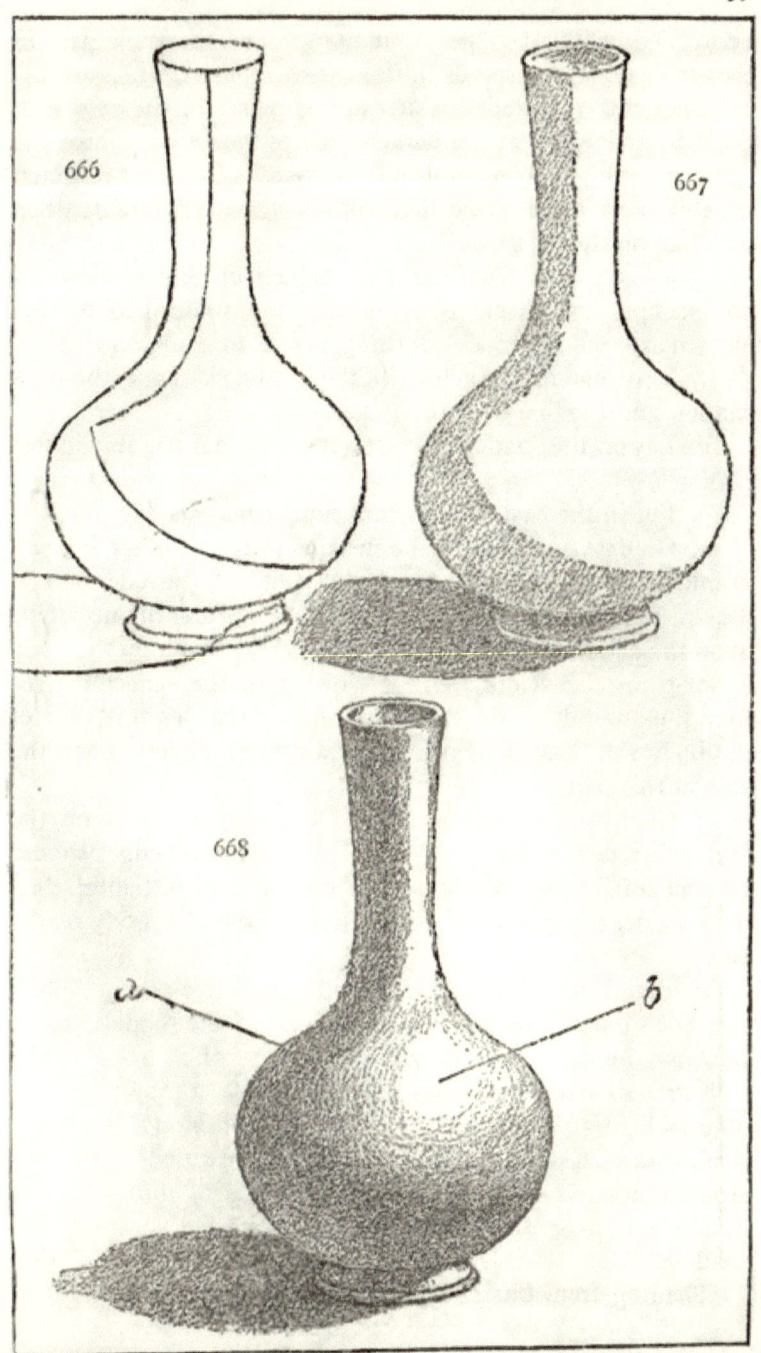

258 *The Teaching of Drawing*

common objects and casts of ornament. In most schools the group of models would probably be taken. Casts of ornament in plaster of Paris may be obtained at a very cheap rate from D. Brucciani & Co., 40 Russell St., Covent Garden, W.C., the agents to the Department. Ten casts of elementary ornament suitable for Standard VII, or for the elementary stage of light and shade, may be obtained for 1*l*.

669

Light and Shade. Standard VII 259

Method of Shading the Cast.—Three drawings showing an ordinary cast in three stages of development are given.

Fig. 669.—1. Place the cast in an upright position against the wall, and about level with the pupil's eye. Begin by drawing the slab upon which the ornament is placed, as this will help the pupil to draw the outline more easily.

670

2. Draw the middle line and fix the position of the top and bottom of the ornament (*a* and *b*).

3. Find the position of *c* and draw the line *de*. In the same manner obtain *fg*.

4. Draw the curves from these points.

5. Draw the other big curves after obtaining their position as shown by the construction lines.

671

6. Complete the drawing and very lightly indicate the cast shadows.

Notes.—1. It is not at all necessary that the student should draw all the horizontal lines shown on the figure, as the rubbing out of these lines will spoil the surface of the paper. It will be sufficient in most cases to carry the pencil across and mark the point.

2. Sketch the cast very lightly, as alterations may then be easily made.

Fig. 670.—1. Very lightly shade the background with an almost clean stump. When there is a large surface to cover, the forefinger, covered with a piece of wash leather very faintly charged with chalk and well rubbed on trial paper, may be used with advantage for this purpose. The portions close to the drawing can be filled up afterwards with the stump. By putting in the background first the student is better able to judge the degree of shade necessary for the various parts of the cast. The light parts will be lighter than the background and will stand out better from it.

2. Put on the main shades and the cast shadows. Where a shade on a curved portion approaches the lighter part, be careful to let it die away gradually.

Fig. 671.—1. Gradate the parts in shade by darkening them towards the left, where they approach the high light. Continue the shade over the lighter parts where needed, leaving the highest light white.

2. Darken the shadow where it approaches the cast. Be careful to keep the edges of the shadow soft, letting them die away somewhat gradually into the surface of the slab.

CHAPTER XII

THE ELEMENTARY DRAWING CERTIFICATE

As all teachers of **boys'** schools are required to **teach** drawing it is very necessary that they should qualify **themselves** by obtaining the certificate. This certificate covers the work required from the standards, and the Education **Code, 1893,** art. 60, states that '*No teachers, passing* **the second** *year's examination after December,* 1896, *will be recognised as certificated* **teachers unless,** *or until, they have* **obtained the** *First or Second Class Elementary Drawing Certificate.*' This applies to all teachers, both male and female.

Those teachers who **may be partially** qualified **and** wish to obtain their certificate should procure information from the Science and Art Department as to what subjects they must take to complete it.

The requirements at present for the **First Class Certificate** are *a First Class in* :—(*a*) *the Elementary Stage of Freehand Drawing* (**subject** *2b*) ; (*b*) *the Elementary Stage of Model Drawing* (*subject 3a*) ; (*c*) *the Elementary Stage of Shading from Casts* (*subject 5b*) ; *and* (*d*) *a pass in the Elementary Stage of Practical Plane and Solid Geometry.*

For the Second Class Certificate :—(*a*) *a pass in the Elementary Stage of Practical Plane and Solid Geometry ;* (*b*) *a second class in the Elementary Stage of Model Drawing ;* (*c*) *a second class in the Elementary Stage of Freehand Drawing.*

'Pupil teachers may, after August 31, 1893, be examined at their schools in the Elementary Stage of Freehand, of Model, of Shading from Casts, and of Perspective. Teachers wishing to be examined in Geometrical Drawing must sit for examination in that subject at the May examinations of Science and Art schools and classes, and the examination in Geometrical Drawing at elementary schools will cease.'

A few hints and directions are given with regard to each subject. If the method of working explained in the previous chapters be thoroughly understood and well practised, the teacher should not experience any great difficulty in doing the work required.

Elementary Stage Freehand.—The instructions for examination are :—That the *leading lines of the whole figure* must be sketched in, and that the drawing should fairly fill the paper supplied ($\frac{1}{4}$ imperial sheet, 15$\frac{1}{2}$in. by 11$\frac{1}{2}$in.). When this is done, carry the drawing to completion, as far as possible in clear outline.

The object is clearly to ascertain whether the proper method of drawing a copy is understood. Figs. 377, 378, 379, 380, show the leading lines of the figures they accompany and are suitable for preliminary practice. Two recent examination tests are also given, from which the student may see the character of the copies set and the proper method of drawing them.

Figs. 672 and 674 show the copies as set, slightly reduced in size.

Fig. 673 shows the construction and leading lines of fig. 672. The left side is carried a little further towards completion than the right.

Fig. 675 shows the construction and leading lines of fig. 674. The student will have no difficulty in following after studying the figure. In both copies begin with the spiral curves and the circles containing the flower, leaving the detail until last. The copies would require enlarging to about 2$\frac{1}{2}$ times the given size.

Elementary Stage Model.—Practise the methods of drawing the models and vases given in Chapter X., and especially notice the remarks concerning the arrangement of the group in fig. 651.

It is usual to give three models in the group for examination, which are frequently required to be drawn with the board upon which they may be placed.

672

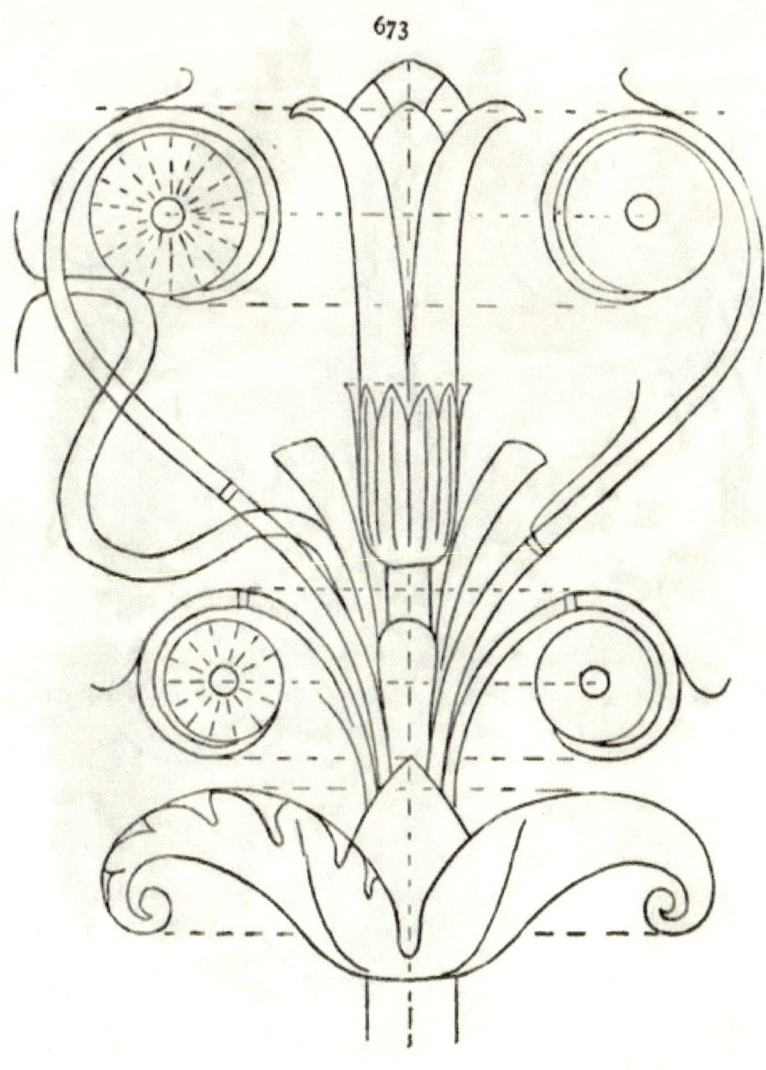

673

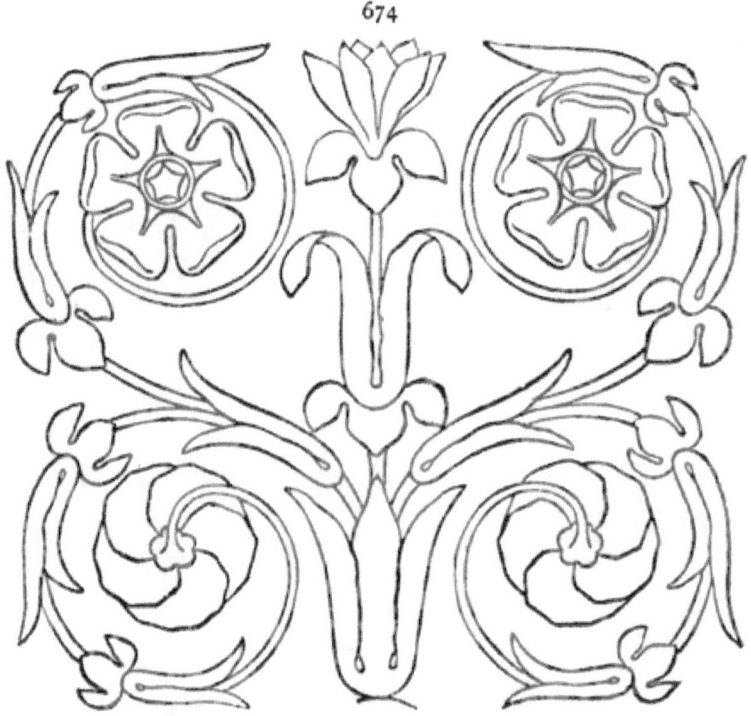

674

The examination is now confined to groups composed from the following models and vases prescribed by the Science and Art Department, and which are all dealt with in Chapter X. *The cube, square prism,* **square pyramid,** *triangular prism,* **hexagonal prism,** *cylinder, cylindrical ring,* **and cone,** *together with* **the bottle** *from the three objects of form (figs.* 338, 648, *and* 649) *and the* **large terra cotta vase** *(figs.* 645–647*).*

Practise groups of these models, paying special attention to the method of drawing; as, if the group be correctly drawn, even though not finished, the student would undoubtedly get through. To secure a first-class the group should be correctly drawn and completed in the hour allowed.

Elementary Stage of Shading from Casts.—The student is required to make a drawing in chalk, from a cast in *low relief*, in three hours. The cast shown in figs. 669–671 is suitable for the purpose and is one in common use. The

675

Illustrated Syllabus also shows two casts such as are set for this stage.

Read over the directions given in Chapter XI., and then draw a variety of casts, as success largely depends upon the amount of practice bestowed upon the subject. At the same time the student will find that more useful knowledge of shading will be obtained by well finishing two or three casts, than by making rough drawings of a large number.

Elementary **Stage of Practical Plane and Solid Geometry.**—The course indicated for Standards VI. and VII. forms a good introduction. The student who thoroughly understands the principles there dealt with will be able to take up the Elementary Stage without much difficulty. 'Practical Plane and Solid Geometry,' by I. H. Morris (Longmans & Co., two shillings and sixpence), amply covers the requirements.

www.ingramcontent.com/pod-product-compliance
Lightning Source LLC
Chambersburg PA
CBHW031941230426
43672CB00010B/2000